ALL THE
COUNTRIES
WE'VE EVER
INVADED

ALL THE COUNTRIES WE'VE EVER INVADED

AND THE FEW WE NEVER GOT ROUND TO

STUART LAYCOCK

942

First published 2012

The History Press
The Mill, Brimscombe Port
Stroud, Gloucestershire, GL5 2QG
www.thehistorypress.co.uk

British Library Cataloguing in Publication Data.
A catalogue record for this book is available from the British Library.

ISBN 978 0 7524 7969 9

Typesetting and origination by The History Press
Printed and bound by CPI Group (UK) Ltd, Croydon, CR0 4YY

CONTENTS

INTRODUCTION

If someone asked you how many countries we've invaded over the centuries, what would you say? Forty? Fifty? Sixty? What if I told you that we've invaded, had some control over or fought conflicts in the territory of something like 171 out of 193 UN member states in the world today (and maybe more)? Because that's exactly what we've done. It may come as a shock, but it's true. Writing this book has changed the way I think about who we are as a nation, and in that sense about who I am. Maybe it will change the way you think about yourself too.

This book sprang from my son Fred asking me about countries that we have invaded. Once I started compiling in my mind a list of them for him, I found the list growing longer and longer. In fact, it turns out that there are relatively few countries on the planet that we haven't invaded at least once, and there are quite a few countries that our forces have visited on more than one occasion, sometimes a lot more than one occasion.

A lot of people are vaguely aware that a quarter of the globe was once coloured pink to represent British-held territories, but that's not even half the story. Sometimes, because we're used to it, we forget quite how unique our story is. When you read how many times we've invaded, for instance, China or Egypt or Russia, ask yourself how many times Chinese or Egyptian or Russian forces have invaded Britain. We're a stroppy, dynamic, irrepressible nation, and this is a story of how we have changed the world, even, often, when it didn't ask to be changed.

I've tried to be objective, but sometimes the question of what constitutes an invasion can be a little subjective.

The book is, in some sense, focused on British forces actually setting foot in foreign countries, but it would be unfair to ignore the question of times we have invaded the maritime territory or airspace of other countries. Since we were long a massive naval power and have used sea power as a deliberate method of enforcing British influence, it would be wrong to exclude naval actions in other countries' waters. Air raids in recent years have played a similar role. However, air raids, being individually of comparatively short duration, somehow seem less of an invasion (even though those underneath them may disagree), than naval or land action, so I have not concentrated on these.

There are many instances where we have negotiated and sometimes paid for our initial toehold in a land, and then gradually gone on to develop and expand our control of the territory. Even though there may have been no actual violence in the initial arrival of armed Brits, it seems reasonable to include such instances.

Similarly, there have been instances where our military incursions into a territory have been in support of the locals, rather than against them, but as with the D-Day invasion of France, it would be wrong to exclude these too.

I've not generally included military actions by British soldiers in foreign armies (of which there have been over the centuries far, far more than the average Briton is now aware), unless they seem of particular interest, or unless they were in some way fighting with British government encouragement. When it comes to questions of, for instance, pirates, privateers and armed explorers, the question becomes a little more complex, but it seems fair to include some of the more interesting efforts by privateers operating with official approval.

In this book, I'm basically looking at invasions of other countries by the current United Kingdom of England, Scotland, Wales and Northern Ireland, and predecessor political entities, or by bodies that in some significant sense represent them. So, there is a section on invasions of the current territory of the Republic of Ireland in here, but not on invasions of the current territory of Scotland and Wales. Similarly, I haven't covered our existing other territories such as the Falklands, Gibraltar, and so on.

In the same way that your family history, with both the good bits and the bad bits, is part of who you are, so, too, is your country's history also part of who you are. This book is probably primarily going to be sold in the United Kingdom to Britons, so I don't apologise for using the word 'we' when I refer to something past Brits have done.

As well as British, I'm also English, and therefore you will find me using the word 'we' about something done just by England and the English, not by Brits as a whole. I have tried to minimise this, because this book is supposed to be mainly about Britain's record of invading the world, rather than just England's, but I know I have done it sometimes.

I also hope anyone in Northern Ireland who is a citizen of the United Kingdom of Great Britain and Northern Ireland, but does not regard themselves as a Brit, will forgive me for sometimes using the terms Brits, Britons and Britain as shorthand for the whole UK and its citizens.

Similarly, I am well aware of the contribution made throughout Britain's history by immigrants, some of whom may not have been under the laws then, officially British. And I am also aware of the huge contribution to British military efforts made over the centuries by people from other parts of the empire and Commonwealth, as well as Great Britain and Northern Ireland. Again, I hope that my use of the terms Brits, Britons and Britain as shorthand, often to include the hugely significant contributions from these sources, does not in any way detract from their importance.

We are a nation with a long and spectacular history, so it is clearly impractical to give detailed accounts of every invasion we have ever carried out. For that reason, I have concentrated on the more interesting and more unusual ones, with a tendency to concentrate on the less well-known ones. D-Day, for instance, is hugely interesting but it is well known and covered in great detail in a large number of books, so there seems little point in focusing on it too much in this modest little book. Equally, the stories of our involvement with what were some of the major elements of the British Empire, like India or Australia, are fascinating ones, but have received comparatively extensive coverage in British books and media over the years, so I have not focused too extensively on them in this book. Even then, with interesting, unusual and less well-known invasions it is still not possible in a small book like this to give anything more than brief details. This isn't so much supposed to be an account of our invasions, rather it's intended to whet the readers' appetites to go in search of more information elsewhere.

I have divided the book into sections based on today's national boundaries, under the names of today's countries. Clearly, many of these national boundaries did not apply at the time of many of the invasions in question, but it seemed the simplest and clearest way to approach the aim of this book. Modern country names and boundaries are what today's readers understand best. Using them is the quickest and easiest way to grasp the enormity of our military influence and what a truly awe-inspiring power, for bad and for good, our country has been right across the world. And anyway, a change of country name rarely implies widespread change to a region's people, its towns, cities or landscape. Moscow did not stop being Moscow when it went from being the capital of the Soviet Union, to being the capital of Russia.

Using modern boundaries also makes it easier to trace common themes in our activities over the centuries in particular areas. When we go into places like Iraq and Afghanistan, we are not going there for the first time. Even if a large section of our population is not aware of that fact, you can be fairly sure that a large percentage of the populations of the countries that we're going into are well aware of our past appearances in their country, and while we do not have to agree with others' views of us, it is always wise to be aware of them. We have been to almost all these places before, and we have made mistakes as well as had successes. Both past mistakes and past successes are worth considering when it comes to the present and future.

In terms of countries, I've included a section on every one of the world's nations because there are only a few where people from Britain haven't conducted some kind of armed operation, and even in those cases where they haven't, there is usually something worth saying.

In terms of 'what is a country', the simplest method seemed to be to treat as a country those entities that the UK government recognises as separate independent sovereign states. So, I've looked at UN member states, plus the Vatican City and Kosovo, which even though they aren't UN member states, are recognised by the UK government as independent states. There are some places around the world that some readers will feel should be countries or believe are countries, even though the UK government does not recognise them as independent sovereign states. Conversely, there are some places that some readers will feel should not be countries and believe are not countries, even though the UK does recognise them as independent sovereign states, but this little book is not the place to explore such questions.

Sometimes I've briefly written indications of where a country is located. This is not in any way a suggestion that these countries are in any sense less important than other countries. It is simply an acknowledgement that many Brits today, myself included, know less about the map of the world than they really should, and can also often be confused by countries that have similar names to other countries.

This book is most definitely not intended to be any kind of moral judgement on Britain's history or the British Empire. From a British perspective it is still very easy to see our empire as a civilising force spreading democracy and moderation across the world, and there is, of course, some truth in that view. But as you read in these pages endless stories of raids and invasions, it is also easy to see another view, one that would perhaps be more easily accepted outside our borders.

In this view, the British Empire was almost like the last and by far the most successful of the Viking kingdoms, an empire which continued a North European tradition of using our knowledge and expertise at sea, gained from an inevitable close association with it, to leave behind a land of limited agricultural space with an often unattractive climate and sail away in search of loot, trade and power in warmer countries that seemed militarily vulnerable. The Saxons, Angles and Jutes had something of this in them after all. We had Viking kings of England like Cnut, and the word Norman is an abbreviation of Norseman.

It seems to me that some of the things we have done around the world are self-evidently wrong (like our deep involvement in the slave trade, which our later campaign against slavery in the nineteenth century only makes up for to a small extent), some are self-evidently right and there is a wide range in between. In some small way it's a bit like your own life: there are things you've done that you're ashamed of; there are things you've done that you're proud of; there are things you've done that seemed like a good idea at the time, but don't now; and there are things you've done that seemed like a good idea at the time and still seem like a good idea.

Whether wrong or right, *all* are interesting because they are our history, the history of a nation that dragged itself out of a small, cold, wet island somewhere off the mainland of Europe to make a mark, for better or worse, on every corner of the globe.

This little book is a modest attempt to tackle what is an absolutely enormous and complex subject. It is inevitable that it will not be a completely perfect attempt. Our country's history belongs to all of us, so if you feel I've missed out any essential details or got something badly wrong, do please let me know. I'd like to know anyway, for my own benefit, and if there's ever a new edition of the book, then I'll try to get it right next time! Similarly, our armed forces are still in action on a regular basis and it may be that by the time you read this book, or even by the time it's published, one or two or a few sections may be out of date. If so, again, as and when and if the book is reprinted, I'll correct that.

For world maps, please see pp. 253–256.

1

AFGHANISTAN TO BURUNDI

Afghanistan

We start with Afghanistan because in English it's the country that comes first alphabetically, but it's an appropriate place to start due to our long history of involvement in the country.

The Soviet war in Afghanistan in the 1980s was the first time that many Britons alive today became much aware of the country. A lot of our early involvement with Afghanistan has to do with the country's strategic (and from the point of view of being invaded, let's face it, unfortunate) location between areas of Russian control and influence to the north, and areas of British control to the south. This is the so-called 'Great Game', the battle for domination of Central Asia that was such a preoccupation with the Victorians. They called it a game, but it was the kind of game where people ended up dead in large numbers rather than just, for instance, being given a stern word by the referee or getting sent off.

Our first venture into the Great Game as far as Afghanistan is concerned could not, however, be described as a great success. Early signs of spreading Russian influence, plus a failure to conclude a British alliance with the emir of Afghanistan, Dost Muhammad, led to a British attempt at regime change. In 1838, a British army of 21,000 men set out from the Punjab to replace Dost Muhammad with a previous pro-British ruler of Afghanistan, Shah Shuja. The army successfully took Kandahar and advanced north. Eventually, Shah Shuja was installed as the new ruler in Kabul and over half the army left Afghanistan. Dost Muhammad was captured and sent to India. But the final whistle hadn't blown. This wasn't the end of this particular episode of the Great Game. It was only half time, and in the second half things went downhill spectacularly from a British point of view.

Shah Shuja was unfortunately fairly heavily reliant on British arms and British payments to tribal warlords to stay in power, and as it became apparent that the British were settling in for a long occupation, the Afghans weren't too keen on the whole idea. A senior British officer and his aides ended up getting killed in a riot and when the local British agent, William Hay Macnaghten, tried to restore the situation by negotiating with Dost Muhammad's son, Macnaghten was also killed and his body dragged through Kabul before being displayed in the Grand Bazaar. Not at all the sort of thing you want to see when you go shopping.

As the situation deteriorated almost as fast as the weather, the British commander in Kabul decided, in January 1842, that his situation was untenable and tried to negotiate safe passage out of the country for his force and the British civilians there. Instead of this, the retreating column was forced to try to make its way through snowbound gorges and passes in the face of heavy attacks. In the end, only a single Briton, a surgeon, Dr William Brydon, made it as far as the comparative safety of Jalalabad.

After this disaster there were plans to reoccupy Kabul, but a new government came to power in London determined to end the war and, instead, we made do with destroying Kabul's Grand Bazaar as a reprisal, and withdrew back to India. Dost Muhammad was subsequently released and returned to power in Kabul.

After such a disastrous start, you would almost have thought that we might have left Afghanistan alone, but the Great Game continued so another round was almost inevitable. This time around, it all went a lot more smoothly for Britain. Well it would have been pretty unfortunate if we'd ended up with a disaster as bad as the first one on *two* occasions.

By 1878 Dost Muhammad's son, Sher Ali Khan, was, after a spot of family feuding with his brother, now emir of Afghanistan. When a Russian diplomatic mission arrived in Kabul, Britain insisted that, as a balance, a British diplomatic mission should also be allowed there. The British mission was duly dispatched and was duly not allowed beyond the Khyber Pass. So we reckoned it was time we sent in the troops again.

This time an army of roughly 40,000 men, divided into three columns, invaded Afghanistan. Initial Afghan resistance soon crumbled, with the collapse aided by the death of Sher Ali Khan at Mazar e Sharif in 1879. After this, to prevent Britain occupying Afghanistan, Sher Ali's son, Mohammad Yaqub Khan, signed the Treaty of Gandamak, handing over control of the country's foreign affairs to Britain. Then, it will probably come as no surprise to you that the situation began to get complicated again.

In September 1879, mutinous Afghan troops killed the British representative in Kabul, Sir Pierre Cavagnari. And in the aftermath of this, General Sir Frederick Roberts led an army into central Afghanistan, defeated the Afghan army at Char Asiab and occupied Kabul yet again. That was then followed by yet another uprising against the British presence in Kabul, which was eventually put down, but by this time Britain had had enough of Yaqub Khan and decided that more regime change was needed. Splitting the country up was discussed, as were other options, before we finally made Yaqub's cousin, Abdur Rahman Khan, emir instead. Then there was yet another insurgency, this time in Herat, which led to a British victory at the Battle of Maiwand, and finally, with Abdur Rahman Khan still in power and the Treaty of Gandamak still in force, the British Army managed to make a timely exit from Afghanistan. Glad to be out, no doubt.

Subsequently, Abdur Rahman Khan ruled Afghanistan with a heavy hand, but at least managed, on the whole, to prevent competition between Russia and Britain causing him too many problems. In 1919, though, his son and successor, Habibullah Khan, was assassinated and a power struggle ensued between his brother and his son, Amanullah. Eventually, Amanullah had his uncle arrested and decided that what was needed, in order to quell domestic trouble, was a nice little foreign war. So he invaded India.

At first sight this seems like a total mismatch, with Afghanistan up against the entire might of the British Empire, but in fact the situation was nothing like that simple. In 1919, Britain was exhausted after the First World War. What is more, just as today, cross-border loyalties there made it a difficult area for outsiders to operate in. However, like today, and unlike previous occasions, Britain now at least had an air force to assist it.

On 3 May 1919, the Afghan army crossed the border and captured Bagh. The Afghans hoped that an insurgency against Britain in Peshawar would help them, but we reacted quickly and managed to contain any possibility of rebellion. Eventually, on 11 May, British forces, including the use of planes, managed to push the Afghans out of Bagh and back across the border. Then Britain invaded Afghan territory again, and occupied the town of Dakka. But fighting was fierce and the situation was deteriorating behind the British advance. The Khyber Rifles became mutinous and began to desert. British Handley-Page bombers attacked Kabul, but the intended British advance to Jalalabad ground to a halt and things worsened when the South Waziristan Militia mutinied as well. Eventually, forces under Brigadier General Dyer pushed back Afghan army units and Amanullah offered an armistice which the British accepted. The war was in many ways inconclusive, but it did effectively mean we gave up on trying to control Afghan foreign policy. Instead it left us concentrating on the equally insoluble problem of trying to control the long-running and bitter insurgency in the North-West Frontier area that dragged on pretty much for as long as the Raj. As Great Games go, our venture into Afghanistan hadn't proved to be such a great one from our point of view. Mind you the Russians haven't exactly had a lot of fun in Afghanistan either. And, of course, it's all brought a lot of misery to the Afghans. So not a Great Game from anybody's point of view.

Now we are back in Afghanistan. Names like Kabul, Kandahar and Mazar e Sharif have once again become regular features of the news. After the 9/11 attacks in 2001, we joined the US-led Operation Enduring Freedom to topple the Taleban regime and remove Al-Qaeda from Afghanistan. At the time of writing, we are still intending to be there at least a little bit longer, attempting to crush the Taleban insurgency and help establish a stable and democratic Afghanistan. Let's hope it ends better than some of our previous efforts in the country.

Albania

Ah, Albania, Land of the Eagles (see flag), but also, until not long ago, the land of the less than attractive dictator Enver Hoxha and place where you could spot a statue of Stalin as recently as 1980. This was a land so scared of invasion that it had large numbers of concrete pillboxes scattered across the countryside in a slightly bizarre and surprising fashion.

During the Cold War, most of Eastern Europe seemed remote and cut off to West Europeans. But Albania seemed remote and cut off even to most East Europeans. If you'd asked a selection of Brits in 1975 where Albania was, I suspect a fair percentage wouldn't even have guessed it was in Europe. In fact, for anyone who grew up in the Cold War period, Albania was such a mysterious, closed land that it seems almost inconceivable that Britain's armed forces could have a history of operations in the area, but, in fact, they do.

We tend to think of Trafalgar and Waterloo when we think of the Napoleonic Wars, which in some sense is fair enough, but we actually fought the French in all sorts of places, one of them being the Adriatic. The Albanian coast saw assorted actions by the Royal Navy during the Napoleonic Wars, including, for instance, the capture of the French corvette *Var* at the Albanian port of Valona (now Vlorë) in 1809 by HMS *Belle Poule*. You'll come across some rather fabulous names for Royal Navy warships in this book. I know our modern Royal Navy doesn't have that many ships to name, but when they do have new ones to name, it would be nice if they resurrected some of the more jolly ones from the past. The rather unusual name of this particular ship comes from the fact that she was a French ship until we captured her in 1806.

In the First World War, in December 1915, the Austro-Hungarian navy, aiming to impede the evacuation of Serbian troops retreating in front of the enemy onslaught (see Serbia), sent a naval force to attack Durazzo (Durres, Albania's main port) which was then in Allied hands. British ships, including HMS *Dartmouth* and HMS *Weymouth*, stalwartly helped to repel the attack. And British troops landed in Albania to help the epic evacuation of the retreating Serbian army across a narrow stretch of sea to Corfu. Thinking of Corfu today, as the holiday island it is, you might be tempted to be jealous of people being evacuated to it, but this was before the days of sun-and-sand package tours. The retreat was long and bitter, and the evacuation was sort of Serbia's Dunkirk. The brave men of the Royal Navy's Danube Flotilla, who had made the long and grim retreat with the Serbian army, were also rescued.

Then in October 1918, with Durazzo now in Austro-Hungarian hands (so much for our efforts the first time round), Royal Navy ships, including HMS *Weymouth*, took part, along with, Italian, Australian and American warships, in the Second Battle of Durazzo. Shore batteries and assorted other buildings were destroyed, and a squadron of Austro-Hungarian patrol craft was defeated. Shortly afterwards, Austria-Hungary lost the war and HMS *Weymouth* could go off and do something else.

Early in the Second World War, we were back in the area. In 1940 and 1941, the Royal Navy and the Royal Air Force (RAF) launched operations to try to help Greek troops by attacking Valona, treading in the footsteps or sailing in the wake of HMS *Belle Poule* almost 150 years earlier. For instance, on 19 December 1940, HMS *Warspite* and HMS *Valiant* (good names but much more obvious than *Belle Poule*) shelled Valona, destroying Italian planes. The Special Operations Executive (SOE), also got in on the act and conducted assorted operations here during the war, with the aim of assisting resistance.

In October 1944, sailing from Brindisi in Italy, Number Two Army Commando and 40 Commando, with help from a Royal Navy bombardment, fought their way into the southern Albanian port of Saranda, opposite Corfu, and took it from the German defenders.

Brits found themselves fighting alongside Albanian Communists during the Second World War, but such close ties were not to last. Shortly after the end of the war, relations between Britain and Albania were plunged into crisis over incidents involving the Royal Navy in the Corfu Channel.

Algeria

We don't tend to think of Algeria as an area of British influence, so it may come as something of a surprise to find out that our forces have been in action here many times.

In the early centuries this mainly had to do with Algerian pirates. Britain, of course, has a long history of producing pre-eminent pirates and privateers, but we do tend to object when others play the game too well. The so-called Barbary Corsairs played it exceptionally well. They didn't even just attack targets in the Mediterranean; they attacked ships and raided coastal areas as far north as Britain itself. All in all we didn't like Barbary Corsairs. And some of the most successful North African pirates worked from the area around Algiers.

We tried to deal with the problem with a mixture of diplomacy and rather less subtle violence. By the 1630s we had partially effective treaties in force, but then things got messy and a treaty signed in 1671 broke down into open warfare. Defeats by British naval forces under Arthur Herbert forced Algiers to sign another treaty in 1682.

It's worth pointing out at this stage, that even though we do have quite a record of attacking places around the world, it wasn't just us having trouble with Algiers. Frankly, the city seems to have been a rather unsafe place to live at the time and you have to wonder what happened to the house prices. The French bombarded Algiers on a number of occasions, including in 1682, 1683 and 1688. So did the Spanish on a number of occasions, including in 1783 and 1784. In 1770, the Danish-Norwegian fleet had a go. Even the Americans, rather far from home, got in on the act by sending ships to Algiers in 1815.

We tend to think of military interventions on humanitarian grounds as a modern invention, but in 1816 we carried out what can, in some sense, be seen in these terms. It was our turn to bombard Algiers. With Napoleon finally defeated, we decided that it was time to do something (yet again) about the slave industry in North Africa. Admittedly, in this instance Britain was mainly concerned with preventing Europeans and Christians being enslaved, but it was perhaps better than nothing.

So Lord Exmouth set off for the North African coast to persuade the locals to stop their bad habits. And he took a small squadron of naval ships with him to make his arguments even more convincing. Indeed, the Deys of Tripoli and Tunis found Exmouth's arguments, or at least the sight of the British Navy, thoroughly convincing and agreed to do as demanded by Exmouth. However, things proved a little more difficult in Algiers. Exmouth thought he'd succeeded only for events to end with a massacre of European fishermen we thought we were protecting.

Not surprisingly, people in Britain weren't exactly happy about how it had all worked out, so Exmouth was sent back to drop a few less subtle hints on the Dey of Algiers, along with the threat of some even less subtle cannon fire.

For his mission, Exmouth took along assorted ships of the line, frigates and various other vessels. In Gibraltar, a Dutch squadron also joined the mission. Just as today, the safety of diplomats could be a problem in such situations, and the day before the attack a party from the frigate *Prometheus* tried to rescue the British consul and his wife, only to be captured. Not a huge success.

When the fleet was finally in position for the bombardment, an Algerian gun started the battle and a flotilla of small Algerian boats full of men tried to reach the British ships and board them. Neither Algerian guns nor the boarding parties achieved much and, instead, Exmouth fired at both ships in the harbour and the Dey's military installations before withdrawing and demanding the Dey fulfil his demands about slaves and slavery. The Dey now finally complied.

In 1825, however, we ended up bombarding Algiers again. In some ways it's surprising that people chose to remain living in Algiers, particularly since, in 1830, the French bombarded it yet again. Oh, and then invaded it as well. Which meant that the next time we returned to the area, it wasn't the Barbary Consairs we were bombarding any more.

Mers-El-Kebir is situated in western Algeria, near Oran. In July 1940, a large number of French warships were concentrated here and Britain feared that because of the Vichy government's relations with Nazi Germany, these ships could at some stage be used against us. So we shelled them.

In 1942 we were headed back to Algiers yet again, this time for Operation Torch. This operation involved landings in Vichy-controlled Morocco and Algeria, and a lot of the forces involved were American, but British forces also played major roles. The Eastern Task Force aimed at Algiers was commanded by British Lieutenant General Kenneth Anderson and included troops from the British 78th Infantry Division and two commando units, No. 1 and No. 6 Commando.

French Resistance forces staged a coup in Algiers, and when the Allied troops arrived they met little local resistance from Vichy forces. The heaviest fighting took place in the port of Algiers where HMS *Malcolm* and HMS *Broke* launched Operation Terminal to try to prevent Vichy forces destroying the port facilities. Both ships came under heavy artillery fire in the port and were badly damaged, but HMS *Broke* managed to land the American troops it was carrying, before withdrawing. HMS *Broke* was, it turned out tragically, indeed broken, and eventually sank from the damage it received in the operation. The American troops who had landed were eventually forced to surrender, but, at least, the port was not totally destroyed.

Andorra

A small country that regularly gets loads of British visitors, particularly skiers, these days (I've been there myself), but so far I can't find any evidence we've ever invaded with troops. During the Second World War, some British airmen did use Andorra as a route to escape from occupied France, but that's maybe the closest we've come to sending British troops into Andorra. If anyone knows differently, let me know. Small countries make for small targets and have a disproportionately high representation in the short list of places we've never really invaded.

Angola

A land that has seen a lot of devastation from war in its history, but very little of it has been down to us. During the colonial era this was an area largely of Portuguese influence and since we have a long-standing friendship with Portugal, we've thoughtfully tended to steer clear of invading places like Angola.

Early on we did take a bit of interest in Cabinda, a slightly detached part of Angola, but a part of Angola nonetheless. Cabinda has a strategic location at the mouth of the Congo, so it was inevitable that we would be interested in it. Britain's Royal African Company built a fort there, only to have it destroyed by the Portuguese who weren't too keen on us getting a share of the region's trade, even if we were supposed to be friends.

Then when we finally stopped being a slave-trading nation and started actively fighting the slave trade, the seas around Angola saw plenty of Royal Navy activity. The 4th Division of the Royal Navy's West Africa station covered from Cape Lopez in Gabon to Luanda in Angola. And the 5th Division covered the area south of Luanda.

In the largest British deployment to Southern Africa on active service since the 1960s, 650 British troops on UN duty set foot in Angola in 1995 as part of Operation Chantress to help protect a ceasefire. A friendly invasion.

Antigua and Barbuda

From the point of view of Brits invading it, Antigua has a nice straightforward history. English settlers turned up on Antigua in 1632 and first England then Britain controlled it all the way through until 1981.

Except for 1666 – a bad year for us in many ways. Not only did we have the Great Fire of London and the Great Plague (great in the size sense rather than the 'Ooh, fire and plague, Great!' sense), but as if all that wasn't bad enough, the French turned up and briefly occupied Antigua. When you look at a list of governors of Antigua, your eye runs down the British names until you get to one 'Robert le Fichot des Friches, sieur de Clodoré'. I don't know if there ever has been an English branch of Robert's (pronounced Robaire) family, but he at least was most definitely French.

We had a little more trouble with Barbuda. Our first invasion wasn't a huge success, well at least not for the Brits involved. It was a bit more of a success for the locals already living on the island.

By 1685, however, Christopher and John Codrington, who were involved with sugar estates on Antigua, were granted a lease on Barbuda by Charles II. Barbuda was the scene of a number of uprisings by slaves in the eighteenth century.

Argentina

Yes, they invaded the Falklands. Yes, we'd already invaded Argentina a long time before that. Equally unsuccessfully, though.

We're all aware of the failed Argentinian invasion of the Falklands in 1982. One thing most Brits are a lot less aware of is the failed British invasions of Buenos Aires in 1806 and 1807.

Argentinian waters saw a fair number of armed British ships between the sixteenth and eighteenth centuries, but it was in the nineteenth century that we took a really serious interest in the area.

We had long harboured ambitions in South America and since we were yet again fighting Spain, which then controlled the territory of present-day Argentina, Major General William Beresford, prompted by Admiral Sir Home Riggs Popham, decided that even though there were no official orders from the British government to do so, it would be a good idea to invade Buenos Aires. It wasn't a good idea. It was a terrible idea, in fact.

There had been a sort of concept in Britain that the locals might welcome getting rid of the Spanish, but it didn't entirely work out like that. We took Buenos Aires easily enough in June 1806, and some locals were pleased to see us, but quite a lot were not. One Santiago de Liniers helped organise a fight-back against us and raised militia forces, eventually leading to bitter fighting and Beresford's surrender in August. It was all highly embarrassing and more than a little humiliating. Our occupation of Buenos Aires had lasted forty-six days, even less than the Argentinian occupation of the Falklands.

In 1807 we were back, but things went even worse this time round. In July, Lieutenant-General John Whitelocke led our second attempt to take Buenos Aires. From the start our forces met stiff local resistance and, once again, a British commander was forced to sign another humiliating deal over Buenos Aires. When he got back to Britain, Whitelocke was court-martialed and dismissed from the service.

You'd think somehow after two such major disasters we might have left the area alone, but we were back in Argentinian waters later in the nineteenth century. We occupied an Argentinian island, Martín García, for a time and conducted the British and French Blockade of the Rio de la Plata, the British part in this lasting from 1845 to 1849. We don't seem to have achieved anything very much with that effort either.

Armenia

British troops were active in parts of current day Armenia in the chaotic era after the Russian Revolution and around the end of the First World War, and after that. We operated in the area of what is now the border between Turkey and Armenia, with a garrison at Kars just inside Turkey, but also with units active in Armenia in the area around what was then Alexandropol, now Gyumri. For instance, 27th Division's Southern Command area included Armenia's capital, Yerevan. We dived in with high hopes and then failed to solve loads of the major political and ethnic conflicts affecting the area at the time. The troops were eventually pulled out from the Caucasus when it was felt that the cost of maintaining them there was no longer justified by what they were achieving, and lots of people at home were sick of the venture anyway.

Australia

In the seventeenth century, the Dutch were the first Europeans to reach Australia and map it. A Brit named William Dampier landed here briefly in 1688 and again in 1699. Then along came Cook in 1770 and claimed a big chunk of the land for Britain. He was followed, in 1788, by Captain Arthur Phillip with the First Fleet and its contingent of convicts into Port Jackson to set up a settlement at Sydney Cove on 26 January. The colony of New South Wales was declared on 7 February. Another fleet of convicts arrived in 1790 and a third in 1791. By 1793, free, non-convict settlers were also arriving. Slowly we began to take control of the whole of Australia.

In 1803 a settlement was attempted on Tasmania, and in 1804 Hobart was founded.

The Swan River Colony, which was to become Western Australia, was declared in 1829. And in 1836 South Australia was declared. Victoria was established in 1851 and Queensland in 1859. The Northern Territory came into being in 1911.

There was some local resistance. For example, a man called Pemulwuy organised resistance to the settlers between about 1790 and 1802. In 1797 he led about 100 men against British troops at the Battle of Parramatta. He was killed in 1802. In 1824, with conflict breaking out between settlers who had crossed the Blue Mountains and the local Wiradjuri warriors, martial law was declared for a period of some months.

Between 1828 and 1830 there was resistance to the British on Tasmania.

In the 1830s, Yagan, a warrior of the Noongar people, was to engage in clashes with settlers in the area around Perth. After he was killed, his head was cut off and brought back to Britain. It was only returned to Australia in 1997.

Examples of resistance continued. The Kalkadoon people kept settlers out of Western Queensland for up to a decade until their defeat at Battle Mountain in 1884.

Australia became independent from Britain through a series of steps that gradually gave it more and more control over its affairs.

Austria

It's strange isn't it? Somehow, today we tend to think of Austria as almost not a military country, in the sense that we don't now particularly associate it with fighting wars (though according to the Afghanistan ISAF website at the time of writing it has three troops in ISAF). A bit like Switzerland, perhaps it's all those mountains and snow, and lederhosen (though, apparently, lederhosen aren't a big Swiss tradition). But, of course, Austria has a huge military history, a fair bit of it involving us.

In many ways, Austria is one of those countries that some Brits might think we've invaded more than we actually have. After all, it's a part of the world that was on the opposite side to us in both world wars. But in reality we also spent a lot of time fighting on the same side as the Austrians prior to the twentieth century. And it's quite a long way away from both Britain and from the sea.

In the First World War, in a little-known part of our war, we had divisions fighting the Austro-Hungarian army, but almost all the fighting was done on Italian soil. By the armistice, which in this region was on 4 November 1918, not 11 November, our 48th South Midland Division had pushed to a position 8 miles north-west of a place then in Austria, called Löweneck. But when borders changed after the First World War, the area went to Italy and its name today is Levico.

In the Second World War, once again our troops were mainly approaching Austria from Italy (the main push into Austria from the west being conducted by US troops). This time we arrived in Austria just about the time the war ended. The big British push into Austria began on 8 May 1945 with 6th Armoured Division leading and Klagenfurt a major objective.

Having said that, after 8 May our troops moved in force into Austria. A lot of people have heard of our post-war presence in Germany, but our occupation of Austria isn't so widely known. In July 1945, Austria was split into four zones, one each for us, the Americans, the French and the Soviets. We got Carinthia, East Tyrol and Styria. Vienna was similarly divided, plus the centre of the city was a separate zone under combined control. We had troops in Austria all the way through until 1955, enjoying the outstanding scenery. And perhaps, on occasion, the lederhosen.

Azerbaijan

Azerbaijan, found in the Caucasus with the Caspian Sea to the east, is one of those countries that is so far away from us, so far away from the open seas, and so far from what we tend to think of as our normal zones of influence that you may think we can't possibly have invaded it. But if you think that, you'd be wrong.

By mid-1918, after the Russian Revolution, the Caucasus was a surprisingly confusing place. We tend to think of control of oilfields as a modern strategic goal, but already by that time, control of Azerbaijan's oilfields was vitally important. A surprising number of players were competing for control of the oil, and for control of the Caucasus more widely. Obviously there were the locals and the Russians, but there was also, with the Ottoman Empire still in the First World War at this stage, the Ottoman Third Army trying to push up from the south. There was (bizarrely since you wouldn't expect Germans here, but then, to be fair, I suppose, equally you wouldn't expect Brits either) a German Expeditionary Force, independent of the Ottoman forces, that had come across the Black Sea from the Crimea, heading for the region after Georgia signed the Treaty of Poti with Germany. And there was us, with the imaginatively named Dunsterforce, commanded by one General Dunsterville (Dunsterforce does sound a little more crisp and dynamic than Dunstervilleforce, and imagine being an army clerk having to write Dunstervilleforce all the time). This included British and other Empire troops and some armoured cars, which had arrived in the area from Hamadan in what is now Iran.

Their original goal to counter German influence in the region turned into a mission to seize and defend the oilfields around Baku. After a few problems with Bolshevik troops, they made it across the Caspian to Baku, but their problems had only just started. Once in Baku, they were caught up in defending the city against an attacking army of Ottomans (and their allies in the Caucasus). In the ferocious Battle of Baku, lasting from August into September, Dunsterforce was eventually forced to withdraw from Baku in a dramatic night-time evacuation under fire. Probably spectacular to watch, but not much fun to be part of.

But we weren't gone for long. Elsewhere, the war was going very badly for the Ottomans, and by late 1918, with the Ottoman Empire defeated, it was the turn of Ottoman troops to pull out of Baku and for us to return. British troops under General Thomson arrived in the capital of Azerbaijan on 17 November 1918 and imposed martial law. Gradually we handed over control to an Azerbaijani government, and by August 1919 we were leaving Baku again.

Bahamas

Columbus was probably the first European to hit the Bahamas. From our point of view, things sort of started in 1629 when Charles I granted the islands to Robert Heath, Attorney-General of England at the time. It was a bit of a cheap grant in many ways, since Charles didn't actually control them and the man who was awarded the grant doesn't seem to have done anything with them either. So, not much of an invasion at that point.

Finally, in 1648, William Sayle seems to have turned up from Bermuda with some English Puritans to found a settlement called Eleuthera, Greek for 'free'. A settlement on New Providence followed and in 1670 Charles II granted the islands to the Duke of Albemarle and five others.

But it all became a bit of a mess with pirates and privateers running rampant and foreign powers joining in the chaos. In 1702–03, Nassau was briefly occupied by the French and Spanish.

The British crown took over control of the islands in 1717 and stamped out piracy, but our grip was still pretty tenuous at times. Well, in fact, more than tenuous, because we lost the islands occasionally and had to get them back. The Spanish attacked in 1720; in 1776 US marines occupied Nassau briefly; and in 1782 the Spanish turned up again and took control. At least this provided us with one really good story about invading the Bahamas.

The main character in the story is one Andrew Deveaux, who had an extraordinary career. He had been born in Beaufort, South Carolina. When the American Revolution came, he had originally joined the American rebels, but then had reverted to the loyalist side. He'd been given the rank of colonel by the British and raised a force of irregulars to fight for them. The traditional account is that when the Bahamas fell to the Spanish in 1783, he set off from St Augustine, Florida, with only seventy men to recapture the islands. He recruited another 170 men to his cause in the Bahamas themselves, and so with only 240 men, and even fewer guns, he faced a much larger Spanish occupation force, yet managed to persuade the Spanish commander Don Antonio Claraco Sauz to surrender.

The Bahamas became independent in 1971.

Bahrain

We have, of course, long had contact with the Gulf States, among them Bahrain.

In the early days, one of our main priorities was combating sea raiders in the area. So in 1820 the East India Company got the sheikhs of Bahrain to sign an anti-piracy treaty.

By 1861, we had also prevailed on Bahrain to sign a treaty which gave us control over its foreign affairs in return for protection.

But still we weren't always entirely happy with the way everything was going here, and in 1868, after a conflict between Bahrain and Qatar, the gunboats *Clyde* and *Huge Rose* of Her Majesty's Indian Navy destroyed the fort at al-Muharraq in Bahrain. In 1869, British gunboats were sailing into Bahrain to change rulers and put 21-year-old Sheikh Isa into power.

There were further treaties in the late nineteenth century between Britain and Bahrain. Bahrain became fully independent in 1971.

Bangladesh

Bangladesh consists of the eastern part of what used to be undivided Bengal. The western part is now in India and some of the key events in the history of Britain taking control of the territory that is today Bangladesh took place in modern day India.

As early as the late seventeenth century we were trying to take control in Bengal. But failing.

In 1620, the East India Company had a presence in Bengal, and in 1666 it set up a base in Dhaka. In 1682, William Hedges from the East India Company arrived in Bengal to talk to the Mughal governor there. Hedges was looking for trading privileges, but negotiations got a bit difficult and an English fleet arrived under Admiral Nicholson. What followed is sometimes called Child's War (not much to do with kids, more to do with Sir Josiah Child, head of the East India Company) or the Anglo-Mughal war. But Child's War wasn't child's play (see what I've done there?). It lasted from 1686 to 1690, during which we seized ships and bombarded towns. In the end, though, we lost and had to make concessions to the Mughal emperor, and pay compensation before we could re-establish commercial operations.

By the middle of the eighteenth century we were ready to have another go. In 1756 the new, young nawab of Bengal, Siraj ud Daulah, decided to exert control over the British base in Calcutta (Kolkata) in what is now West Bengal in India. With overwhelming forces he quickly captured it. In response, Colonel Clive and Admiral Watson were sent with the aim of re-establishing the British presence and getting reparation for its losses. After fighting outside Calcutta in January 1757, a peace deal was signed, and we turned our attention to the French, and not in a friendly way, attacking the town of Chandannagar, north of Calcutta. Chandannagar fell, but now Siraj ud Daulah started negotiations with the French, while we started secret negotiations with one Mir Jafar with the aim of replacing Siraj ud Daulah. Then Clive set off with a force to confront Siraj ud Daulah. The two armies met at the Battle of Plassey, or Palashi, in June 1757. Siraj ud Daulah had French help, but he lost. Clive then made Mir Jafar nawab, and when he got too close to the Dutch for our liking, we made Mir Qasim nawab instead.

Victory over Mir Qasim's army and other allied forces at the Battle of Buxar in 1765 gave the East India Company control over Bengal in many ways. In 1793 the company took control of judicial administration in the territory as well.

William Heath had attempted to take control of Chittagong for the East India Company as early as 1688. In 1766 the company finally took control of the city. We were also given control of areas around Chittagong in the east of what is now Bangladesh, and a period of prolonged fighting followed against the region's Chakma kings. The Chittagong Hill Tracts became an area where British control faced assorted challenges and was not always solid.

We left Bengal in 1947, when part of it became East Pakistan. The country became independent as Bangladesh in 1971.

Barbados

Barbados means 'the bearded ones', though nobody seems to know quite which bearded ones are being referred to, whether it was bearded locals, or the bearded fig tree that grows on the island, or something else. Bearded something anyway.

Our history of invading Barbados isn't a hugely complex and dramatic one. The first English ship arrived here in 1625 under one John Powell and about two years later his younger brother turned up and started a settlement. And from then on it was basically under English and then British control until independence in 1966.

In fact, the only time we invaded it after 1625 was when we invaded it against ourselves, if you see what I mean. It sort of got sucked into the heavily armed disagreement, or civil war, that we had at home, starting in 1642. In the period after the execution of Charles I in 1649, bucking the trend in England, Royalists took over control of the government of Barbados, with the exception of the governor who stayed loyal to Parliament. So in 1651 the English Commonwealth sent an invasion force under Sir George Ayscue, and after a bit of fighting the Royalists surrendered. Invasion completed and succeeded.

Belarus

Big country, but unhelpfully for us, from the invading point of view, it doesn't have a coastline and because of that, and assorted other quirks of history, we've not had that much to do with it militarily. If you know otherwise, let me know.

As far as I can work out, the closest we've got to invading Belarus is an assortment of English knights who led expeditions to fight alongside the Teutonic Knights in the fourteenth century. At the height of their power, the Teutonic Knights extended their control as far inland as Grodno in Belarus, so it's possible some of our lot may have made it that far as well. Certainly some were active in besieging Vilnius (see Lithuania), which isn't much more than 20 miles from the border with Belarus.

There were, however, in an interesting bit of history that deserves to be better known, a number of Scots playing a major role in Russian armies around the end of the seventeenth century and the beginning of the eighteenth century. About fifteen generals of Scottish origin were working with the Russians in this period and, generally speaking, the Scots seem to have played a more significant role than any other nation in Russian forces at this time. Some of them operated in what is now Belarus. Marshal Baron George Ogilvie, for instance, commanded an army in the Grodno region in this period. Grodno seems to have been relatively popular with armies.

Belgium

Belgium has famously only existed as a country since the nineteenth century, and still sometimes doesn't seem entirely sure where its future as a country lies. But there were armed Brits roaming on what is now its territory a lot earlier than that.

I think Belgium is a bit of a hidden gem. It's a place a lot of Brits seem to know very little about today, and yet it's just across the Channel and has some fabulous towns, cities, scenery, history and beer. Go see it. Our troops of the past certainly did, regularly. And while their visits did not always leave the towns, cities and scenery unscathed, they certainly contributed to the history and no doubt enjoyed the beer.

Often had rather friendly relations with the area, rather friendlier, for instance, than with their next-door neighbours in France.

So often, as with Portugal, we've been involved with the area, trying to help (at least some of) the locals rather than harm them. Not surprisingly, it's been us and them against the French. For example, the English were already fighting alongside Flemish troops against the French at the Battle of Bouvines (just on the French side of today's French/Belgian border) in 1214. Again in 1297, Edward I led a brief and not hugely successful campaign in Flanders against the French.

When the Hundred Years War broke out, England was yet again trying to help the Flemish against the French, and in 1340 Edward III turned up with a fleet and anchored at Blankenberge (now in Belgium), while his wife Philippa (this is Philippa of Hainault and therefore, in modern terms, basically Belgian herself) was safe in Bruges. He then smashed the French fleet at the Battle of Sluys (fought just on the Dutch side of what is now the Belgian/Dutch border, but don't worry we'll get to battles on Belgian territory very shortly). Their son, John of Gaunt, was not called that because he had a particularly gaunt look, but because he was actually born in Ghent in what is now Belgium. John of Gaunt is John of Ghent.

Later in the fourteenth century we invaded the area, again supporting the Flemish against the French and this time adding a religious element, siding with Pope Urban VI in Rome against anti-pope Clement VII in Avignon. This is what has become known as Despenser's Crusade. Sounds like something to do with pharmacists, but in fact it was in honour of Henry le Despenser, Bishop of Norwich, who was a major leading figure in the crusade. Actually, when we say 'in honour of', it's more like 'in dishonour of' because it was all a bit of a disaster. Or quite a lot of a disaster. The force set off from Sandwich and landed at Calais. Then it headed up the coast, took Gravelines and set off to besiege Ypres, a town many Brits were to fight in more recently, albeit to defend it instead of attacking it as Despenser's lot were. The siege was not a success and Despenser's Crusade fell apart. When it was all over Despenser, was put on trial.

The rise of the United Provinces (Netherlands) as a significant regional power had a major impact on the power politics of the area and in the late sixteenth century Brits were back. English troops repulsed the Duke of Parma's forces in fighting near Aarschot in what is now Belgium. And in 1580 English soldiers sacked Mechelen in what became known as the 'English Fury'. In fact, as it turned out, assorted armed Brits were to spend quite a lot of time wandering around what is now Belgium in the late sixteenth century and early seventeenth century. Horace Vere, for instance, could be found, along with Scottish and English troops, on the victorious side at the Battle of Nieuwpoort in 1600 and then in 1601 he was defending Ostende. Well, we've always loved the Channel ports.

By the middle of the seventeenth century we were back invading what is now Belgium yet again. This time English forces, for a change, were allied with the French and fighting the Spanish. But, not everything had changed. After victory at the Battle of the Dunes in 1658, they still ended up besieging Ypres.

Then at the end of the seventeenth century we were back roaming around what is now Belgium in the Nine Years War. This time we were fighting the French and allied with the Dutch. Despite our troops fighting bravely in the victory at the Battle of Walcourt in 1689, it wasn't an entirely successful venture, including defeat at the Battle of Leuze in 1691.

With a new century came a new war, the War of the Spanish Succession 1701–14, and this time we had a really thorough go at invading what is now Belgium. This is Marlborough's war. Early on he captured Liège. In 1706 he beat the French decisively at the Battle of Ramillies in Belgium and after that took Antwerp. On 11 July 1708, he crushed another French army, this time at the Battle of Oudenarde, again in Belgium. Ramillies and Oudenarde are two of those names that I remember clearly from school history, but I have to admit that until writing this book I didn't really have any concept of where they actually were. Oudenarde at least sounds Belgian or Dutch, but the name Ramillies doesn't particularly. The way it was pronounced at school sounded more like Rameses than anything, which didn't help in giving a sense of where it actually was. In case you're interested, Ramillies is near Namur and Oudenarde is sort of south of Ghent and west of Brussels.

With the War of the Austrian Succession we once again had troops fighting in Belgium. This time, sadly from our point of view, it wasn't such a string of victories. In fact, in 1745 the Duke of Cumberland suffered a serious defeat by the French at the Battle of Fontenoy in Belgium. Oh and they had already taken Ypres before that. And things didn't get much better as the war ground towards an unsuccessful end. British forces were on the losing side at the Battle of Rocoux near Liège in 1746 and again at the Battle of Lauffeld in 1747.

With the arrival of the French Revolutionary Wars and the Napoleonic Wars, we had troops on the ground here yet again. Against the French, obviously. In the 1790s, for instance, British troops were involved in heavy fighting in the Flanders region as part of an allied force trying to push into France. After early successes, things went into reverse and we found ourselves back fighting on Belgian soil. There were still some successes like the Battle of Willems in 1794, but Austrian support for the alliance wavered and the British and allied front in Flanders collapsed, with our troops retreating through the Netherlands, all the way back to be eventually evacuated from Bremen. That's a *long* retreat. In 1809 the Walcheren Expedition failed to take Antwerp. But who could forget the final, decisive victory at Waterloo in 1815? This, of course, was won not far from Brussels and, famously, the Duchess of Richmond's ball. This was held in Brussels on 15 June and was attended by numerous officers from our army, before being interrupted by news of the approach of Napoleon's army.

In 1830, after a revolt aimed at separation from the Netherlands, the sovereign state of Belgium was formed and we sort of gave it a king. We came up with Leopold of Saxe Coburg Gotha, uncle of Queen Victoria and widower of Princess Charlotte of Wales, only legitimate child of the Prince Regent, as a candidate for the throne. And he got the job.

The twentieth century saw many, many Brits fighting to help the people of Belgium. In 1914 we went to war to protect Belgium when Germany violated its neutrality and for four long, bitter years, British troops bravely fought on Belgian soil. The Belgian city of Ypres, with the Menin Gate commemorating men whose bodies were never identified, and the Belgian village of Passchendaele, have become synonymous with that struggle. The course of the First World War also saw courageous ventures into occupied Belgium, such as the raid on Zeebrugge on 23 April 1918, when the Royal Navy attempted to hinder German ships and submarines using the port by sinking old British ships in appropriate places. Our last soldier of the war to die was George Edwin Ellison from Leeds, serving in the 5th Royal Irish Lancers, who was killed about an hour-and-a-half before the armistice came into effect. He had fought near Mons in Belgium in 1914 and died near Mons in Belgium in 1918.

In 1940, during the Second World War, British forces fought in Belgium before being forced to withdraw by the German advance. In 1944, less then three months after D-Day, they were back. On 3 September we liberated Brussels, and on 4 September Antwerp.

Belize

I've long sort of vaguely wondered where the name Belize comes from. One explanation, which is so jolly that it ought to be true even if it's not, is that it derives from the Spanish pronunciation of the name of Peter Wallace, a Scottish buccaneer who, so the traditional story goes, used to operate in these parts.

Anyway, whatever the origin of the name it does seem to have been British buccaneers who were the first Brits to arrive in what is now Belize. They came in the early seventeenth century, looking for a base to carry on their buccaneering operations against Spanish shipping, but eventually found by the late seventeenth century that they could make a better and more secure living chopping down trees than chopping up sailors. They were called Baymen (seems reasonable since they were living on a bay).

The Spanish, viewing this area as very much their patch, were less than keen on the British log-choppers and there was plenty of tension and conflict, as well as some log chopping. Somehow the Baymen seemed to hang on in there or come back after the Spanish had withdrawn. By the 1763 Treaty of Paris, the Brits got the right to cut logwood even though the Spanish still had the right to sovereignty.

But the Spanish still didn't love the Baymen. In 1779, the Spanish captured St George's Caye and we didn't get back into the area until after the 1783 Treaty of Paris (another Treaty of Paris). Things came to a head again in 1798, when the Spanish invaded from Mexico.

A naval confrontation was to ensue and it's worth listing the names of our key ships: *Merlin* and *Mermaid*, *Towser* and *Tickler*, *Swinger* and *Teazer*. I particularly like the trio, *Tickler*, *Teazer* and *Swinger*. It sounds like some Georgian sex party.

The Spanish were approaching with significant forces and the Baymen decided to arm slaves to help fight the attackers. On 10 September the two forces clashed in the Battle of St George's Caye. It went on for two hours, and by the end of it the Spanish had had enough and retreated. The victory is still celebrated in Belize as an annual holiday. This was the final Spanish attempt to take control of the area.

In 1862 we formally declared it a Crown colony called British Honduras.

Relations with the neighbours haven't always been too friendly. In February 1948, there were fears of a Guatemalan invasion and a company from the Gloucestershire Regiment was rushed to the border. In 1958, the Hampshires intercepted a group from the Belize Liberation Army that had crossed the border. While in 1975 the Guatemalans moved troops to the border and we, of course, responded again.

Belize gained full independence in 1981.

Benin

Somewhat confusingly, the modern country of Benin has no connection to the impressive Benin bronzes that we seized from the Kingdom of Benin (located in present-day Nigeria), which we captured in 1897.

Modern-day Benin used to be known as Dahomey after the Kingdom of Dahomey. An interesting kingdom, it gained a reputation among European explorers as a kind of African Sparta, with a society that was in many ways geared to war. Boys were, for instance, often trained by older soldiers from a young age to be warriors, and there was also an elite female military unit.

Benin has only a comparatively short coastline, on which stands Ouidah, which was for a long time a major port for the slave trade. In the seventeenth century the English Fort William was built and there was a British presence in the fort up until 1812, which came under occasional attack from local forces.

Then when Britain had switched from being a slaving country to an anti-slaving country, the Royal Navy started running patrols off Ouidah trying to stop slaving vessels operating.

In the east, Benin borders on Nigeria. In the late nineteenth century, as the European powers carved up Africa, it took some time to work out which bits of the area the French would take control of, and which Britain would take. At one point, in 1894, one Frederick Lugard signed a treaty with the King of Nikki which theoretically gave us control over the foreign affairs of his kingdom. However, by the Anglo-French Convention of 1898, the town of Nikki fell under French control and today is part of Benin.

So armed Brits have operated on its soil and in its waters.

Bhutan

Bhutan isn't a country we hear much about in Britain, and some Brits might be tempted to think it's a kingdom of legend. But, in fact, it's perfectly real, lying up in the Himalayas sandwiched between India and China. Its capital is Thimpu.

Really, it's to our shame if we don't know much about it, because Brits were getting involved with Bhutan very early on. And in this context that 'involved' included 'invaded'. In fact, we first invaded Bhutan in the eighteenth century. Bhutan had been doing a bit of empire-building itself. Nothing on our scale clearly, but it had effectively taken control of Cooch Behar. However, in a battle for control of the Cooch Behar throne, the rival to the Bhutanese nominee decided his best bet was to apply for the support of an even bigger power than the Bhutanese – Britain. So in 1772 Captain Jones arrived in Cooch Behar, expelled the Bhutanese and pursued them into their own territory. Eventually a peace treaty was signed between Bhutan and the East India Company in 1774.

But the peace between us and Bhutan was not always a calm and easy one and in the middle of the nineteenth century we ended up invading Bhutan again. There was a border dispute over control of the Bengal Duars, so not unreasonably the war is sometimes known as the Duar War, or, if you like, the Bhutanese War. The issue was complicated by an internal conflict in Bhutan, which is worth mentioning here for the cast of characters. The secular head of Bhutan was called the Druk Desi. And in this conflict the Dzongpon of Punakha had established his own Druk Desi as rival to the established Druk Desi who was hoping for support from the Penlop of Paro. Don't worry, I expect a lot of British names sound exotic to the Bhutanese, but these Bhutanese names are impressive.

Most Brits have never ever heard of the war, and it wasn't exactly our finest hour. We were up against forces that consisted of assorted people carrying a variety of weapons from matchlocks to bows and arrows, and some of them wearing helmets and chain mail. They still managed to surprise us at Dewangiri (now known as Deothang) in Bhutan. But inevitably we won in the end and destroyed the fort at Dewangiri.

Finally, in 1910, we signed the Treaty of Punakha with the Bhutanese, which gave us control of Bhutan's foreign affairs. And that situation continued until we left India in 1947.

Bolivia

As far as I know, we've never invaded Bolivia, but according to one story, we came perilously close to it. I haven't been able to find the source of this story and it may just be one of those jolly fictions that crop up occasionally and are accepted as fact by some people. But if it isn't actually true, then it's such a fun story that it really should be.

According to the tale, in 1868 Bolivia's then president, General Mariano Melgarejo, invited a British diplomat to a reception honouring his new mistress. The diplomat, viewing such an event as unfitting to one of his status refused the invitation, only to find himself being tied facing backwards on top of a donkey and carried three times round La Paz's central square. Queen Victoria was, as one might expect, 'not amused'. In fact, she was so not amused that it had to be pointed out to her that sadly Bolivia was too far from the sea for British gunboats to be sent.

As with many other South American countries, volunteers from the British Isles did genuinely play a fascinating and little-known role in the liberation of Bolivia at the beginning of the nineteenth century. Irishman O'Connor, for instance, was a lieutenant in the Albion Regiment of British and Irish volunteers, and after years of fighting ended up as Minister of War in Bolivia. Colonel Sir Belford Hinton Wilson, who after some years at Sandhurst had joined Bolivar's forces in 1822, was even given the task of delivering Bolivia's new constitution, as penned by Bolivar, to the new country.

Bosnia and Herzegovina

This area during the Second World War saw some of the fiercest fighting between German forces, and their local allies and Yugoslav resistance forces. And Brits were part of it. Most famously, Fitzroy Maclean led a British liaison mission to Tito and spent time with him at assorted locations in Bosnia, including Drvar and Jajce. Maclean helped to establish and run the RAF's Balkan Air Force, which provided significant assistance to the partisans.

Recently we were back in Bosnia and Herzegovina, trying both to alleviate the suffering caused by the war there during the 1990s and, ultimately, to help bring it to an end.

British units played a major role in the initial UN operation in Bosnia. Much of their work included escorting aid and maintaining supply routes, but there were also occasions when the British units deployed open fire in pursuit of their mission. British soldiers died and British soldiers killed during the UN mission in Bosnia.

British units also formed part of the NATO forces in their operations during the Bosnian War. For instance, on 16 April 1994, a British Sea Harrier was shot down by Bosnian Serb forces over Gorazde while targeting a Bosnian Serb tank, and on 22 September 1994, two British Jaguar aircraft destroyed a Bosnian Serb tank in the Sarajevo area.

In 1995 both the RAF and British artillery on the ground in Bosnia assisted with Operation Deliberate Force against Bosnian Serb targets.

By the way, Herzegovina is the southern bit of Bosnia and Herzegovina.

Botswana

Not one of our more spectacular invasions.

In 1884, we were afraid that the Germans might expand their influence into Bechuanaland and link up with the Boers who were opposed to us. Consequently, we sent the Warren Expedition north to assert British control. Major General Charles Warren (later to head the London Metropolitan Police and be criticised for its failure to catch Jack the Ripper) marched north from Cape Town with a force of 4,000 British and local troops, plus the very first three observation balloons that the British Army had ever used in the field.

The Warren Expedition turned up and achieved its objective without firing a shot, though presumably not without sending up a balloon.

Botswana became independent on 30 September 1966.

Brazil

Since Brazil was a Portuguese colony and Portugal our long-time ally, we have tended to steer clear of invading it too much. At least we've invaded it less than many other places.

Some British expeditions did make it to Brazil in the early period. An expedition under William and Richard Hawkins, for example, explored the Brazilian coast in the 1580s.

In the early nineteenth century, the Royal Navy headed for Brazilian waters, but on this occasion on the rather friendlier mission of escorting the Portuguese royal family here, after they escaped from Napoleon's forces in Portugal itself.

However, things did become a little more tense at one point after Brazil became independent from Portugal. By this stage, despite Britain's earlier major involvement with it, we had abolished slavery and were taking some measures to see that it was abolished elsewhere. In 1826, we pressured Brazil into agreeing to outlaw the transatlantic slave trade. Instead, the trade increased. In 1845, we passed the Aberdeen Act, which allowed the Royal Navy to chase suspected slaving vessels right into Brazilian ports. This they did on a number of occasions until finally, in 1850, Brazil outlawed the importation of slaves into Brazil.

Our efforts were rather less successful the next time we clashed with Brazil. In 1862, when a bunch of British sailors were arrested, British warships were ordered to blockade Rio de Janeiro for six days. Brazil stood firm, and when we refused to apologise and pay compensation, they decided to break off diplomatic links and we decided to become a lot more conciliatory.

Brunei

Our early involvement with Brunei and the surrounding territory is intimately linked with the extraordinary story of the White Rajahs of Sarawak, which is also mentioned in the Malaysia section. Briefly, a man named James Brooke, born to British parents in India, became governor and eventually rajah of the territory of Sarawak, due to help he offered the Sultan of Brunei. Sarawak is now part of Malaysia, bordering Brunei, but previously was controlled by Brunei. It's a rather exotic story for someone with the not hugely exotic name of James Brooke, who is now buried in St Leonard's Church in Sheepstor on Dartmoor, which, while very pretty and with some views, is not the most hugely exotic of locations either.

In the 1840s, Captain Keppel of the Royal Navy with HMS *Dido* and Brooke with his ship the *Jolly Bachelor*, which sounds more like a pub, were involved in fighting pirates in the region. Brooke and the Royal Navy also teamed up to intervene in Brunei's internal politics in 1846. Two of Brooke's allies in Brunei had ended up dead because the sultan was suspicious of their closeness to the British, and to Brooke, and Brooke was determined this should not go unpunished. Admiral Cochrane turned up and the steamer *Phlegethon* was sent upriver to attack the forts there.

In 1888, Brunei became a British protectorate. Unfortunately we couldn't do much to protect it against the Japanese when they invaded in December 1941.

However, in 1945 we were back. Or to be more accurate, the Australians were, liberating the territory from the Japanese in the delightfully named Operation Oboe Six. Subsequently, an interim government was formed under the British Military Administration, which took control before civilian administration was re-established.

Then in December 1962 British forces were in action in Brunei again when the Brunei Rebellion broke out. Ghurkas were rushed by air from Singapore to assist the sultan, and with the help of subsequent British reinforcements and local support, the rebellion was eventually beaten. In one of the more dramatic moments of the action, marines of 42 Commando arrived in landing craft to raid Limbang and free prisoners taken by the rebels.

Brunei became independent from Britain on 1 January 1984.

Bulgaria

Bulgaria's a lovely country in many ways but, for whatever reason, it doesn't seem to have attracted much attention from British invaders. Not that I imagine it's disappointed about that fact.

There is a rather confusing reference in a text to the presence of 1,000 English knights at the Battle of Nicopolis in Bulgaria in 1396. Nothing much confusing about the battle itself. The Turks had been making their presence felt in Bulgaria and a crusade was announced. But when the crusaders finally arrived to besiege Turkish-occupied Nicopolis, a Turkish army arrived to fight them and the crusaders suffered a crushing defeat. The confusion lies in the fact that there doesn't seem to be much evidence in England of 1,000 English knights, plus all their assorted baggage and hangers-on heading east for sunny Bulgaria at the time. And frankly you'd think someone would have noticed, particularly if a large chunk of them had never returned from the battlefield.

We were definitely in Bulgaria during the Crimean War (1853–56) because on the way to the Crimea our forces popped into the country for about three months to help the Turks, who by this stage were our allies and controlled Bulgaria against the Russians, who had a Bulgarian Legion on their own side during the war. All very confusing but presumably our leaders at the time understood it. Varna became a major naval base, and even today you can see a memorial to all the Britons who died there of cholera during the Crimean War. So, not the happiest of times for our folks.

By the First World War, the Russians, who had been our enemies, were now our allies and the Turks, who had been our allies, were our enemies. Got that? The Bulgarians, at least, were still on the other side. Most emphatically. We fought a bitter campaign against them in northern Greece, of which more in the Greece section, but by 25 September 1918 the British 26th Division was poised to cross the Serbian-Bulgarian boundary. This they did and Bulgaria surrendered two days later. The 27th Division meanwhile advanced into Bulgaria as far as Krupnik and beyond.

After it was all over, we had troops stationed here for the occupation of Bulgaria for a bit.

Burkina Faso

It used to be called Upper Volta. Many Brits didn't know much about the country as Upper Volta, and changing the name to Burkina Faso hasn't altered things in that respect. It's a landlocked country in West Africa. If you're ever in a quiz where you're being asked about countries that border lots of other countries, Burkina Faso is worth a thought because it has six neighbouring countries: Mali, Niger, Benin, Togo, Ghana and Ivory Coast.

When the French occupied the area that is today Burkina Faso, they took control of territory previously controlled by a number of kingdoms with interesting histories and cultures that deserve to be much better known.

In 1898, we had the opportunity to come to the aid of the ruler of the Mossi kingdom, Wobogo. The French were attacking Ougadougou, and Wobogo requested our help. Wobogo was forced to retreat and launch a guerrilla war against the French, and we then sent an expedition under Colonel Northcott to take Ougadougou back. Our forces were only a short way from Ougadougou, however, when they received news that the British government had agreed with the French at the Conference of Paris that the area would be in the French sphere of influence. Northcott thereupon withdrew. Invasion over and Wobogo was abandoned by us.

Burma

Did you know that in the nineteenth century we fought not one, not two, but three wars against Burma? Yes, there was a First Burma War, a Second Burma War and a Third as well.

The first war was a bitter and bloody affair. The Burmese Empire had been expanding west into areas such as Assam, while British influence had been expanding eastwards from India. A clash between the two was perhaps inevitable.

Early in the war, Burmese forces advanced further, and even managed to capture Cox's Bazar (still the name of a town in Bangladesh) and cause some panic in Calcutta (Kolkata). We decided to strike back deep inside Burma, landing an expeditionary force at the port of Yangon (Rangoon) in 1824. Bitter fighting followed and cost both sides heavily, but with our forces slowly pushing the Burmese back, a month's armistice resulted in September 1825. We demanded assorted territorial concessions and, among other demands, a £2 million indemnity, in the days when £2 million was a huge amount of money. Eventually negotiations broke down and the Burmese tried one more military move. This was repelled with the aid of a flotilla of gunboats at the Battle of Prome. Finally, in 1826, the Burmese agreed to a peace deal, in which the indemnity had been reduced to £1 million, still a vast amount at the time.

In 1852 we were back. The Second Burma War started in extremely dubious circumstances, which have led to accusations that Brits deliberately provoked it. We occupied Rangoon on 12 April and Prome in October. Even though no peace treaty was ever officially signed, we effectively won and annexed a chunk of southern Burma. During the war, Rear Admiral Charles Austen died of cholera at Prome. He's a naval officer with an interesting career in his own right, but as the brother of author Jane Austen, it seems strange there hasn't been more focus on him. Perhaps a biopic starring Colin Firth is in order.

In 1885 we were involved in the Third Burma war. We had been getting nervous about increasing French influence in the country and there was also a legal dispute over the amount of teak being extracted. We gave the Burmese an ultimatum. They rejected it. We invaded. And invaded quickly. In November, in a lightning advance, under the spectacularly named Major General Harry North Dalrymple Prendergast, a force moved along the Irrawaddy River and captured the Burmese capital at Mandalay and the Burmese king. On 1 January 1886 we annexed Burma. With our annexation of the country a resistance war started that dragged on for years.

Then in January 1942, the Japanese invaded Burma. They rapidly took Rangoon and our forces had to make an exhausting and grim withdrawal through Burma up the Irrawaddy. Despite the desperation of the situation, Lieutenant General William Slim managed to hold the Burma Corps together and, by May 1942, the withdrawal had come to an end. In late 1942 we struck back, attacking into the Arakan. Sadly the attack didn't make much progress. But Orde Wingate's first Chindit campaign managed to hit back at the Japanese far behind the front line. In 1944, the Japanese launched a desperate assault into India to try to take Imphal and Kohima. After bitter fighting the Japanese were thrown back, and Slim's Fourteenth Army began to pursue them through Burma, while behind their lines the Japanese suffered continued Chindit attacks. Meanwhile, some Burmese nationalists who had previously sided with the Japanese in the hope of winning independence had already become disenchanted with them, and as the Japanese fell back, these Burmese switched sides. Aung San, the father of Aung San Suu Kyi, brought his Burmese National Army over to us. Rangoon fell in the interestingly named Operation Dracula in May 1945 after a Gurkha parachute battalion dropped on Elephant Point and the 26th Indian Infantry Division landed from ships.

After the Second World War, Aung San helped negotiate the shape of an independent Burma but was assassinated in 1947. Burma became independent in 1948.

Burundi

Burundi is one of those countries that may have to be classified as a bit of a near miss for us on the invasion front. In 1856, a British Indian Army officer, Hanning Speke, became part of a British expedition to explore the area of Central Africa where Burundi is situated, and he is sometimes quoted as being one of the first Europeans, or indeed, the first European to enter Burundi. But instead of becoming part of the British Empire as the European powers carved up Africa, the area eventually went to Germany.

In the First World War, the region became a battle zone between the European powers. A British naval force did see action on Lake Tanganikya and it may have operated in what are now Burundi's waters and against targets on the shore, but so far I don't have any evidence for that. Of course, if you do, please let me know.

British forces also advanced south from what is now Uganda to Bukoba (in Tanzania) on the shores of Lake Victoria, but it was the Belgians advancing from the then Belgian Congo to the west who occupied Burundi. After the war Belgium took control of the territories as a League of Nations Mandate. We got the Bugufi area, which according to some evidence was administered by the Germans as part of Urundi, the forerunner to Burundi, to incorporate into Tanganikya. However, since the area in question stayed part of Tanganikya and is now part of Tanzania, it doesn't really qualify as an invasion of Burundi.

2

CAMBODIA TO DOMINICAN REPUBLIC

Cambodia

I grew up in the 1970s seeing images of death and destruction in Cambodia on TV.

When we think of violence and Cambodia, we tend to think of the Khmer Rouge and the horrors of their period in power. And many people will know of America's war efforts here prior to that period, but it's not a place many associate with the British Army. Yet we have been here.

During the Second World War, a Vichy French administration ran the country until March 1945, when the Japanese ended French control and interned many of the members of the French administration. In August, Japan surrendered, and in October 1945 our Lieutenant Colonel E.D. Murray moved into Phnom Penh with a detachment of Gurkhas to supervise the surrender and disarming of the Japanese troops.

In November 1945, our troops were involved in an operation with the cooperation of surrendered Japanese troops to take much-needed food supplies from Phnom Penh to Saigon. And by 25 November, the security situation was sufficiently under control for Murray to start formal surrender procedures.

The French were keen to return to Cambodia, and we assisted them. Shortly after our forces arrived in Cambodia, the French resumed control, though not for long. The fact is that, as we see later, particularly in the case of Vietnam, our occupation of this region did play a significant role in its dramatic history.

Cameroon

The country lies on the west coast of Africa, east of Nigeria. As with many other African countries, Britain took an early interest in this one because it wanted slaves it could transport across the Atlantic. And, again, as with a lot of other African countries, once we had turned against the slave trade we took an interest in suppressing it here, attempting to enforce a number of slavery abolition treaties.

However, it was the Germans who took over Cameroon, establishing their rule here in 1884. They weren't to control it for long, though.

In 1914 we were at war with Germany and Cameroon was an early target for us, and we probably thought a pretty easy one. It wasn't that easy. Things didn't start well from our point of view. Three columns sent into Cameroon all ran into trouble due to difficult terrain and German ambushes. But the French and Belgians were also advancing from other directions. With British and French ships shelling targets ashore, Douala fell on 27 September 1914. Garoua fell to our forces in June 1915. But this, a fiercely fought and little-known war, did not finally end until 1916. After the First World War, Cameroon became a League of Nations Mandate territory and was split into a British-controlled part and a French-controlled part.

We sort of almost helped to invade Cameroon again during the Second World War. On 27 August 1940, the Free French emissaries LeClerc and Boislambert set off from the British Cameroons to the French Cameroons by canoe to take control of the territory. And after the disastrous episode of Dakar (see Senegal), in 1940, the British and Free French flotilla headed south to Cameroon instead. But when it got to the Wouri River in Cameroon, our ships were called elsewhere, and so it was without us that De Gaulle and the rest of his Free French contingent landed in Douala to popular acclaim on 8 October. It was a huge step on De Gaulle's road to building up the Free French. A huge step he ultimately took without us.

In 1960, the French part of Cameroon became independent and in 1961 the UN organised a plebiscite in the British-controlled part. Under this plebiscite the northern part of the territory we controlled opted to become part of Nigeria, while the southern part opted to become part of Cameroon.

Canada

Bearing in mind the significant numbers of French speakers in Canada today, it won't come as a surprise that much of Canada's history has involved a competition for power between us and the French.

Having said that, the first Europeans who reached what is now Canada were probably Vikings. Some claim that Irish Saint Brendan, Welsh Prince Madoc and Scottish Prince Henry Sinclair may also have visited. And the Portuguese definitely had a go at it as well. Labrador, for instance, is named after a Portuguese explorer Lavrador, and assorted Portuguese turned up in the area in the early sixteenth century, either claiming bits of it or just going fishing for cod. Would a Portuguese Canada be a very different place? Probably, but we'll never know. Perhaps, being used to the Algarve and all that, they just found Canada's climate in winter a bit too challenging. Anyway, for whatever reason, they subsequently focused their attention elsewhere.

Instead, it was the French who started taking a serious (and from our point of view unwelcome) interest in the area. In 1534, Cartier turned up and claimed a chunk for France, and by 1608 Champlain was founding Quebec City.

And we were keen on the area, too. After all, we're not used to Algarve-style weather in this country. John Cabot had already visited Newfoundland at the end of the fifteenth century, and in 1583 Sir Humphrey Gilbert occupied a part of Newfoundland (which curiously enough was 'Land Newly Found by Europeans', although it had been found a long time beforehand by both the locals and the Vikings) and established St John's. By 1610, Henry Hudson was lurking in Hudson's Bay. It's good that he's remembered through the bay because his immediate future after 1610 wasn't a particularly bright one. In fact it was pretty grim. Well, very grim. In 1611, his crew mutinied and dumped him and a few others in a small boat never to be seen again. In the 1620s, the Scots tried to settle in Nova Scotia (New Scotland), but found the French (and the locals) weren't too keen on the idea. Then in 1670 the Hudson Bay Company was founded.

There was a lot of fighting against both French and locals ahead before we could take control of the whole of Canada. Already in the mid-seventeenth century the Beaver Wars erupted in parts of what is now the USA and Canada. These wars in some sense sound amusing, but in fact they were a bloody conflict between the Iroquois Confederation, backed by us, and the Algonquin, backed by the French, for control of the fur trade. And then there were numerous wars with us and our local allies fighting the French and their local allies, some of which were part of wider wars with different names and some of which have different names even in North America. It can be quite confusing.

Thus, the first war from 1689 to 1697, which we'll call King William's War, has also been called St Castin's War and the Second Indian War, and it happens to also be the North American section of the Nine Years' War which is also known as the War of the League of Augsburg or the War of the Grand Alliance. Confused? You should be. Anyway, King William's War was a sort of draw, in which, after assorted fighting, everyone pretty much ended up back where they began.

Queen Anne's War ran from 1702 to 1713. When it was over, the French accepted our claims to the areas of Hudson's Bay, Acadia and Newfoundland (but not Cape Breton) at the Treaty of Utrecht.

The next war is Father Rale's War (also known as Dummer's War, Lovewell's War and Gray Lock's War – always nice to have a choice). Father Rale was a missionary who was connected with the start of the war, and in it we faced locals rather than the French. We sort of won on the mainland, but weren't so successful in Nova Scotia and were forced to make concessions to the Mi'kmaq.

Then there was King George's War from 1744 to 1748. In 1745, after a six-week siege, we took Louisbourg (on Cape Breton Island, Nova Scotia) only to hand it back at the end of the war in return for Madras in India, a global swap that, understandably, didn't go down too well with the local New Englanders who had fought to capture it.

Anyway, the war didn't really end in 1748 because in some sense it dragged on into Father le Loutre's War of 1749–55. This was us against the Mi'kmaq and the Wabanaki Confederacy, who had French support. Our founding of Halifax sort of started the war and it ended with our victory at the Battle of Fort Beausejour.

But just as King George's War led into Father le Loutre's War, so that war led into the French and Indian War of 1754–63. In 1755 we started expelling the French-speaking Acadians and continued doing so after the siege of Louisbourg in 1758. By 1760, following assorted battles, including the Battle of the Plains of Abraham and the Battle of the Thousand Islands, we had taken control of Quebec and Montreal. After the treaty that ended the war, all France had left in what is now Canada were the small islands of St Pierre and Miquelon.

Across on the other side of the land, it was us against the Spanish, rather then the French. The Spanish had taken an early interest in Canada's Pacific coast, but we soon started competing with them and we almost went to war with Spain over our respective interests in the area during the Nootka Crisis in the late eighteenth century. Eventually it was, yet again, us that became the dominant European power in the area.

The imposition of our control over the central parts of Canada did not come without local resistance, like the Red River Rebellion of 1869 and the North-West Rebellion of 1885.

Canada became independent from Britain through a series of steps that gradually gave it more and more control over its affairs.

Cape Verde

The Cape Verde Republic has ten islands nestling in the Atlantic, off the west coast of Africa. Not everybody in Britain knows where they are. Unfortunately for the locals, Francis Drake did, and he attacked the then capital of Cape Verde, Ribeira Grande (now Cidade Velha) in 1585. Drake's men stayed in the town for a couple of weeks. Finally, one of his men was killed and he set light to the town as a reprisal. At least he spared the hospital. The fort in the town was built in 1590, no doubt because of Drake's efforts.

In 1781, we fought a fairly inconclusive sea battle against the French in the roadstead of Porto Praya in the Cape Verde Islands.

Darwin was a rather more peaceful British visitor in 1832.

Central African Republic

The Central African Republic is, not surprisingly, pretty centrally placed in Africa. As such, it somewhat fulfils the role that Mongolia plays in Asia, that Bolivia plays in South America, and Hungary in

Europe, in terms of our armed globe-trotting. It's just too far away from the sea to have received our attention.

Nevertheless, we have operated on its borders, for example in the Bahr el Ghazal region of South Sudan to its east, which we controlled for a long time, so in the fluid state of affairs in the late nineteenth and early twentieth century it's certainly possible our troops crossed the present border at some stage. There is some evidence that in the early twentieth century, British troops were asked to assist the French against local rebels that were active in what is now the Central African Republic.

Chad

A lot of Brits would probably struggle to say exactly where Chad is, so it's perhaps no surprise that it's one of those countries we haven't had a lot to do with on the invading front. Having said that, Chad does play an interesting and, at one point, vital role in British military history.

In the 1820s, a small British expedition reached Lake Chad, the first Europeans to reach it, and elements of the expedition seem to have ventured into what is now Chad.

In the nineteenth-century imperial carve-up of Africa, however, Chad went to France. The border was undefined for a while, so again it's possible British troops may have been on the other side of it at some stage. You will probably have heard of Darfur, now sandwiched between Chad to the west and the rest of Sudan to the east (South Sudan), well it was Britain that first brought that troubled region to the notice of the Western world. Up until the First World War, the region had been mainly independent, but by 1916, as we fought the Turks, we were afraid that the ruler of Darfur might side with the Ottomans, who were looking for Muslim allies, against us. Consequently, we started by arming Arab tribes, who promptly used their weapons to advance across Darfur and fight tribes inside Chad. We then sent a British and Egyptian invasion force into Darfur to occupy the region.

In the Second World War, Chad from the start sided with the Free French against Vichy in our conflict with Vichy, so we didn't get an opportunity to invade it then. Instead, it was to become a vital part of our war against the Axis powers in North Africa.

For instance, early in the war the Long Range Desert Group used Chad as a base to launch attacks, with the Free French, against Italian garrisons across the border in southern Libya. On one occasion they attacked the Italian garrison at Murzuq and destroyed the airfield there, before heading for Zouar in French-controlled Chad.

Of rather more overall strategic importance, though, was something called the Takoradi Route, or more officially, the West African Reinforcement Route, because of which Chad became vital to British airpower in North Africa and the Middle East, and was consequently vital to victory both in the area and in the Second World War itself. It's one of the Second World War's great but little-known stories.

Early in the war, with most of Europe and North Africa in German, Italian or Vichy French hands, there was no safe way to get planes to our forces in the Middle East and North Africa, except by hugely lengthy sea voyages. So, planes were shipped from Britain in kit form and reassembled at Takoradi in Ghana. They were then flown via a series of landing strips across Africa to Khartoum. And one of the stops on the way was at Fort Lamy (now N'Djamena, the capital) in, you guessed it, Chad.

Chile

Chile is an enormously long, thin country. It has a coastline that stretches all the way from the bottom of South America, where it can be very chilly indeed, and north to Peru

With such a long coastline and with Chile long a part of the Spanish Empire, it was hardly likely to escape attacks by us, and it didn't.

Pretty much as soon as we made it round Cape Horn, we had our eyes set on the Chilean coast and not in a friendly way.

Francis Drake dropped in to sack Valparaiso on 5 December 1578 and capture a ship laden with gold and wine, which must have been handy. Perhaps even handier, he also got hold of the ship's pilot who happened to have a map of the coast. Then, in the 1590s, Richard Hawkins popped in for a spot of looting and plundering. And George Anson, on his amazing round-the-world mission (see Peru), was to cruise along the Chilean coast in the eighteenth century.

In 1814, we fought the Battle of Valparaiso, but not, interestingly, against the Spanish or Chileans. No, instead it was against the Americans. With the War of 1812 still blazing (since confusingly it wasn't just a War of 1812, but also a War of 1813, 1814 and 1815) on land far to the north, the frigate USS *Essex* had headed south to raid British whaling fleets. The frigate HMS *Phoebe* and the sloop HMS *Cherub* were dispatched to find the Americans and finally cornered them in Valparaiso. Eventually, the USS *Essex* and the sloop USS *Essex Junior* were brought to battle and the US ships were captured.

In 1810, a national junta had proclaimed Chile an independent state within the Spanish monarchy. By 1818, it was proclaimed an independent republic and by December of that year, a British veteran of the Napeolonic wars, Thomas Cochrane, was in command of the newly created Chilean navy and hiring large numbers of British sailors and organising it along British lines. He led this navy in the dramatic capture of the powerfully fortified Chilean city of Valdivia (from the Spanish) in 1820.

Soon after Chilean independence, instead of invading Valparaiso, we took to having a base here. It's a fascinating but comparatively little-known fact about the Royal Navy that from about 1826 to 1837 its South America Station, and from 1837 to 1865 its Pacific Station, had their headquarters at Valparaiso, the place Drake had raided all those years before. HMS *Beagle* dropped in here in 1834 on its second voyage. In 1854, a number of ships, including HMS *President*, HMS *Amphitrite*, HMS *Pique*, HMS *Trincomalee* (now located at Hartlepool) and HMS *Virago* set sail from here to attack Petropavlovsk in Kamchatka during the Crimean War (see Russia).

Today, a large and impressive arch, the Arco Británico, in Valparaiso, commemorates people like Cochrane who fought on behalf of Chile.

China

People who grew up during the Cold War, when the threat of nuclear war seemed so very real, might be tempted to think that we have never invaded China, simply because during the Cold War such an act would have been basically asking to be nuked. But, of course, we have invaded China on a number of occasions, as many Chinese are very well aware.

Already by 1637 we were invading China. In that year, four heavily armed ships sent by Sir William Courteen turned up in Macao and proceeded to capture one of the Bogue forts, annoying quite a few people before departing again.

It wasn't the best of starts to our relations with China, but there was worse, much worse, to come.

By 1711, British merchants were being given permission to enter Guangzhou to buy tea. Nothing wrong with that, except that eventually we started dealing in much less pleasant commodities, in particular opium. We began to send large quantities of opium to China from India. The Chinese government tried to put a stop to this with assorted measures. However, some local British authorities saw these measures as an unacceptable infringement on the rights of British merchants and the First Opium War broke out. British and Chinese warships clashed and in 1840 an expeditionary force landed in China. We fought the Battle of Amoy, took the Bogue forts at the mouth of the Pearl River, occupied Shanghai and in the last big battle of the war took what is now Zhenjiang in July 1842. This was not our finest hour, but it's worth pointing out that, even at the time, some Brits knew that. Gladstone, for instance, loudly denounced the war and the trade it was protecting.

After the war ended, our winnings from the Chinese included a lot of money, Hong Kong Island and the opening up of assorted trade ports, such as Shanghai.

The peace wasn't to last. By 1856 we were attacking China again. This was the Second Opium War, also known as the Arrow War, because of a dispute over a ship called the *Arrow*. Soon the French joined in on our side, and the Americans and Russians, keen to get involved in China too, gave us support. In June 1859 the Treaties of Tientsin gave the four powers pretty much what they wanted. However, in the wake of this treaty, the Chinese emperor decided to take a tougher line and when, in June 1859, a British military expedition tried to escort British and French envoys to Beijing, fighting broke out again. The result was that in 1860 a large British and French force headed for Beijing. The Chinese defenders were decisively defeated at the Battle of Palikao in September, and in October we entered Beijing and burned the Summer Palace. From the negotiations that ended the war we got even more from the Chinese, including Kowloon.

Relations continued to be tense. For instance, in 1868 the Yangzhou riot prompted the British consul in Shanghai to sail up the Yangtze to Nanjing with Royal Marines in a show of force.

In 1898 we considerably expanded the territory we controlled in China. We leased the New Territories around Hong Kong for ninety-nine years, and we also picked up another bit of territory that few people are aware of today, Weihai, which was far up the Chinese coast towards the Korean Peninsula. We held that until 1930.

In 1899, things once again started getting very tense. This was the Boxer Uprising, and by the summer of 1900 a bunch of foreigners, including diplomats, civilians and soldiers, were under siege in the Legation Quarter in Beijing. The siege lasted fifty-five days. An international relief force under our Vice Admiral Edward Seymour was stopped and surrounded. But a second international force under our Lieutenant-General Alfred Gaselee finally made it through, defeated the Chinese forces opposing them and captured Beijing. The peace treaty imposed heavy penalties on the Chinese.

In 1904, fearful of spreading Russian influence, we invaded Tibet. We had many more lethal weapons than the Tibetans, and we killed a large number of them.

In the years between the First and Second World Wars, British forces were involved in yet another series of incidents in China. For example, in 1926 there was the Battle of Wanhsien involving HMS *Cockchafer* and HMS *Widgeon*, and in 1927 we sent significant troops to Shanghai to protect the international settlement there.

With the arrival of the Second World War, we found ourselves fighting on the same side as the Chinese. After that, there were to be yet more difficulties in the relationship, but our days of invading China were finally over.

Colombia

Colombia has a lengthy coastline, is handy for the Caribbean, and has been controlled for quite long periods by Spain, so, as you would expect, it has received quite a few unfriendly visits from us.

As often in this part of the world, privateers, pirates and raiders led the way. In 1568 Sir John Hawkins allegedly had a cunning idea to take Cartagena, a port built by the Spanish on the Colombian coast, by persuading the governor to open up a foreign fair in the city, with Hawkins then planning to sack the city afterwards. The plan failed, and so did Hawkins' subsequent attack on the town.

In 1586 the English returned. This time it was Sir Francis Drake leading the attack, and this time Cartagena wasn't so lucky. The attack caused considerable damage and the Spanish had to pay Drake an enormous ransom to get their town back.

Then in the early seventeenth century we even had our own colony on what is now Colombian territory. From 1631 to 1641, the Providence Island Company ran a settlement on, you guessed it, Providence Island, now called Providencia or Old Providence. John Pym, later to find fame in the English Civil War, was its treasurer and, in fact, the company was to help bring together a number of people who would be leading figures on the Parliamentary side in the conflict of the 1640s. Things went downhill for the Providence Island Company in 1641, though, when a Spanish fleet overran it. And by that stage, people in England were slightly distracted by other issues, such as looming civil war and slaughter.

And as so often where privateers, pirates and raiders first went, the British Navy followed. Not always terribly successfully, of course. For instance, we found ourselves fighting the French off Cartagena in the so-called Action of August 1702, which took place, you won't be surprised to know, in August 1702. The British commander, Vice Admiral Benbow, was wounded and eventually died from his wounds, but not before he had ordered the court-martialing of some captains on a variety of charges, with two of them eventually being shot for cowardice.

And we didn't have a lot more luck in 1741. Admiral Edward Vernon mounted a major invasion, attempting to take Cartagena. Vernon had 186 ships, and from Britain and America 23,600 men, 12,000 of them infantry. Somewhere in there was George Washington's brother, Lawrence Washington. But after weeks of heavy fighting and losing men both to the defenders and disease, Vernon was forced to abandon the siege.

In the nineteenth century, we probably made our most significant military effort in Colombia. This, however, was unofficial or semi-official rather than official. With the battle under way to free South America from Spain, significant numbers of Britons went to the continent to fight in the liberation wars. Many of these were experienced veterans of the Napoleonic Wars and the British government gave tacit support to the effort. Eventually, most Brits fighting for Simon Bolivar against the Spanish were combined into a brigade called the British Legions. At the Battle of Boyaca in 1819, which led to the liberation of Colombia, they carried banners featuring the British flag, and Bolivar credited them with playing a significant role in the eventual victory in Colombia.

Comoros Islands

The Comoros are an archipelago lying between north-eastern Mozambique and north-western Madagascar. They have never been a British colony, but have had armed Brits set foot on them.

One of the more unusual British visitors was one William Kidd. Now you may know Kidd as a pirate, and indeed he was hanged as a pirate. In fact, the rope having broken the first time round, he was hanged twice as a pirate. Not something many people can, or indeed, would wish to claim.

However, when he landed on the Comoros in 1697, he was on a fairly official mission, ironically enough to capture pirates. With the backing of a number of powerful figures, including the First Lord of the Admiralty, Kidd had set off from London in 1696 in the appropriately named *Adventure Galley*. After assorted adventures, he ended up in New York to recruit more crew, and then returned across the Atlantic and rounded the Cape of Good Hope.

In early 1697 he had made it to Mohéli in the Comoros. Not the happiest of times for him or his crew, because fifty of his men got sick and died in just a week. And things didn't get too much better for Kidd on the pirate-hunting front. Instead, he turned to apprehending non-pirate ships and eventually reached the gallows. Twice.

In the nineteenth century we posted a consul to Anjouan and the Royal Navy used coaling facilities at Pomony. It was, however, the French who became the dominant European power in the Comoros. This meant that when the islands sided with Vichy in the Second

World War, we got a chance to officially invade them. In 1942 we sent troops to seize the Comoros, which they did successfully.

Congo, Democratic Republic of the

The area around the Congo River was strongly connected to slaving and, as elswhere after we had changed from a nation strongly connected with slaving to one opposing it, the anti-slaving patrols of our navy's West Africa squadron carried out a number of operations in the vicinity of the Congo in the first half of the nineteenth century.

In 1875 we dispatched two Royal Navy expeditions aimed at tackling Congo pirates. And in December 1875, Commander Hewett and three gunboats made it 73 miles inland from the mouth of the Congo River as far as the port of Boma.

The same year we also came close to having a Congo empire of our own, but passed up the opportunity. A certain Lieutenant Cameron had been assiduously following in the footsteps of the explorer David Livingstone and in the process he had also been just as assiduously signing treaties along the way with assorted local chiefs, so much so that by 1875 he could proudly declare that the lands of the Congo Basin were now British. Much to Cameron's chagrin, however, our government decided that they weren't British, and that it wasn't an area the government would be choosing to focus on. So the explorer Henry Morton Stanley, who had also failed to interest us in the area, helped the Belgians take it over instead.

In 1887, however, Stanley and assorted Brits formed part of the Emin Pasha Relief Expedition which came up the Congo and through what is now Kinshasa on its way to what is now South Sudan. During the process, Stanley attacked the village at Yambuya in what is now the Democratic Republic of the Congo, and took it over as a base.

In the First World War, although we weren't invading the then Belgian Congo (since the Belgians were our allies it would have been both impolite and pointless), the Royal Navy did find itself having to trek through large parts of it to get the gunboats HMS *Mimi* and HMS *Toutou* onto Lake Tanganyika to face German ships there. They went as far as they could on the railway from South Africa and disembarked on 6 August 1915. It then took them until 26 October to reach the lake.

Congo, Republic of the

The Republic of the Congo is not, confusingly to some, the same place as the Democratic Republic of the Congo. You could sort of call the Democratic Republic 'South Congo', and the Republic 'North Congo', and that might make it easier to understand because the Republic is a bit more north and the Democratic Republic is a bit more south. Both territories are next to the Congo River and while the Belgians used to control what became the Democratic Republic of the Congo, the French used to control this bit.

As we have already noted, the anti-slaving patrols of our navy's West Africa squadron spent a fair amount of time focusing on the Congo area, and also operated along the coast of what is now the Republic of Congo.

The area was controlled by France from the late nineteenth century through much of the twentieth century, but it was never Vichy-controlled, so we didn't invade it.

We did have about 350 British soldiers stationed in Brazzaville in May 1997, but not as any kind of force invading the Republic of Congo. They were there to get Commonwealth and European citizens out of Kinshasa, capital of the neighbouring country of Zaire as it then was, or the Democratic Republic of Congo as it now is, if a crisis there worsened.

Costa Rica

Costa Rica lies north of Panama and south of Nicaragua. When part of the Spanish Empire, it seems to have received a lot less attention from us than other parts of Spain's American Empire. Not, I expect, that the locals were disappointed about that.

Nevertheless, armed Brits have spent time in and around it. Sir Francis Drake sailed the waters off Costa Rica's Pacific coast in the late sixteenth century. His ship, the *Golden Hind*, was beached for a week at Cano Island and the nearby Drake Bay is, not surprisingly, named after him. Assorted privateers and pirates from Britain spent time in the area doing what pirates do. George Shelvocke, for instance, dropped in on Cano Island in 1721.

We've also seen action on Costa Rica's Caribbean Coast. In 1747, for instance, a force of English baymen and locals from the Mosquito Coast attacked and destroyed Fort San Fernando in the Matina area of Costa Rica.

Croatia

As you lie in the heat of the summer sunshine, gazing out at the turquoise Adriatic Sea, the UK seems such a long way away and it is hard to imagine that British armed forces could ever have made part of Croatia their home. We're used to the idea of the Venetians running up and down the coast building in that amazing golden local stone, but if we associate the country with Britons and war at all, we tend to think of blue berets and the recent break up of Yugoslavia. There were indeed British forces in Croatia at that time, including, for instance, a unit based at Divulje airbase at Split, whose hospitality I enjoyed on at least one occasion.

In fact, Britain has a much longer military association with Croatia and, improbable though it sounds, there is a small bit of Croatia that has been, at least for a while, British.

As early as the fourth century, Magnus Maximus, who was later to enter Welsh legend as Macsen Wledig, led an army from Britain into mainland Europe to seize the imperial throne. And he specifically recruited more Brits for an attempted invasion of Italy. But the forces of Theodosius advancing from the east won a significant victory over forces from the army of Maximus at Siscia, present-day Sisak in Croatia, and Magnus Maximus himself was captured and killed at Aquileia in northern Italy shortly afterwards.

Many British holidaymakers know the beautiful Croatian islands, and will have their favourite spot. Vis lies one of the furthest from the Croatian mainland, and it is perhaps for this reason that on two occasions in our history we have chosen to make it a British base.

During the Napoleonic Wars, the Adriatic was a vital strategic area both commercially, because of the trade routes that ran through it, and strategically, because of its location on the southern flank of Napoleon's extending power base. It was too tempting a target for the Royal Navy. In 1807 we seized control of the 14-mile-long island of Vis, or Lissa as it was then known, and built a naval base at Port St George.

Using Vis as a base we then proceeded to raid French positions and allies in and around the Adriatic, occupying a few that took our fancy, such as the Ionian Islands (see Greece). Unsurprisingly, the French found this rather irksome and, in March 1811, a leading French naval commander, Rear Admiral Bernard Dubourdieu, led a sizeable task force of six frigates, plus other ships and hundreds of soldiers, towards Lissa with the intention of ending Britain's stay on the island. Perhaps unwisely, Dubourdieu decided personally to lead a boarding attempt on the British commander's ship HMS *Amphion*. The British then launched a load of musket balls at point blank range at the French, which killed Dubourdieu and many of his officers, rather weighting the odds against the French. The result of the battle was a decisive victory for Britain, leaving us free to roam up and down the Adriatic at will for the rest of the war, working with our Austrian allies to destroy French influence in the area. In May 1811, *Alceste* and *Belle Poule* chased a French brig into Porec harbour and landed men and guns on a nearby island to fire on and sink the brig. In August 1813, landing parties from HMS *Eagle* and HMS *Bacchante* attacked Rovinj and captured or destroyed twenty-one vessels there. And in 1814, we forced the surrender of lots of prime real estate along the Adriatic coast at Zadar, Kotor (see Montenegro) and even Dubrovnik, something to think about if you ever wander through Dubrovnik's gorgeous streets today.

This was not to be our last stay on Vis. The nineteenth century turned into the twentieth century, and another little corporal set off on his own European tour. In 1941, Hitler's blitzkrieg smashed its way through Yugoslavia, of which Croatia was then a part. It was the beginning of our return to Vis, in what was to become one of the most interesting, but least known aspects of our Second World War effort. We've all heard about the invasions of France and Sicily, but who knows about our landing in Croatia?

Up until 1943, the Italians had been the occupying power. When Italy dropped out of the war, Tito's partisans took over a number of the Croatian islands and, to prevent the Germans moving in, we decided to base forces again on our old home, Vis. This time round our forces consisted of a couple of commando units, the Highland Light Infantry and some other troops. Together, they were rather grandly known as Land Forces Adriatic. There were also the motor gunboats of the 61 Motor Gun Boat (MGB) Flotilla, and Allied planes flying off an airstrip carved out of the vine-covered countryside.

The base was the same as in the Napoleonic Wars and, in many ways the mission was similar. The gunboats spent much of their time attacking and sometimes just seizing supply ships. The Royal Navy also transported commandos and partisans in assorted raids on targets up and down the coast that many Britons have more recently visited on holiday. Operation Detained targeted Solta; Operation Endowment went to Hvar; Operation Farrier attacked Mljet; and the delightfully named Operation Flounced was aimed at Brac. Several more ambitious plans for attacks in the Adriatic area were formulated and then shelved as the focus of the war shifted elsewhere; nevertheless, at a crucial period of the war, British forces on Vis had distracted the enemy, made him feel unsafe in what was then his own backyard and ultimately played a key role in facilitating the final partisan victory in Yugoslavia.

It's all well worth thinking about, if you ever get to wander today though the vineyards, pine trees and citrus orchards of Vis.

One final slightly random effect of the Second World War was that we ended up occupying the beautiful Croatian city of Pula, with its lovely stone buildings and Roman amphitheatre, for a couple of years after the war, as part of the process to settle border disputes with Italy. A British battalion of the 26th Guards Brigade helped US troops control the territory.

The last time we attacked targets in Croatia was during the war after Croatia declared independence. For instance, on 21 November 1994, two Jaguars from 54 Squadron bombed Udbina air base, at that time held by rebel Croatian Serbs.

Cuba

We're so used to thinking of Cuba and Castro, and perhaps of the Bay of Pigs invasion, that many will be surprised to know that not only did we once launch a full-scale invasion of Cuba, but that we actually once controlled a part of Cuba. Not for very long, admittedly, but we did control it for a time.

We had already had plenty of practice at attacking Cuba by the time we took it over.

Drake was sailing the waters off Cuba in the sixteenth century and, rather bizarrely, he may be linked to the mojito. The origins of the mojito are hotly debated, or at least as hotly as you can debate the origins of a cocktail. Some suggest it may be derived from a nineteenth-century drink called El Draque, perhaps named after Drake, and others go as far as suggesting that Drake himself invented it. I personally have no idea whether any of this is true, but they're jolly stories and the idea of Drake stylishly sipping a cocktail makes a change from all that looting, burning and pillaging.

Talking of which, in 1662, English admiral and pirate Christopher Myngs, who could probably fairly be called Myngs the Merciless due to his rather unsavoury reputation, captured, looted, sacked and briefly occupied Santiago de Cuba.

And in 1741, guess where we invaded? Yes, we stormed ashore at Guantanamo Bay itself. Obviously this was before all the barbed wire and orange prisoner suits. Admiral Edward Vernon arrived with 4,000 soldiers and eight warships, intending to march on Santiago de Cuba again. We even briefly renamed it Cumberland Bay. Imagine if the Americans were running a facility at Cumberland Bay; it would sound more like a bed and breakfast. But the locals weren't very friendly to us, nor were the local diseases, and Vernon was forced to withdraw.

In 1748 we were back again. In the Battle of Santiago de Cuba, Rear Admiral Sir Charles Knowles tried to send his squadron straight into the harbour of Santiago de Cuba and the Spanish defenders, not surprisingly, expressed their lack of enthusiasm through the medium of artillery. With two ships disabled, hundreds of men dead and 200 wounded, Knowles limped off. Later in the year he was back in Cuban waters for the Battle of Havana. Though it wasn't quite as disastrous as the Battle of Santiago de Cuba, it wasn't a glowing success either, and Knowles ended up being reprimanded in a court-martial. After that there were assorted duels involving Knowles and some of his subordinates.

Finally, in 1762 our time had come at last. On 6 June (yes, 6 June, just like D-Day) a huge British fleet arrived off Havana with large numbers of ships, and thousands of sailors and soldiers. The expeditionary force landed and we rapidly realised we had a problem with the heavily defended Morro fortress. A bitter and fiercely fought siege, with attacks and counter-attacks, dragged on through June and July, until finally Havana surrendered in August. We lost thousands of men in the fighting and even more were killed on this expedition by disease. Out of the 11,000 men who first landed and the subsequent 3,000 reinforcements, only 3,000 were available for action by the end.

A big chunk of Cuba was ours. But only until the year after. In 1763, in a bit of an anti-climax on the Cuban invasion front, we gave it and Manila (see Philippines) back to the Spanish in exchange for Florida and Minorca.

Cyprus

Yes, we've still got troops on the island of Cyprus, and yes it's a beautiful place with a complex and sometimes troubled history. But did you know Richard the Lionheart invaded Cyprus?

In April 1191, Richard was heading for the Holy Land when he was hit by a storm and his fleet was scattered. In the days before modern communications this, as you can imagine, was a major problem, especially since he'd lost his treasure ship, and his sister and his bride-to-be, Berengaria. We don't know whether he was more upset about losing the treasure or his bride-to-be. Anyway, when he finally discovered where they all were, it turned out they were off Cyprus, so, not surprisingly, that was where he went.

The local ruler was a not very nice man called Isaac Comnenos, a minor Byzantine royal who had rebelled against the Byzantine Empire and who reputedly enjoyed the traditional warlord hobbies of raping, defiling and robbing. He had made (as it would turn out, from Isaac's point of view) the unfortunate decision to be less than respectful and helpful to assorted members of Richard's fleet and Berengaria herself. Richard was unamused. He arrived in Limassol in May 1191 and eventually took the whole island. According to tradition, Richard had Isaac bound in silver chains because he had said he wouldn't bind him in iron chains. Richard married Berengaria on 12 May 1191 in the Chapel of St George at Limassol, and she was crowned the same day. Maybe it was not the happiest of marriages though, since when Richard finally got back to England, Berengaria didn't join him. So, one for the pub quizzes here as Berengaria is traditionally known as 'the only English queen who never set foot in England'.

Our first period in control of Cyprus was about as illustrious as Richard and Berengaria's love life. Richard left on 5 June, after a shorter stay on the island than some British tourists go for these days, and rapidly decided to sell the island to the Knights Templar. After a rebellion in 1192, the knights sold the island to Guy de Lusignan.

Our second period in control was quite a lot longer and had some better bits, although quite a few difficult bits as well. It all came about because the Ottoman Turks, who controlled the island at the time, needed our help against the Russians. In 1878 they handed over control of the island to us, though technically it remained part of the Ottoman Empire. The first British forces landed in Larnaca on 8–9 July 1878 and by 12 July we had reached Nicosia. Technically, Cyprus remained part of the Ottoman Empire, but in 1914, with us and the Turks at war, we dropped the 'technically part of the Ottoman Empire' and annexed it.

Cyprus became independent in 1960.

Czech Republic

Generally, armed Brits haven't spent that much time roaming the area of what is now the Czech Republic, but we have spent some time there.

For instance, we didn't get officially involved in the Thirty Years War that ravaged central Europe for, well, about thirty years, but plenty of Brits did get involved on a semi-official level with some government support. For example, in 1620 a Scot, Sir Andrew Gray, started raising a regiment in London and Scotland to fight with the Bohemian-Moravian army. He ended up with ten companies, including 2,500 musketeers. They then headed for Bohemia to fight off the advancing Imperial and Bavarian troops, not, unfortunately for them, with huge success. They lost a lot of men, and Gray's regiment consisted of only 300 troops by the time they left and headed for Upper Palatinate.

During the Second World War, we spent quite a lot of time bombing targets in occupied Czech territory linked to the German war effort, such as the Škoda works near Plzen. SOE also dispatched many missions to the area. Chicheley Hall (in Buckinghamshire) was SOE's Special Training School No. 46 and was used from 1942 to 1943 to train Czechoslovaks. The most well known of SOE's Czech operations was the assassination of Reinhard Heydrich in Prague in 1942 during Operation Anthropoid. After the killing, the Nazis murdered many and conducted the notorious massacre at Lidice.

Denmark

There have, of course, been plenty of Danes who have invaded Britain over the centuries. But there has been a certain amount of traffic in the other direction as well. In 1700, for example, we bombarded Copenhagen with our allies. And while pretty much everybody knows of Wellington and Waterloo, what a lot of people don't know is that, before heading off to Spain, Wellington had some urgent business in Copenhagen to attend to.

The trouble all began with Napoleon and something rather delightfully called The League of Armed Neutrality. Basically, in our war with Napoleon we reckoned we had the right to board any-body's ships to check for French contraband. However, the League of Armed Neutrality (or Second League of Armed Neutrality since there was something similar going on during the American War of Independence) disagreed. Strongly. With Denmark joining the league, and with many European ports closed to British trade due to an embargo encouraged by France, we got a bit nervous and told the Danes to get out of the league. The Danes refused and the Royal Navy was on its way. In the Battle of Copengahen in 1801, Admiral Sir Hyde Parker's fleet, with Nelson playing a prominent role, defeated the Danish fleet, and soon after the Danes became more interested in negotiations.

The situation remained fluid, and by 1807 we were nervous again. This time, with Napoleon's advance across Europe, we were afraid that Napoleon might drop in on the Danes and use Denmark and its navy against us. We decided we would get in first. We assem-bled a fleet and an army of 25,000 men, and demanded Denmark form an alliance with us, while Napoleon told the Danes to fight Britain or he would invade. The Danes refused our demands and our second attack on Denmark in a decade was on. Wellington, or Arthur Wellesley as he then was, and the British troops landed and we defeated the Danes at the Battle of Køge. Then, when the Danes still refused to give up, the Royal Navy bombarded Copenhagen with guns and rockets, killing over 2,000 civilians and destroying large numbers of buildings. Eventually, the Danes were forced to agree to surrender their navy.

However, this was far from the last action between Britain and Denmark. In the so-called Gunboat War in the early nineteenth century, so-called, not surprisingly, because the Danes took to using smaller gunboats against us, there was a series of actions, including for instance, our invasion and occupation of the Island of Anholt in order to control its lighthouse, until the Treaty of Kiel finally ended hostilities in 1814.

Denmark was invaded and occupied by Germany on 9 April 1940. A few days later Britain occupied the Faroe Islands, which were then part of Denmark and are now self-governing under the sovereignty of the Kingdom of Denmark. The British operation was called Operation Valentine and it seems a reasonable name, since apart from an official protest, the occupation was met with little resistance. British veterans have put up a plaque in Tórshavn Cathedral thanking the locals for their hospitality and a fair number of British soldiers married local girls. The occupation lasted until 1945.

During the Second World War, British ships saw action in the seas off Greenland, which is also autonomous within the Kingdom of Denmark. In the Battle of the Denmark Strait, the strait between Iceland and Greenland, HMS *Hood* was sunk by the *Bismarck* on 24 May 1941. And in the Denmark Strait again, in March 1943, HMS *Glasgow* intercepted the German blockade runner *Regensburg*. We did not, however, get involved in the slightly bizarre and little-known war on Greenland itself, in which US troops and Greenland's own army, the North-East Greenland Sledge Patrol, battled Nazis who had landed several times to set up clandestine weather stations on Greenland's east coast, which in the days before satellites would have given them vital meteorological information for their war effort.

The RAF conducted assorted operations over Denmark during the war and SOE worked with the Danish Resistance.

In May 1945, our army marched into Denmark again, but this time it was to a warm welcome from the citizens, as we were there to help supervise the German surrender and work with the Danes, not against them.

Djibouti

Little Djibouti, tucked away on Africa's eastern coast near the mouth of the Red Sea, has in some ways a fairly eccentric history. It was the site of an attempt by Imperial Russia to create an African empire to match those of other nineteenth-century European imperial powers. In 1889, a bunch of Russians led by one Nikolai Ivanovitch Achinov decided it would be a good idea to establish a colony at Sagallo. The French disagreed, since they were also busy establishing their presence in the area, and shelled the Russians until they surrendered.

British interest in the area comes in the Second World War. After the Fall of France in 1940, French Somaliland, as Djibouti was then known, came under Vichy control. And it stayed that way for a surprisingly long time. Even after British forces had wiped out Italian resistance in the surrounding regions and started to blockade the country, French Somaliland remained under Vichy control. In fact, when its governor, Dupoont, surrendered in December 1942, after a blockade of 101 days, it held the unenviable record of the being the last French African colony to abandon Vichy. After the surrender, Free French forces supported by British armoured cars moved into Djibouti to take control.

Dominica

One of a line of islands in the Caribbean running north from South America, some Brits tend to confuse Dominica with the much bigger, but similarly named, Dominican Republic.

In 1493, Christopher Columbus named the island after Sunday (*Dies Dominica* being Church Latin for Sunday and *Domenica* being Sunday in Italian), because that's the day he discovered it. To be fair to him, I guess he wasn't thinking too much about potentially confused people in the twenty-first century.

Dominica is part of the Lesser Antilles. The Antilles are nothing to do with antelopes or anteaters as some children, and maybe some grown-ups probably think. The name comes from the mythical island of Antilia, meaning the Island Opposite, which was a sort of Atlantis-like island that people used to stick on maps opposite Europe when they weren't entirely sure what was out there.

For a long time after being discovered by Europeans, though, they only dropped in occasionally, usually while on their way somewhere else. For example, in 1606 George Percy called by before heading off elsewhere, and the same year Captain Henry Challons, heading for Virginia, rescued a marooned Spanish friar from the island. In 1607, Captain John Smith visited on his way to establish Jamestown.

Then in 1627 we launched a sort of virtual invasion. Charles I granted the island to the Earl of Carlisle without anything very much being done about it. Subsequently, in 1635, the French claimed it, but they didn't do very much about it either, and in 1660 we agreed with them that Dominica shouldn't be settled and should be left to the Caribs.

Inevitably, some English pirates turned up, but so did English and French foresters looking for wood.

Finally, in the 1720s the French took control of Dominica. The scene was thus set for the British Invasion of Dominica in 1761. After the successful invasion of Canada we had a lot of spare troops with time on their hands. Pitt wanted to seize something to look good 'at home and abroad'. Thus, on 6 June, a day usually remembered for a rather different invasion, the British fleet under Lord Rollo arrived at Dominica. At 1pm Rollo told the locals he was about to land and demanded they surrender. When by 4pm nothing much had happened, we landed 700 men. Firing broke out and eventually we stormed a French battery, with two of our troops being killed in the process. In the morning the locals surrendered and our troops were authorised to plunder until noon.

Thus we took control of Dominica. The Treaty of Paris in 1763 confirmed our control, but then the French took it back from us in 1778 during the American War of Independence, invading the island before our forces there even knew that the French were at war with us. Not very sporting. In 1783, we got it back under the 1783 Treaty of Paris (another Treaty of Paris), but not all the locals were that keen on our return and we ended up fighting some of those who had been armed by the French.

Dominica became independent in 1978.

Dominican Republic

New Year's Day 1586 wasn't a particularly happy New Year's Day for the people of Santo Domingo. In fact, it was a pretty miserable one. Francis Drake turned up and attacked the city. While

Drake distracted the defenders by firing at the city and pretending to attempt a landing, a landing party of 800 men under Carleill attacked the town from the west, scattering the defenders they met. Fairly quickly, Carleill's men got inside the defences and, after that, Santo Domingo was theirs. For a time. Drake's men set about looting it, and then Drake set about putting the town up for ransom. He started off by demanding 1 million ducats, and when the Spanish refused, Drake ordered his men to start destroying buildings as a bargaining tactic. The final price agreed was a mere 25,000 ducats – even today British tourists aren't particularly renowned for their bargaining skills abroad.

Where Drake had gone, other English ships would follow.

In 1655, we were back, and back in strength, for what would turn out to be a major military fiasco. Cromwell had decided to strike a major blow against Spain and dispatched Venables and Penn with a massive expeditionary force to the Caribbean to do something about it. On 14 April they landed on the island, but some 30 miles from their target Santo Domingo. They had no water bottles and they needed them. Four days later, they had almost made it as far as their objective when they were ambushed by a few hundred locals. It was all a bit of a disaster from an English point of view.

Eventually, after bombarding the city and some other rather ineffective actions, the expedition sailed away to capture Jamaica instead.

By the end of the eighteenth century, the French had taken control of Santo Domingo. In 1809, after assorted actions in the area, the British Army under the command of Major General Hugh Lyle Carmichael helped the locals take it back from the French. Santo Domingo surrendered on 6 July 1809.

3

EAST TIMOR TO FRANCE

East Timor

East Timor was controlled by the Portuguese, and since the Portuguese have long been our friends, it's not a place where armed Britons have spent much time. But they have spent some time there.

There was a possibility of conflict during the Napoleonic Wars. In 1812 we temporarily took over the part of Timor controlled by the Dutch. The problem was that the Dutch and Portuguese didn't always entirely agree where the boundary lay between the bits of Timor they controlled. And since we had temporarily taken over the Dutch bit of Timor, we had also temporarily taken over its border disputes as well. This led to some encounters with our Portuguese friends that, as it turns out, were rather less than friendly. In 1812, a Dutchman had been dispatched in a ship with a British flag to inform people in some areas that they were now under British instead of Dutch control. He was trying to reach Maubara, a disputed region claimed by both sides (now in East Timor), but when he encountered the Portuguese commander at Batugade, he was told that he could not go there and that it was Portuguese. The commander, clearly no diplomat, underlined his message by pointing to the British flag on the boat and saying that it was only good for wiping their backsides.

During the Second World War, Portugal was neutral. However, after the attack on Pearl Harbor, to help protect the flank of the Dutch-controlled part of Timor, a combined Dutch and Australian force took control of the Portuguese part of Timor on 17 December 1941. In February 1942, the Japanese invaded and the Allied troops with local Timorese volunteers fought back in a bitter and brave year-long guerrilla campaign. In 1943, most of the remaining Allied troops were evacuated, and an American submarine, the USS *Gudgeon*, took off twenty-eight men – Australian, English, Portuguese and Filipino – pretty much the final survivors, on 10 February. After this evacuation, some of the Timorese fought on against the Japanese. The Australian Brigadier Dyke, commander of Timforce, arrived in Dili on 22 September 1945 to help organise the Japanese surrender.

In 1974 a left-wing coup succeeded in Portugal, and Portugal announced that it would withdraw from East Timor. In 1975, Indonesia invaded East Timor. A long guerrilla campaign ensued against the Indonesians, and in August 1999 a referendum showed a majority of East Timorese in favour of independence. Violence errupted and in September 1999 INTERFET, the International Force for East Timor, arrived to help restore order. Units of the British armed forces played key roles. With HMS *Glasgow* offshore, British Army Gurkhas and SBS Royal Marines moved in with the vanguard of INTERFET on 20 September. British troops helped to secure the airport, harbour and key road junctions. On 1 October, a Gurkha patrol fired the first shots of the mission, helping to free refugees.

Ecuador

Ecuador has avoided official British invasion, but in its early period, when under Spanish control, it did receive a fair amount of semi-official and unofficial British attention.

The Galapagos Islands, part of Ecuador, were first unintentionally discovered by a Bishop of Panama who was somewhat off-course. But it was British buccaneers and privateers who were among the first permanent or semi-permanent settlers. It was a British buccaneer, William Ambrose Cowley, who first charted the islands and gave them British names like James, Charles, Albemarle and Narborough. While they weren't engaged in such cartographic pursuits, the Brits spent some time invading the mainland of Ecuador. A particularly favourite destination was, perhaps inevitably, Ecuador's main port, Guayaquil. In 1687, British pirates under George d'Hout attacked the port. And again in 1709, because we were at war with Spain, Rogers, Courtney and Dampier – not in this case an

advertising agency or law firm, but in fact, another bunch of privateers – looted the town and demanded ransom, only to have second
thoughts and depart hastily when there was an outbreak of yellow
fever. Rogers also managed to rescue Alexander Selkirk, the reputed
model for Robinson Crusoe, and Rogers himself later became the
first royal governor of the Bahamas.

Another Brit, Darwin, famously did less military things with
finches on the Galapagos Islands in the nineteenth century.

As with Colombia, Brits played a crucial role in the liberation
of Ecuador. For instance, English, Scots and Irish volunteers of the
Albion unit, who had been protecting the ammunition train at the
Battle of Pichincha, outside Quito, in 1822, arrived in the battle just
at the crucial time when a veteran Spanish unit, the Aragon, looked
likely to smash the rebel lines. Instead, largely thanks to the Albion, it
was the Aragon who suddenly found themselves in deep trouble and
shortly afterwards the rebels were able to advance towards Quito.

Egypt

We have invaded Egypt quite frequently, starting first with the
Crusades. People tend to think of the Crusades as purely happening
in the Holy Land, but there was quite a lot going on elsewhere at
times. And Egypt's one of the places Brits invaded.

An English contingent in 1249 decided to join the Seventh
Crusade, led by Louis IX. It wasn't a wise decision, and the English
knights would have lived to regret it. That is, if they had lived.
First, when they arrived at the port of Damietta, they fell out with
the French, but the quarrel was patched up in time for the English
to join the march south towards Cairo. The leader of the English
contingent was one William Longsword. Longsword but perhaps
not quite long enough, since, along with all but about one of his
followers, he was cut down at the Battle of Mansourah in February
1250. Mind you, the French didn't do much better there. In fact,
they had an even worse time. Thousands were killed or captured in
the battle and the pursuit after it, and Louis IX himself ended up
as a prisoner.

We left Egypt alone after that, but by the late eighteenth century
we were back. To be fair, it was Napoloen who started it. He decided

he would invade Egypt partly as a way of getting at British India. It does rather make you wonder about Napoleon, since it is still a long, long way from Egypt to India.

Anyway, Napoleon took Egypt fairly easily, in 1798, but then Nelson destroyed his fleet at the Battle of Abukir Bay, or Battle of the Nile, on 1 August. Nelson managed to get his ships on both sides of the French fleet, which from the French point of view was definitely a bad thing. After failure at the Siege of Acre, Napoleon returned to France, and then it was our turn to invade Egypt. Our Admiral Keith cooperated with the Mamelukes to attack the remaining French troops, and even though the French won the Battle of Heliopolis, they lost a land battle to us at Abukir when we landed a British army under General Abercromby there. Eventually, the French surrendered to us and we got the Rosetta Stone as well, which was handy from an Egyptology point of view.

We invaded Egypt again in March 1807, but, in the face of opposition from locals, we didn't achieve very much.

Then we were back in 1840. In the Syrian war (or second Syrian war, or Egyptian-Ottoman war, or second Egyptian-Ottoman war – why have one name for a war when you can have several?) our naval forces helped push back the Egyptian forces that had taken a lot of ground from the Ottoman forces (hence the Egyptian-Ottoman thing) in Syria (hence the Syrian thing, though quite a lot of it was in what is now Lebanon) and the coast to the south (see Israel). Commodore Charles Napier followed this by turning up at Alexandria with his squadron in November 1840 and blockading it before negotiating a peace treaty.

In 1854, the Frenchman Ferdinand de Lesseps was granted permission to build the Suez Canal, and its opening in 1869 gave us a whole new strategic interest in Egypt. In 1875, with the Khedive of Egypt in serious financial difficulties, Disraeli stepped in to buy the Khedive's Suez Canal company shares. Gradually, British and French influence over Egypt increased, and in 1881 there was a national uprising. On 11 July 1882, British ships opened fire on the defences at Alexandria with HMS *Alexandra* firing the first shot. The defences were silenced, but a resulting fire in the city destroyed many buildings. In August 1882, a British force under Lieutenant-General Garnet Wolseley landed and took control of the Canal Zone before destroying the rebel forces at the Battle of Tel el-Kebir.

Prince Arthur, son of Victoria and Albert, was present at both the action at Mahuta and at Tel el-Kebir in command of the 1st Guards Brigade. Cairo was taken the next day. To a great extent we now controlled Egypt, even though there was still a Khedive. Sorry if this all sounds a bit condensed, but, as you can see, the story of our involvement with Egypt is a big one, and this is only a modest book.

In 1914, the Khedive was pro-Ottoman, so we chucked him out and put a Khedive more friendly to us in power. And when the Turks invaded Egypt we pushed them out. But after riots in 1922 we gave Egypt independence. Sort of. Then in the Second World War, we had to push the Italians and Germans out of Egypt on the other side. In the period after the Second World War relations between Britain and Egypt became increasingly tense, with Britain keen to hang on to control of the Suez Canal and Egyptians keen to see us depart.

In 1954, Nasser came to power and an agreement was reached between Britain and Egypt for Britain to withdraw its forces from the Canal Zone in 1956. This went ahead, but a separate crisis had developed over funding of the construction of the Aswan Dam. When Britain and the US withdrew their contributions to the dam project, Nasser retaliated by nationalising the canal. On 29 October 1956, Israel attacked Egypt from the east. On 5 November, we and the French launched our invasion of Suez. Air attacks targeted the Egyptian air force and British and French paratroopers went in. On 6 November there were sea and helicopter landings. Militarily, the British and French invasion was on its way to being a success. Diplomatically, though, it was a disaster. UN pressure forced a ceasefire at midnight on 6 November and pressure from the UN, US and the Soviet Union forced Britain and France to withdraw their forces.

El Salvador

El Salvador is on the Pacific side of the Isthmus of Panama, southeast of Mexico, with Guatemala separating the two. It's a little way away from some of our more usual spheres of military operation, but we have been in action in its waters and, on one occasion, we even got somebody else to invade it for us.

Sir Francis Drake, for instance, captured a ship near Sonsonate in El Salvador and took cloth and Chinese porcelain from it, and on 19 July 1587 Thomas Cavendish captured a 120-ton prize off Acajutla.

In 1721, a bunch of British privateers seem to have conducted a rather belated invasion of the area, belated in the sense that, by the time they invaded, the war was already over. Under Captain George Shelvocke, they arrived in Acajutla with a prize ship *La Sacra Familia*, which they had captured off the port. They were then informed by the local authorities that since the war of the Quadruple Alliance was over, they were now to be treated as pirates. Shelvocke eventually got back to London in 1722 and ended up being tried for piracy there.

In 1932, during a peasant rebellion in El Salvador, fearful for the safety of British nationals, we persuaded the Canadian government to send two destroyers, *Skeena* and *Vancouver*, to anchor off Acajutla, El Salvador's main port. A heavily armed landing party was sent ashore and a compromise was reached with reluctant port officials, who didn't want any foreign troops ashore, whereby the Canadians were at least allowed to fortify the land end of the pier. Eventually, El Salvador's government persuaded us there that was no threat to British nationals and the landing party returned to *Skeena*; invasion finished and not too much harm done really.

Equatorial Guinea

Confusingly, none of the land of Equatorial Guinea actually lies on the equator, it's all north of the line, except for a little island that lies to the south.

In 1778, Portugal ceded the territory of Equatorial Guinea to Spain, and in the nineteenth century we set up an anti-slaving base on the island of Bioko, then known as Fernando Po. In 1827, Spain abandoned the island and we took control. It wasn't really much of an invasion since we leased the base from Spain, but we did make ourselves at home. We named the base Port Clarence after the Duke of Clarence, and William Fitzwilliam Owen conducted vigorous anti-slaving operations so that in three years his forces freed 2,500 slaves and detained twenty ships.

In 1840, the naval ship *Wolverine*, under Wilham Tucker, captured the Island of Corisco, off what is now Equatorial Guinea, and destroyed the slaving establishments there. The fighting must have been fierce because of the landing party of forty, ten were killed or wounded.

Gradually, from 1843 onwards, Spanish control was re-asserted over Bioko, and our lease finally ended in 1855.

Eritrea

Many Brits today would struggle to find Eritrea quickly on a map, but there is a clue in the name. The Red Sea used to be called the Erythraean Sea, from the ancient Greek word for red, *erythros*, and Eritrea has a long Red Sea coast.

Despite the haziness of the knowledge of many modern Brits regarding Eritrea, we have invaded it a couple of times, and we have been intimately connected with some key stages in its history.

Our first invasion was actually aimed at the Emperor of Ethiopia, Tewodros, who had taken some Brits prisoner and refused to release them, so we will deal again with this invasion in the section on Ethiopia. But let's just note here that the British expeditionary force commanded by Sir Robert Napier landed in 1867 at Zula, about 30 miles south of Massawa, Eritrea's main port. In an impressive feat of engineering, they rapidly built new piers (of the cargo kind rather than the promenade up-and-down kind) and started building a railway heading inland and roads for the force, which included a number of elephants to carry the heavy guns. What expedition would be complete without elephants I hear you asking? The expedition was a great success from the Victorians' point of view, though clearly not from Tewodros' point of view as he ended up dead.

At about the same time as Napier's expedition, the Khedive of Egypt was conducting his own invasions of parts of Ethiopia, or Abyssinia as it then was. In the process he leased the port of Massawa from the sultan. Subsequently, we ended up with troops there as part of our Egyptian operations, but frankly we weren't very interested in it, so in 1885, to prevent the French getting it, we handed it over to the Italians.

This, as it turns out, may not have been a very wise move and shows the problems of always assuming that your former enemies will also be your future enemies and that your former friends will always be your future friends. Massawa became a key element in the Italian colony of Eritrea, which the Italians put together in the late nineteenth century and which then became a key element in Mussolini's African Empire, with which we were at war by 1940.

In January 1941 we were ready to invade Eritrea, and British and Commonwealth units, particularly Indian troops, crossed the border into Eritrea on 19 January. The key battle in the campaign was the bitter Battle of Keren, which lasted from 5 February until 27 March as two opposing forces in many ways quite well matched fought it out. Finally, our side won and Keren fell. Massawa fell shortly afterwards and in June, Assab, a port in southern Eritrea, was also captured. Though after that, and until Italy itself signed an armistice with the Allies in 1943, Italians, with some local support, conducted a guerrilla campaign against British forces.

We continued to administer Eritrea until 1951 when it was federated with Ethiopia. In 1993, after a long guerrilla war against Ethiopia, and after a UN-supervised referendum, Eritrea was internationally recognised as independent.

Estonia

Estonia is the northernmost of the Baltic trio of Lithuania, Latvia and Estonia. It's right next to Russia, and indeed the territory has spent long periods under Russian domination. Bearing in mind that Britain and Russia haven't always been exactly the best of friends, it's no surprise then that we've spent a fair bit of time roaming around Estonian waters on military business.

During the Napoleonic period when we clashed with Russia, some of the action took place in the waters off Estonia (then controlled by Russia). For instance, in June 1808, assorted encounters took place off the Estonian port of Rogervik. The same year, *Victory* herself, as part of an operation to blockade the Russian fleet, took control of the island of Nargen, finding a useful supply of wood there. And our Admiral Saumarez, when he was in charge of operations in the Baltic, spent a certain amount of time blockading Russian ships in Rogervik.

With the Crimean War in the 1850s, we were back in Estonian waters reconnoitring Reval (Tallinn) for signs of the Russian fleet, and imposing a blockade (again) in the area. Again, our ships spent time hanging around 'off Nargen', obviously a popular Royal Navy destination. We also landed on and captured Arensburg on the Estonian island of Saaremaa, then called Ösel.

We were fighting in the area again during the First World War, but this time, for a change, alongside the Russians as opposed to against them. The British submarine flotilla in the Baltic is one of those less well-known stories that is still, in many ways, fascinating. Some of the submarines reached Russian-controlled territory via a route that went round the North Cape, but others bravely made their way there through the Baltic under the noses of the German navy. The flotilla was based in Reval and saw a fair amount of action. HMS *C32*, for instance, was lost while trying to counter the German invasion of three Estonian islands. And the wreck of HMS *E18* was discovered off Estonia just recently.

With the revolution in Russia, the situation changed again, and by the end of 1918 we were helping the Estonians fight assorted Russians. On 26 December, we captured two Bolshevik destroyers, *Avtroil* and *Spartak*, that had been shelling Tallinn and handed them over to the Estonians to use, and broadly we gave naval and some air support to Estonian land operations.

On 2 February 1920, under the Treaty of Tartu, Russia recognised Estonia's independence. After the Second World War, Estonia would once again find itself under Russian control, and once again today it is independent. But we have played a significant role on the way in Estonia's history.

Ethiopia

Ethiopia is a fascinating country with a fascinating history that deserves to be much better known, and we, not surprisingly, have played something of a role in it.

As far back as the early fifteenth century we have a letter from Henry IV intended for the King of Abyssinia. It wasn't until the nineteenth century, however, that we became a major player in the region. By 1855, we were signing a treaty with Abyssinia and by 1868 we were invading it.

Emperor Tewodros (sounds an exotic name to the average Brit, but it's basically Theodore), mentioned in the Eritrea section, was having a spot of trouble with local rebels and wrote to assorted European powers requesting their assistance in the matter. When he didn't get the answers he was looking for, he took the unwise step of grabbing some hostages. After various negotiations had failed we sent in the troops.

Lieutenant General Sir Robert Napier and an expeditionary force from the Bombay Army was given the job. After extensive preparations had been made on the Red Sea Coast (see Eritrea), the force moved inland to face the emperor. Tewodros failed to unite the Abyssinians (Ethiopians) against us, and when his remaining forces faced Napier's outside Magdala, his capital, on 10 April 1868, for the loss of just two dead from our side, the emperor's forces were crushed and the hostages were released. Shortly afterwards Tewodros was dead.

With the war over and having got his title (Napier was soon to become Baron Napier of Magdala, imaginatively enough), Napier withdrew his troops, in the process handing over a lot of expensive military kit to a helpful (to us) local leader, Ras Kassai, who then used it to help himself to become emperor as Yohannes IV. He also picked up a British military adviser, one John Kirkham.

In the following period, Abyssinia (Ethiopia) had rather more to fear from other directions apart from us. For example, we were on its side against Muhammad Ahmed (see Sudan). It was Italy that started taking a rather intense and unwelcome interest in the area. This culminated in Mussolini's invasion of Abyssinia in 1935, bringing it under Italian control in 1936.

The good news is that Italian control wasn't to last long. In the summer of 1940, the Italians picked a fight with us in the region, with a series of probing attacks followed by their conquest of British Somaliland in August.

We, however, were not going to let Mussolini take over. We soon struck back both in Somaliland and elsewhere, including Ethiopia. Our invasion of Ethiopia was to come from a number of directions. In the south, units advanced into southern Ethiopia from Kenya. In the north, units advanced south from Eritrea after its fall. In addition, Emperor Selassie himself crossed into Ethiopia to lead patriot Ethiopian forces in alliance with Gideon Force, led by Orde Wingate, in a sort of precursor to the role played by Wingate and the famous Chindits later in Burma.

On 6 April 1941, General Cunningham's forces advancing from the south took Addis Ababa. On 5 May 1936, the Italians had taken Addis Ababa from Haile Selassie, then on 5 May 1941, five years later, it was Haile Selassie who was entering the city. In July, the Italian stronghold at Jimma fell and finally, in November, the Italians at Gondar also surrendered to British, Commonwealth and Ethiopian troops.

Fiji

Ah, Fiji.

Europeans first started settling permanently on Fiji in the nineteenth century. In 1858, under pressure from other chiefs and from the Americans, King Cakobau offered to sell us the islands. We turned down the offer, partly because we weren't actually convinced that all of the islands were Cakobau's to sell, since not everybody recognised him as king of all Fiji.

By 1871, Cakobau had been made constitutional monarch of Fiji, though a lot of power actually rested with Australian settlers in the cabinet and legislature. Things did not entirely go well, however, with the new kingdom running up heavy debts, and by 1872 we got another offer to take over the islands.

So eventually, in 1874, Fiji became a British colony. Cakobau himself became Fiji's second most important chief, but allowed Queen Victoria to become Paramount Chief of Fiji. He died in 1883 and Queen Victoria lasted a bit longer.

Fiji became independent in 1970.

Finland

We saw action in Finnish waters in our war against Russia of 1807–12, one of those wars set amid the chaos of Napoleonic Europe, in which we were temporarily at war with people who at other times were instead fighting the French alongside us.

There were assorted naval actions. For instance, on 25 July 1809, *Princess Caroline*, *Minotaur*, *Cerberus* and *Prometheus*, not in this case the cast of some mythological movie, but a British naval squadron, fought a battle with four Russian gunboats and a brig near Hamina. After nineteen Britons and twenty-eight Russians were killed, the Russian boats were captured by the princess and her mythological friends.

The Russians, not surprisingly, moved fairly fast to end the war when Napoleon invaded them in 1812.

With the arrival of the Crimean War in the 1850s, we were invading Finnish waters again. We spent quite a lot of time bombarding Russian fortifications from the sea, but in the most dramatic of the incidents we landed and took hundreds of Finnish prisoners (Finnish prisoners from the Russian army, since the Russians controlled the area at the time). This was the Battle of Bomarsund, or rather two Battles of Bomarsund. The first battle was more of a bombardment of the Russian fortress at Bomarsund and notable because Charles Davis Lucas threw a live shell off the ship, performing the earliest act of bravery to be rewarded with a Victoria Cross.

The Second Battle of Bomarsund was a more dramatic affair. On 13 August 1854, a British fleet landed thousands of French troops and then shelled the fortress until it surrendered. After the surrender, British and French forces made the fortress unusable. About 300 mainly Finnish grenadiers, with Russian officers, were taken to Britain and held prisoner in Lewes, where you can now see the so-called Russian Memorial commemorating twenty-eight Finnish soldiers who died here. The story of their incarceration also makes an interesting aside, with the officers going out riding and shooting, and the soldiers becoming a tourist attraction for some Brits, while other Brits complained that the prisoners were being too well treated.

Then, bizarrely when you consider that we had been fighting Russians in what is now Finland, about the only time we have attacked Finland, we attacked it in what was then Finland but is now Russia. Confusing eh? On 30 July 1941, to show Churchill's sudden enthusiasm for Stalin, once the German invasion of Russia had brought him into the war on our side, we managed to get two aircraft carriers into Arctic waters north of Finland and tried to bomb Kirkenes in Norway and Petsamo in Finland (now in Russia). It was a bit of a disaster all round for us, with many Fleet Air Arm planes shot down and not much damage done to the ports.

France

When we think of France and invasions, we tend to think of two things: the Norman invasion of England and, going the opposite way across the Channel, D-Day.

What many Brits are less aware of is the vast number of attacks that went across the Channel into France before that landmark day, 6 June 1944. This is only a small book, but this section on France is going to be quite a big one. It has to be. Our record of sending armed forces south across the Channel has been so persistent over so many centuries that this section can't be anything other than the longest section in the book.

One of the first historical references to Brits is to them fighting in France, or Gaul as it then was. Caesar writes that he regularly came across Brits fighting in France. Now, if Caesar was telling the truth here, rather than just making up an excuse to invade us, then he is talking about Brits allied to Gauls, or even perhaps mercenaries. It has been suggested that the presence in Britain of significant numbers of Gallic gold coins may represent what survives of mercenaries' wages.

Nevertheless, it wasn't to be long at all until we were seriously invading Gaul/France. Towards the end of the second century, Clodius Albinus led an army from Britain, which probably included plenty of Brits, across the Channel in an attempt to seize the imperial throne. He got as far as invading Gaul, but not much further. In February AD197 he was decisively defeated by Septimius Severus at Lyon.

Constantine I tried the same trick, a lot more successfully, in the early fourth century. Again there were probably plenty of Brits in his army. Certainly, Brits would have been in his army in AD312 when he smashed the army of Maxentius at the Battle of the Milvian Bridge outside Rome, before taking it.

In AD383, Magnus Maximus set off on the same path, leading an army across the Channel from Britain into mainland Europe. He was successful for quite a long time, until it all ended in disaster for him at Aquileia in AD388.

And in our last outing to mainland Europe, before we walked out of the Roman Empire entirely, in the early fifth century Constantine III led an army from Britain, this time including a general from Britain, Gerontius, south across the Channel into mainland Europe. In 411, though, Constantine III was dead and Britain had rebelled against Rome and resigned from the empire. Our lack of enthusiasm for one of the world's most famous ancient empires is somewhat ironic, considering how much time we spent building our own in more recent centuries. Or perhaps it just shows we found it more interesting running an empire than being a part of someone else's.

Leaving the empire hadn't removed our interest in invading Gaul, or indeed invading France as it was about to become. The ensuing decades and centuries were to make that very clear.

One of the first actions taken by Brits that we know about after Roman control ended was when a bunch of them set off to invade Gaul/France. In about 470, the Emperor Anthemius invited a British king (probably from Britain itself, but just possibly from Brittany) to help him against the Visigoths in Gaul. So Riothamus sailed with 10,000 men to Gaul. It wasn't our most successful invasion of Gaul/France. In fact, it was definitely one of our less successful ones. After a long and bitter battle, Euric and the Visigoths smashed Riothamus' army and Riothamus took refuge with the Burgundians.

Much more successful was that other British invasion of Gaul at about the same time that we've just alluded to – the creation of Brittany. Sometimes we take the name Brittany for granted, but in French, of course, it is 'Bretagne', the same as Britain itself in the language. And Brittany is called Bretagne today because some time in the fourth, fifth and sixth centuries, a lot of Brits made their way across the sea to Armorica and settled there. We don't now know how much violence was used in the process of establishing Brittany. Maybe there was none at all, or maybe there was sometimes just a threat of violence, or maybe sometimes there were actual clashes. Whatever the case, a lot of Brits ended up in a bit of Gaul and took some kind of control, to the extent that the name of the area was changed.

Of course, about this time, the people back in parts of Britain itself had a few incoming settlers and invaders on their own soil to think about. The Saxons, Angles and Jutes turned up, and after the Anglo-Saxon kingdoms had established themselves, the Vikings turned up as well.

The Vikings didn't only turn up in Britain, they appeared in France as well. And some of them managed to repeat the Briton/Breton feat of changing the name of the region where they settled.

So the Norsemen became Normans and the place where they settled became Normandy. And, shortly after that, they too decided to head over here and invade us.

In some ways, the Norman invasion worked in both directions. Yes, it brought a bunch of people over here from France and meant that the upper classes in England spoke French for a time, but it worked in the opposite direction as well, in the sense that it automatically gave the first Norman king of England a foothold in France and an intimate involvement in its politics. It was, in other words, a perfect recipe for renewing our interest in invading France.

It's worth noting that William, the first Norman king of England, didn't actually die over here. He had already tried to invade Brittany in 1076–77, only to be thwarted by the French King Philip I and eventually he died in France attacking Mantes, in a campaign against allies of the French king. It was in some sense an indication of how much time future English monarchs were going to spend attacking France.

Sure enough, William's successors soon got in on the act. In 1097–98, William Rufus attacked the Vexin and Maine in France. And in 1105, Henry I took an army to France to try to seize back Normandy, then held by his brother. The army landed at Barfleur in the spring and finally, in 1106, Henry triumphed at the Battle of Tinchebrai. Then war broke out between him and Philip's successor, Louis. Henry was victorious at the Battle of Bremule in 1119 and the war ended in 1120.

Henry II's reign opened up new opportunities for English kings to invade bits of France after he inherited Anjou and married Eleanor of Aquitaine. He then gradually extended his lands by selecting from a menu of diplomacy, violence and threat of violence as he saw fit to extend his control. By the time he was finished, he controlled vast parts of western, northern, central and southern France.

So it went on, with varying degress of success. In 1242, Henry III lost the brief Saintonge War to the French. Then along came the Hundred Years War. Confusingly (and, let's face it, somewhat disappointingly for the pedantic), this wasn't a single war lasting exactly 100 years, but was instead a scrappy, messy series of campaigns spread out over a period of more than 100 years in total, separated by periods of non-fighting. I'm not going to go into much detail on the Hundred Years War here, partly because France is already going to be the longest section in this book and partly because it's a war with which many Brits are familiar. So I'll just say that there were some notable English victories, including Crécy (1346) and Agincourt (1415), and some notable English defeats, including Pontvallain (1370), Paty (1429) and Castillon (1453). At times it seemed like we would win the lot, particularly when Henry V, after Agincourt, was supposed to inherit the French throne, but at the end in 1453 we had pretty much lost the lot. By the time it was all over we were left with little more than Calais.

Nevertheless, the English defeat in the Hundred Years War did not end the English appetite for invading France.

Henry VIII, who had a big appetite for other things as well, made several attempts. It's quite possible that he had dreams of starting a whole new phase in the Hundred Years War. In 1513, in an alliance with the Emperor Maximilian against France, he was involved in a battle at Guinegate (or Enguinegatte) in France, which became proudly known in Britain (though no doubt not in France) as the Battle of the Spurs, due to the enthusiastic French use of that particular bit of kit for departing the field hastily. After this, Henry took Therouanne and Tournai.

In 1522, he had another go, in alliance with the Emperor Charles this time, sending troops from Calais out to invade Picardy. And in 1523, a large English army under the Duke of Suffolk advanced through the Somme region, and only halted its advance about 50 miles from Paris.

In 1544, Henry invaded yet again. This time his army besieged and took Boulogne. But, frankly, that was about as far as it all got. It was Henry's last attempt at invading France. Soon his daughter, Mary, would give it a go. She sent an army under the Earl of Pembroke into France to fight alongside the forces of her Spanish husband Philip II against the French.

By contrast, Elizabeth I generally saw Spain as more of a threat than France and therefore spent more time organising military activities against that country instead. Her successor, James I, ordered an invasion of France in the 1620s. It wasn't a success. The Anglo-French War of 1627–29 was pretty disastrous from our point of view. In 1627, the Duke of Buckingham besieged Saint Martin de Ré for three months, but failed to take it. In 1628, two expeditions were supposed to aid the defenders of La Rochelle against the French king, but neither achieved anything of note.

During the middle of the seventeenth century we had other things on our mind, like the Civil War.

However, by 1658, we again had forces fighting in France, and not just fighting in a battle in France, but fighting *on both sides* in a battle in France. This was the so-called Battle of the Dunes near Dunkirk. Allied with the French, on this occasion, were some of Cromwell's forces. While fighting alongside the Spanish was a selection of some of the Royalist Forces of the exiled Charles II. The French and Cromwell's troops won.

By the end of the century, we were back in action in France. The Nine Years War of 1688–97 saw us attack France with rather varied results. We had successes, but there was also the disaster of the attack on Brest, in which a large force landed in an attempt to take Brest, only to find itself unable to advance in the face of heavy fire and unable to retreat either. Losses were heavy.

In the War of the Spanish Succession, 1701–14, we were back once again. In September 1709, the Duke of Marlborough won the bitterly fought battle of Malplacquet and in 1711 he proved that the defensive Lines of Ne Plus Ultra (No Further) were rather misnamed when he crossed them and took Bouchain.

In the War of the Austrian Succession, we were at it yet again. We had another amphibious disaster, landing troops to try and take Lorient, but failing even though the defending forces were weak.

Then there was the Seven Years War, in which (despite some distinctly unhappy previous experiences) we took to 'amphibious descents' with gusto. For instance, we landed forces and attacked both St Malo and Cherbourg.

During the Amercian Revolutionary War, we fought assorted naval actions off the French coast, such as the Battle of Ushant off Brest in 1778.

We come at last to the French Revolutionary Wars and the Napoleonic Wars. I hope I'm not rushing too much, but there is a lot to get through on France. Early on, in 1793, British forces advanced into north-east France. We had some successes, like the Battle of Famars, which allowed us to besiege Valenciennes, and the little battle at Villers-en-Cauchies. But eventually the loss of Austrian support led to the collapse of the campaign and British forces having to retreat all the way to northern Germany, from where they were evacuated by sea. That's a long retreat.

There were a variety of naval and amphibious actions in French waters during the wars: for example, the occupation of Toulon by Hood in 1793, and the landing on Corsica in 1794, which resulted in the brief Anglo-Corsican Kingdom of 1794–76.

It took a long tine to beat Napoleon, but by late 1813, while other Allied armies were advancing from the east, Wellington, having fought his way across Spain, was about to launch his invasion of southern France. In October, at the Battle of the Bidassoa, he smashed his way through Soult's lines and into France. A string of battles followed and by April 1814 he was ready to assault Toulouse, that had once been part of Henry II of England's lands all those centuries ago. Wellington's men suffered heavy casualties in the assault on 10 April, and they didn't take the city that day. But after Soult had withdrawn from the city, Wellington entered it on 12 April and the same day news of Napoleon's abdication arrived.

In 1815, after the Battle of Waterloo, Wellington was to invade France again, this time, for a change, from the north-east, not from the south-west. He entered Paris on 7 July 1815.

This brings us to the twentieth-century battlefields of France.

I'm not really even going to attempt to deal here with the suffering, sacrifice and bravery shown by so many Brits in two world wars in France. It is a subject too vast and important for this modest book. I'll simply mention a few brief details.

We've all heard of some of the First World War battles fought by Brits on French soil. The Somme campaign is the obvious one, but there are others which are less well known and which deserve to be better known. For instance, there was the bitter fighting to stem the German Spring Offensive in 1918 and the dramatic battles in the last Hundred Days offensive of the war, which saw the German Army thrown into retreat and included important actions such as The Pursuit to the River Selle.

Similarly, in the Second World War there are the actions we all know about, like Dunkirk and D-Day. However, there are a large number of other battles involving Brits in France that deserve to be remembered. In this category fall the 1940 Battle of Arras, in which British troops launched a counter-attack against the advancing German forces and gave them a serious shock; the Raid on St Nazaire in March 1942; the tragic Raid on Dieppe, in which so many Canadians and Brits, but particularly Canadians, died; the heavy fighting in Normandy after D-Day; and the invasion of the South of France, in which British paratroopers formed part of the 1st Airborne Task Force.

4

GABON TO HUNGARY

Gabon

Like most of the African coast, Gabon's waters have seen plenty of activity from British ships. In the Battle of Cape Lopez in 1722, for example, HMS *Swallow* under Captain Chaloner Ogle (great name) defeated the only slightly less impressively named pirate Bartholomew Roberts. It was all over rather quickly for Roberts since his ship the *Royal Fortune*, unfortunately for it, rapidly took two massive broadsides from the *Swallow*, killing Roberts. The pirates fought on but eventually 272 were taken prisoner.

When we went from slaving nation to anti-slaving nation, our West Africa squadron intercepted a number of ships in Gabon's waters.

During the Second World War, we helped liberate Gabon, then part of French Equatorial Africa, from Vichy French control. In autumn 1940, while Britain was still fearing German invasion, our navy was in action far to the south. In late October, Free French forces from Cameroon penetrated 70 miles across the border into Gabon. Then on 7 November, HMS *Milford*, with cruisers HMS *Delhi* and HMS *Devonshire*, deployed in support of Free French landings at Libreville. The Vichy French submarine *Poncelet* fired a torpedo at *Milford*. Luckily for us, but unluckily for *Poncelet*, the torpedo failed to explode and when the submarine surfaced it was hit by a shot and the crew were forced to surrender, all except the captain, De Saussine, who went down with his ship. On 9 November, after heavy fighting, Free French troops entered Libreville and on 12 November Vichy French forces in Gabon surrendered.

Gambia, The

The Gambia is now a popular tourist destination for Brits. And it's
been a very popular destination for Britons for rather different reasons for a very long time. Early British visitors primarily were after
gold and slaves, and a route to the fabled riches of Timbuktu.

As early as 1588, we were paying the Portuguese for rights in the
area. And in the 1660s we managed to get hold of James Island, the
home, not surprisingly, of our Fort James. It wasn't actually called
James Island when we took it, but we named it after James, Duke
of York, before he became James II and was thrown off his throne.

The French similarly set up a fort at Albreda in 1681, uncomfort-
ably close to James Island for all Europeans concerned. Ahead lay
a long struggle for control between the two European powers. The
French captured Fort James in 1695. We got it back in 1697. And
then the French took it again in 1702.

In 1779, the French took Fort James yet again, but four years
later the Treaty of Versailles gave the Gambia River area to us, while
keeping Albreda for the French. Finally, in 1857 we got that too.

In 1965, the Gambia became independent and in 2011 James
Island was renamed Kunta Kinteh Island to commemorate the slaves
who passed through the island.

Georgia

Georgia, confusingly, has the same name as an American state and
it's also a girl's name. If you say anything about Georgia, there can
be a slight pause while people work out which one you're talking
about.

The country's profile is probably now on the rise in Britain,
partly due to the fact that its flag features the red on white cross of
St George, and if you're not looking too closely, it can look like the
flag of England.

Georgia is a part of the Caucasus our troops ventured into at the
end of the First World War. At about the same time as our second
occupation of Baku in November 1918 (see Azerbaijan), we sent a
large force to the Georgian Black Sea port of Batumi on the other side
of the Caucasus. It began disembarking just before Christmas 1918.

Inevitably, the force was not to be home by Christmas. Instead it deployed along the railway to Tbilisi and Baku, and an HQ was established at Tbilisi in January 1919. As with the rest of the south Caucasus operation, British government enthusiasm for keeping troops in Georgia in an increasingly beleaguered position and in an unpredictable local political and military situation, gradually waned, and we pulled out.

Germany

When Brits think of the words Germany and invasion, they tend to think of those desperate times in 1940, when it seemed that the German blitzkrieg, after crushing the French forces, would roll on across the Channel and crush us as well; those desperate times when radar and the bravery of our fighter pilots and navy was pretty much all that was keeping us safe.

This invasion, Operation Sea Lion, fortunately ended up as a non-invasion and didn't happen. By comparison, what we don't tend to think so much about is all the times that British forces actually have invaded German territory.

As long ago as the early fourth century, Constantine was leading an army out of Britain and making his temporary capital at Trier in Germany before his push south. And in AD383 Magnus Maximus did exactly the same, even if his attempt was ultimately rather less successful. Or a lot less successful.

Anyway, this section is going to contain a lot about advancing armies and so on, so let's look at a quiet, peaceful and almost forgotten invasion. Who can name the Brit who was elected King of Germany and died at Berkhamsted? Technically, he was King of the Romans, which is an impressive title in itself, although also a confusing one since ruling the Romans wasn't what it was all about. Yes, it was Richard of Cornwall, second son of King John, one of those lesser known but fascinating figures that pepper British history. In a close and extensively bribed election in 1256, he fought off hot competition from Alfonso X of Castile to take the title and was crowned by the Archbishop of Cologne at Aachen in May 1257. He didn't achieve very much as King of the Romans (or as King of the Germans), but it's an interesting little story nonetheless and an early example of our royal connections to Germany.

Assorted minor military operations linked to Germany, or rather to the assorted entities that controlled different parts of what later became Germany, followed after Richard. We clashed with the Hanseatic League, for instance, though most of the clashing was done in the Channel and North Sea. And we sent knights to fight on Crusade with the Teutonic Knights, though most of their fighting was in what's now Poland or Lithuania.

In the seventeenth century, the Thirty Years War devastated Germany. We didn't send armies officially but we did send plenty of volunteers to fight unofficially or semi-officially.

By the beginning of the eighteenth century we had graduated to sending official armies. The War of the Spanish Succession broke out because Spain was about to get a French king unless we moved fast. So we did, along with assorted other people also very unchuffed at the idea, particularly the Dutch and the Austrians. And this, of course, is where John Churchill, Duke of Marlborough, one of our most skilful ever military commanders, comes in. Most of his fighting was done elsewhere, but in 1704 he launched a successful invasion of German territory in support of the Austrians against combined French and Bavarian forces.

What with Blenheim Palace and so on, Blenheim today somehow seems such an English name that it's easy to forget it's actually a place in Bavaria, pronounced not 'Blenim' but 'Blen-heim' or 'Blindheim', because that is what it's called. On 13 August 1704, Marlborough and his allies crushingly defeated the French and Bavarian forces, and knocked Bavaria out of the war. It also enabled us to capture the Moselle Valley. Shame we didn't keep it. Lovely views and some gorgeous wines.

As the eighteenth century wore on, more wars followed and more British armies headed for Germany. There was, for example, the War of the Austrian Succession (the eighteenth century seems to have been a particularly popular time for fighting wars over disputed successions). In 1742, a British army landed at Ostend, still a popular destination for Brits. From here it headed south into Germany in 1743 with a bunch of troops from Hanover. It shouldn't come as a surprise that we had Hanoverians on our side, because our king at this stage, George II, was, of course, one of them. He turned up himself in June 1743 to take command of the army and eventually we ended up fighting the French at Dettingen in Bavaria on 27 June.

It is the last time a British monarch has personally led his troops in battle. Fortunately, he won, and to round things off, Handel composed some victory music to commemorate the day.

Then came the Seven Years War. Again we were teamed up with Hanover. The Duke of Cumberland, who had eventually defeated the Jacobite '45 Rising, found things rather different this time round. He had been sent to defend Hanover against French attack, but instead found himself defeated, retreated and forced into a humiliating peace deal signed at Zeven in northern Germany in 1757. Duke Ferdinand of Brunswick later had to come in to save the day, or at least, save Hanover. In 1759, the British and Hanoverian forces won a major victory at Minden over French and Saxon troops. Due to a famous misunderstanding, British and Hanoverian infantry found themselves advancing, but advancing successfully in this case, against French cavalry. To this day, the victory at Minden is commemorated in the Minden regiments by the wearing of roses on Minden Day, 1 August.

Then there were the wars against Revolutionary France and Napoleon. In 1803, the French finally succeeded in doing what they had been trying to do on and off for some time. They captured Hanover and the Hanoverian army ceased to exist. Although in some ways it didn't – a lot of Hanoverian soldiers joined the King's German Legion, a unit of the British Army that fought throughout the Napoleonic Wars. Included in its list of operations is the deployment to the (now German) island of Rügen in 1807. In other little-known facts about our operations in Germany during the Napoleonic Wars, there was our expedition to northern Germany in 1805 and we had one unit at the massive Battle of Leipzig in 1813 that crushed Napoleon and sent him back to France (a couple of years before we had to defeat him again at Waterloo). It's known as the Battle of the Nations because of all the different countries involved, and we had a Rocket Troop of the Royal Horse Artillery, with Congreve Rockets, attached to the bodyguard of the Crown prince of Sweden. It wasn't exactly the biggest military contribution by a single nation, but we were there.

Anyway, we got Hanover back once Napoleon had been kicked out of it, then in 1837 we lost Hanover forever. Succession in Hanover was under the Salic Law so when we got Victoria as queen, they didn't.

On the subject of our German possessions and the Napoleonic Wars, let's not forget Heligoland. Yes, they are German islands today, and they were Danish islands when our navy turned up during the Napoleonic Wars. From then until 1890 (when we swapped them for Zanzibar), they were British and became a popular seaside resort. After they went back to Germany, they became a not-so-popular (at least with us) German naval base, and we flattened it thoroughly during and after the Second World War.

With the loss of Hanover and unification of Germany in the nineteenth century, we had fewer opportunities to invade it again. We had, of course, to wait for the twentieth century for that.

In the First World War, we conducted assorted naval operations in German waters, including the Battle of Heligoland Bight in 1914, and we built the Vickers Vimy aircraft with the intention of bombing Germany, but the war on land ended before our armies reached the German border and before the Vickers Vimy reached German skies. Nevertheless, following the signing of the armistice, British troops entered Germany in December 1918 as an army of occupation. We took Cologne and the surrounding area to control. Lieutenant General Fergusson, the British military governor, raised the British flag over his headquarters in Cologne at the Hotel Monopol on 11 December 1918. We finally left Cologne in 1926, but we still had troops in Wiesbaden all the way through until 1930. It's a little-known but interesting aspect of our military history and of German history.

Our invasion of Germany in the Second World War is such a vast subject and people know so much more about it than other events in this book, that I'm only going to give very brief details here. We conducted extensive air operations against targets in Germany throughout the war and after fighting our way across Europe after D-Day, in early 1945, Montgomery advanced into German territory with Operations Veritable and Grenade. This was followed in March 1945 when Operation Plunder was launched to cross the Rhine. As German resistance crumbled, Montgomery's troops moved north-east. Our second Army reached the Elbe south of Hamburg on 19 April. It took a week of fierce fighting to take Bremen. On 29 April, we crossed the Elbe. We captured Hamburg on 3 May and, on 4 May, Montgomery accepted the surrender of all German forces in Denmark, Northern Germany and the Netherlands.

After the end of the war, our second British army of occupation in Germany was formed from 21st Army Group. We occupied Hanover (quite appropriately), Saxony and Cologne again, and the Moselle Valley that Marlborough had taken centuries before, and this time a bit of Berlin too. As West Germany got back up and running, the role of the British Army of the Rhine became purely military and rapidly became more focused against a potential threat from Warsaw Pact forces rather than any threat from West Germans.

Ghana

In terms of the land that is now present-day Ghana and our assorted invasions of it, two things come quickly to mind: the Gold Coast and the Ashanti. A bit like many Brits don't know that there have been three Burma Wars, a lot of Brits don't know that there have been not three, but four Ashanti Wars, or even five depending on how you reckon them.

It all started from our point of view with the Gold Coast. This is what we called the area when we first got to know it, unsurprisingly for the reason that there was gold to be had there. But there were other sources of wealth available too, mainly slavery and ivory. The French preferred to call the area the Ivory Coast, or Côte d'Ivoire, which, equally unsurprisingly, explains why that's now the name of the country to the west of Ghana.

As early as the sixteenth century we were getting gold from the Gold Coast, and in the seventeenth century we started grabbing bits of land as well. For example, in the 1660s we established ourselves at Cape Coast Castle (bit of a tongue-twister that). Inevitably, with all the money to be made there, it wasn't just us showing an interest in the area. Lots of Europeans were too. But with our customary relentless dedication, we wore the others down and kicked them out slowly. We had a bit of a rocky start on that front since the Dutch almost managed to chuck us out in the seventeenth century, but things went our way in the competition with the other Europeans and by 1850 we had reached a deal to buy the Danish forts, and finally in the 1870s we got the Dutch forts.

And then there are the Ashanti. A lot of Brits know something about our battles with the Zulus, perhaps because of the movies. But our wars against the Ashanti were even longer. They caused massive suffering to the Ashanti and, on a number of occasions, were pretty tough for the Britons involved too.

The First Ashanti War was something of a shock to us. In 1823, Sir Charles MacCarthy, Governor of Sierra Leone and the Gold Coast, declared war on the Ashanti to win control of Fanti areas. In the end it didn't turn out too well for him and his men. The Ashanti killed almost all of them, and his colonial secretary, Williams, was captured and kept prisoner for months. MacCarthy's skull was later used as a drinking cup by Ashanti rulers. In subsequent fighting, the Ashanti advanced to the coast on more than one occasion, but were in for a bit of a shock themselves from our Congreve Rockets. Eventually a peace treaty was signed in 1831.

More fighting broke out in 1863–64 with the Second Ashanti War. Again we didn't manage to achieve very much, and there were losses on both sides.

Things went better for the British forces with the Third Ashanti War. Once we had got hold of the Dutch forts, we found that we had competition from the Ashanti who also wanted them. The Ashanti attacked and General Garnet Wolseley rushed to deal with them. After the Battle of Amoaful, we entered the Ashanti capital, Kumasi, and looted and burned it. A peace treaty, the Treaty of Fomena, was signed in 1874, making the Ashanti pay us an indemnity and giving us assorted trade advantages.

Then came the Fourth Ashanti War. We were getting a little nervous about the spread of German and French influence and wanted the Ashanti to sign up to be a British protectorate. The Ashanti weren't so keen. By January 1896, citing breaches of the Treaty of Fomena as justification for the war, we had troops in Kumasi. Robert Baden Powell was in there somewhere, as was Prince Henry of Battenberg (like the cake), Queen Victoria's son-in-law. It was not Prince Henry's happiest time, however, since he died on the way back from the expedition. By February it was all over and a treaty of protection was signed and Britain sent some Ashanti leaders into exile on the Seychelles.

Finally, in 1900 came the War of the Golden Stool. This was the Fifth Ashanti War, but with a more interesting name. The Golden Stool was one of the main symbols of Ashanti rule and was sacred to the Ashanti. In 1900 the Governor of the Gold Coast demanded it for Queen Victoria and demanded that he could sit on it. Thus began a war. Eventually we won and more Ashanti leaders were exiled to the Seychelles, and on 1 January 1902 the Ashanti territories became part of the Gold Coast colony.

In 1957, the Gold Coast became independent as Ghana.

Greece

Greece is one of those countries that, even though it has a long and tempestuous history, many Brits probably think we haven't invaded. But, of course, we have.

During the Napoleonic Wars our involvement with Greece was to a certain extent focused on the Ionian Islands lying in the Adriatic to the west of the Greek mainland. France had garrisoned these with French and Neapolitan troops, and we feared that the French would turn the Adriatic into an area from which they could raid our ships in the Mediterranean. We weren't putting up with that.

As the sea war raged in the Adriatic, we set about removing the offending garrisons. On 1 October 1809, a British squadron including HMS *Warrior* landed 1,900 troops under the command of Brigadier General John Oswald on Kefalonia, and within hours the Neapolitan troops there had surrendered. Zante and Ithaca surrendered to us shortly afterwards. Soon after that, troops from HMS *Spartan* seized the island of Kythira, which has connection in legend to the ancient Greek goddess of love, Aphrodite.

And there was love for us. Many Greeks were quite pleased to see us and we set up the 1st Greek Light Infantry under Oswald. And when in March 1810 we invaded the island of Lefkada, our success was helped by the fact that local Greek troops came over to our side. The main fortress surrendered after a siege lasting eight days.

But we had left the big one until last. On Corfu the French had installed a French and Neapolitan garrison consisting of something like 7,400 troops. We had been blockading this with mixed success for some years, but finally, in 1814, the garrison there too gave up and surrendered to us. Hurrah!

The Congress of Vienna placed the islands of Corfu, Kefalonia, Kythira, Ithaca, Paxos, Lefkada and Zakynthos under our protection as the United States of the Ionian Islands. We had only just lost the United States of America, so it must have been nice to get another lot of United States instead, even if they were slightly smaller. Well, quite a lot smaller.

Then in 1827, British ships and a British commander played a key part in gaining Greece independence from the Ottoman Empire. Our naval commander in the Mediterranean, Vice Admiral Sir Edward Codrington, was given the subtle diplomatic task of trying to stop fighting in Greece between Turks and Greeks. Instead, in a rather unsubtle manner, he ended up leading a combined British, French and Russian fleet into a confrontation with the combined Ottoman and Egyptian fleet in Navarino Bay on the west coast of the Peloponnese. This resulted in the last major sea battle in which all ships were powered only by sail, and a crushing defeat for the Ottoman and Egyptian fleet that paved the way for eventual Greek freedom.

Our relations with the newly independent Greece were not entirely smooth, however. In 1850, after Don Pacifico, who had been born in British-held Gibraltar, was attacked in Athens, the Foreign Secretary Palmerston sent a British naval squadron to the Aegean to seize Greek property in compensation for Don Pacifico's losses and to blockade Piraeus. Our actions caused trouble with France and Russia, but Palmerston defended himself in a famous five-hour (five-hour!) speech in which he stated that just as any Roman citizen had once been able to rely on the protection of the Roman Empire, so now any British subject could rely on the protection of Britain.

Though there are still traces of our period in control of the Ionian Islands to be seen today, our time there was not an entirely happy one, and as mainland Greece gained its independence, there was growing local pressure for the islands to be returned to Greek control. In 1862, looking for a new king after getting rid of their last one, the Greek people voted for our very own British Prince Alfred, later to become the Duke of Edinburgh (not Queen Elizabeth II's Duke of Edinburgh, although there's a story of Greek connections there as well). Treaty obligations and the opposition of Queen Victoria apparently wouldn't let him become king, but we felt we owed something to the Greeks for voting for a British candidate and we agreed to hand over the islands. Accordingly on 31 May 1864 Sir Henry Storks and a bunch of British troops finally left Corfu and the Ionian Islands.

In 1885, the Royal Navy again blockaded Greece, since the British government was afraid that the Greeks would defy the Treaty of Berlin. Ironically, our admiral in charge of this blockade was none other than Prince Alfred, Duke of Edinburgh, the one who didn't get to be King of Greece before. Presumably he wouldn't have blockaded himself if he had been King of Greece.

During the First World War we were back in Greek waters and on Greek soil, and in strength. Again, Greek islands played a significant part in the action. For instance, in 1915 Mudros Bay on the island of Lemnos became a key Allied base under British Admiral Rosslyn Wemyss during the Gallipoli campaign, and even after the end of that campaign it remained an important element in the blockade of the Dardanelles.

Things on the mainland got off to a slightly rockier start. It probably didn't help us that the Greek King Constantine was married to the Kaiser's sister. The Allies tried to get Greece to join them in the war and in 1915 we landed troops at Salonika in northern Greece to fight the Bulgarians. Greece became split between those who wanted to join the Allies and those who supported the king and wanted to remain neutral. Things got a bit tense. Well, very tense.

In 1916, when a demand for the Greeks to hand over artillery batteries was rejected, we invaded Athens. A mainly French force, but including sailors from HMS *Exmouth* and HMS *Duncan*, and men from the Royal Marine Light Infantry, landed at Piraeus on 1 December 1916 and headed for Athens. In the ensuing Battle of Athens, both sides suffered casualties, including some British dead, and eventually a compromise deal was reached with some guns being handed over. Things went rather more smoothly for us after the Allies forced King Constantine off the throne and we ended up with a united Greece now on our side. By 1918, British troops were advancing north from Greek territory in an eventually successful campaign against the Bulgarians.

With the Second World War we were back yet again. On 28 October 1940, Italian forces invaded Greece from Albania, bringing Greece into the war. The Greeks did well against the Italians, pushing them back into Albania, but when Germany attacked in April 1941, it was a different story. The Greeks and the British and Commonwealth units fighting with them were unable to hold back the German onslaught. By 30 April, mainland Greece had fallen and in May German paratroopers attacked Crete. After bitter fighting and after taking very heavy losses the Germans captured Crete as well.

As Greek resistance to the Axis occupation developed, we sent in teams to help it grow and to try to direct it towards what we regarded as key objectives. Thus in 1942 Operation Harling saw an SOE team working with guerrillas from both the left-wing ELAS and the right-wing EDES to successfully blow up the Gorgopotamos Viaduct in an attempt to hinder supplies reaching Rommel in North Africa.

In September 1943, as Italy signed an armistice with the Allies, we saw the chance to invade and liberate some of the Greek islands previously held by Italy. Thus began our last major defeat of the Second World War and the Germans' last major victory. Perhaps the result of the Dodecanese Campaign is one reason why comparatively so few Brits know about it.

An initial key target was Rhodes, and we parachuted a team onto it to negotiate with the Italians there, but unfortunately the Germans arrived and took over the island. Nevertheless, with Greek help, we managed to take Kos, Samos, Kalymnos, Leros, Astypalaia and Symi. But soon after that the Germans hit back. On 3 October, in the strangely named Operation Polar Bear, the Germans landed on Kos and forced the British and Italian troops there to surrender. The loss of Kos deprived us of a vital air base. On 12 November, a German invasion force landed on Leros and again the defenders were not able to hold back the German assault. Over 3,000 British prisoners were taken and the remaining British garrisons in the Dodecanese were evacuated.

Less than a year later, the war had turned decisively against the Germans, and in the autumn of 1944 the Germans were retreating under pressure from the Greek resistance and from Soviet advances into the Balkans to the north. We landed on the Greek mainland again. The Special Boat Service (SBS) captured Araxos airfield and on 4 October parachute troops landed at Megara. The rest of General Ronald Scobie's Force 140 arrived soon after and on 13 October our troops entered Athens. A bit like our incursion into Athens in 1916, it wasn't to be the happiest of experiences. We were quickly caught up in the growing conflict over who would rule Greece after the Germans and by December British troops were fighting fierce battles in the streets of Athens.

On 24 December, Churchill flew in to try to sort out a ceasefire, and in January and February of 1945, a ceasefire and political deal were eventually agreed. Sadly, ahead lay the bitterly fought Greek Civil War.

Grenada

We took an early but not hugely successful interest in the island. Then the French had a go in 1649, and after a while got pretty much the same reception from the locals. But the French seem to have been better prepared for such eventualities and after five years the fighting settled down.

By 1762, the Seven Years War was on (not, if you think about it, the most imaginative name for a sort of world war that did indeed last about seven years – it's like calling the Second World War the Six Years War) and we were ready to have another go at Grenada. It wasn't the most dramatic of invasions. Commodore Swanton arrived off the island with some ships and shortly afterwards was joined by more ships and some troops. The governor had already politely refused an invitation from Swanton to surrender, and on 4 March he now did the same to an invitation from Lieutenant Colonel Scott. Some of the population had other ideas and promptly surrendered, leaving the governor to shut himself up in the fort with his garrison. On 5 March, Brigadier General Walsh landed with grenadiers' (grenadiers on Grenada) light infantry and the 27th Regiment. Walsh was just getting ready to assault the fort when the governor decided he had had enough as well and surrendered.

The French struck back in 1779 with a far more violent and noisy invasion of their own. The island surrendered and we had another bit of a disaster at the Battle of Grenada when a British fleet trying for an immediate recapture of the island got mauled by the French fleet because our admiral hadn't really grasped how many French ships there were. Rather a problem that. Anyway, we got the island back under the Treaty of Versailles in 1783.

In 1795, Julien Fedon, inspired by the French Revolution's abolition of slavery, led a rebellion against British rule and thousands of the island's slaves freed themselves and joined him. The rebellion was crushed by the end of 1796.

Grenada became independent in 1974.

Guatemala

Guatemala has Mexico to its west and north, El Salvador to its southeast and Belize to its east.

English privateers like Drake and Cavendish prowled the Pacific coast of Guatemala in the late sixteenth century. Both Drake and Cavendish, for instance, passed through here and attacked Huatulco, across the border in Mexico.

The attractive Castillo de San Felipe was built in 1652 by the Spanish to protect Lake Izabal from the attentions of pirates, many of whom happened to be English. And the Guatemalan town of El Estor allegedly gets its name from English pirates sailing up the Rio Dulce to get stores.

In more recent times, the border between Guatemala and British Honduras, now Belize, has at times been a tense one due to Guatemalan claims to the territory, and British troops have regularly had to respond to crises in the area. In February 1948, there were fears of a Guatemalan invasion and a company from the Gloucestershire Regiment was rushed to the border. In 1958, the Hampshires intercepted a group from the Belize Liberation Army that had crossed the border. In 1975 the Guatemalans moved troops to the border and we responded again.

Guinea

Guinea is a big country with a long stretch of west Africa coastline. In the north of the country, there is a little bit of Guinea-Bissau on the coast, then inland the Guinea border meets up with Senegal. On the coast to the south of Guinea is Sierra Leone.

Guinea became a French colony in the nineteenth century, but as you would expect with a country in this part of the world with a long coastline, Brits have had a go at exerting their control.

Between 1750 and 1790, our main area of activity in the region was on the Îles de Los. And Conakry, the capital of Guinea itself, was started on one of the Îles de Los, Tombo Island, which we handed over to the French in 1887.

In 1885 we turned down the chance to have power over a big chunk of Guinea when we rejected an offer from Samori Toure to take his lands under our protection.

Guinea-Bissau

Guinea-Bissau is on the west coast of Africa with Senegal to the north. The Portuguese were the colonising force on the mainland, but we did have a go at setting ourselves up on the island of Bolama in May 1792. Things didn't exactly start well. Two ships brought 275 colonists, including fifty-seven women and sixty-five children, to Bolama. But an attack by locals scared off most of the would-be colonists leaving fifty-two men, thirteen women and twenty-six children to press on. For a while. By late 1793, only a tiny number of colonists remained and finally in November the last of them packed up and left. In 1814 we gave it another go, but that didn't work either.

In 1860, we decided again we had been a bit premature and declared the island annexed to Sierra Leone, which we controlled. Unfortunately for British hopes, a commission under Ulysses S. Grant (yes, him) decided that the Portuguese should have it, not us, and that was pretty much the end, from our point of view, of trying to grab parts of what is now Guinea-Bissau.

Guyana

Guyana is situated in north-eastern South America, with Suriname to the east, Venezuela to the west and Brazil to the south.

The Dutch used to control Suriname before we took over, and they were in what is now Guyana before we were as well.

They set up two colonies, one known as Essquibo and one known as Berbice. And they brought in slaves to work on the plantations. Then in the mid-eighteenth century they decided to allow Brits to settle in the Demerara (as in the sugar) River area and plenty of Brits accordingly arrived there. From the point of view of the Dutch retaining control of it, this might not have been the most logical move, since the Demerara colony was to act as something of a bridgehead for expanding British interest in and involvement with the area prior to our eventual takeover there.

But it wasn't just Brits and Dutch involved in the area. In 1763 the Berbice Slave Uprising erupted, led by a slave named Cuffy. Eventually, with British and French help, the uprising was crushed.

As with a lot of other Dutch colonies around the world, we saw our chance in this region when Revolutionary France took over in the Netherlands at the end of the eighteenth century. We took control in this area in 1796, and though we briefly gave it back to the Dutch under the Treaty of Amiens, we soon had it back again and kept it at the end of the Napeoleonic Wars.

In the nineteenth century, a massive border dispute developed with Venezuela as we expanded control westwards. But after international arbitration this was largely settled in our favour.

Guyana became independent in 1966.

Haiti

Haiti is a country with a lot of history that deserves to be better known in Britain, and a small percentage of that includes armed Brits roaming the place.

The early years of our involvement with Haiti were mainly to do with English pirates, and one name in particular stands out here – Tortuga.

It's one of those names you may well have heard of, without knowing exactly where it is. It's a Haitian island lying off the north coast and it's big in the history of British pirates. And French pirates. And a few Dutch and other ones. Lots and lots of pirates, in fact. In the early seventeenth century there was a sort of ongoing tug of war here between the Spanish on one side and French and English pirates on the other. The Spanish would intermittently attempt to force the pirates out and the French and English would either resist and/or wait until the Spanish had gone away before returning. In 1654 the Spanish recaptured the island for the fourth and last time, but in 1655 the English and French were back and Colonel William Brayne, acting as military governor on Jamaica, appointed Elias Watts 'governor' of Tortuga. After that, the French took over, although that wasn't the end of English pirates on Tortuga.

Soon, though, it wasn't just pirates heading to Haiti from Britain. As the eighteenth century wore on, we had a number of cracks at what had by now become the French-controlled territory of Saint Domingue. Sir Charles Knowles didn't always have the most successful time at sea (see Cuba), but on 8 March 1784 he attacked the French-held Fort Saint Louis de Sud in Saint Domingue. His squadron bombarded the fort heavily and eventually the garrison was forced to surrender.

In the late eighteenth century, with the French Revolution taking place in France and with France struggling to hold in check rebellion in Haiti, we saw an opportunity. War broke out between Britain and France in 1793 and we installed a naval blockade against the French forces on the island. On 19 September 1793, British forces landed at Jeremie in Haiti. Many of the local white property owners supported their arrival, thinking Britain would restore their position, and by June 1794 British forces held the capital, Port au Prince, and most of the port towns. But British success was not to last. Rebels and the revolutionary French did a deal that would give citizenship to all people on the island of any ethnic background, and the efforts of the French and the rebels, combined with the damage done to British forces and their morale, gradually wore our troops down. The black Haitian leader Toussaint L'Ouverture proved particularly successful in fighting our troops. On 31 August, British General Thomas Maitland signed a deal with him and finally, in October 1798, we withdrew entirely from the country.

Recently, the Royal Navy returned to Haiti in Operation Panlake, with the Royal Fleet Auxiliary supply ship *Largs Bay*, at the request of the UN, helping to move supplies after an earthquake.

Honduras

Honduras is the bit on the Central American isthmus where it makes a sharp 90-degree angle on the Caribbean side, just above Nicaragua.

If you're reading this alphabetically, you'll have already come across the name Honduras, because Belize used to be called British Honduras. This region used to be called Spanish Honduras, but not unreasonably the Spanish bit was dropped after the locals got rid of Spanish control.

Spanish-controlled for a bit and handy for the Caribbean, plus a long coastline: with that combination you would expect pirates from Britain to be active here, and indeed they were. They attacked the port of Trujillo on a number of occasions.

Over the decades we began to become involved on a more serious, official basis in the territory of present-day Honduras. As we'll explore in more detail in the Nicaragua section, we formed an alliance with the Miskito kingdom, which stretched along the coast of Nicaragua and a bit of Honduras. And we also had settlements there. We took an interest in the Honduras Bay Islands, particularly Roatán, and in the 1730s the Black River settlement started.

Relations between us and the Spanish colonial authorities in the area were, inevitably bearing in mind the number of wars we fought with the Spanish, often tense, and when the Spanish joined the American side during the American War of Independence we mounted an invasion of their territory in Honduras.

In October 1779, with twelve ships and 1,200 men, we attacked the fortifications at San Fernando de Omoa. Eventually, some of our men climbed into the fort and opened a gate, and the Spanish subsequently were forced to surrender. Rather fortunately for us, in the harbour there were two Spanish ships holding more than 3 million Spanish dollars of silver. Handy.

Less fortunate for us was that the Spanish counter-attacked, a lot of our men fell ill and by the end of November we withdrew.

Also less fortunate for us was that during the war the Black River settlement was overrun by the Spanish, and though we got it back for a time, we handed it over to them permanently in 1787.

We hung on for longer in Roatán and even declared the Honduras Bay Islands a colony in the 1850s. However, within a decade Britain was handing them over to Honduras, something in itself which led to one last attempt to invade Honduras, with Britons this time involved on both sides.

William Walker is one of those figures from history that when you read about him, you wonder why you have never heard of him before. He is more a part of American and Central American history than British history, so I won't go into big detail here except to say that from 1853 he roamed the region on filibustering or freebooting missions, basically moving into areas with a bunch of like-minded freebooters, including the English adventurer Charles Frederick Henningsen, and taking over. At one stage he even set himself up as President of Nicaragua.

Finally, in 1860, British colonists in Roatán decided that they didn't want to become Honduran and prompted Walker to head for

Honduras. But Walker was in big trouble this time. He landed at Trujillo, only to fall into the hands of Captain Nowell Salmon of the British Navy. Salmon then handed him over to the local authorities, who shot him. End of invasion.

Hungary

Hungary is just a bit too far from the sea to have received very much attention from us. Nevertheless, armed Brits have conducted operations there.

For instance, in the late seventeenth century, assorted volunteers from Britain, including the son of Prince Rupert, fought in the army of Prince Eugene of Savoy as it pushed the Ottomans back through Hungary. Buda was stormed in 1686 and in 1687 the prince won a battle at Mohacs, scene of the decisive Ottoman victory in 1526.

The RAF operated over Hungary in the Second World War. SOE also operated in Hungary, though not extensively. SOE had difficulty establishing a presence in the country, with a couple of failed missions. When Basil Davidson was working as liaison with the Yugoslav partisans, SOE sent him into Hungary to try to organise a rebel movement there, but he realised that it wasn't going to work and eventually crossed back into the Fruska Gora area.

5

ICELAND TO JORDAN

Iceland

Older readers will probably remember the so-called Cod Wars with Iceland in the 1970s, but what many won't be aware of is that some decades before that we actually invaded Iceland.

At the time of the German invasion of Denmark on 9 April 1940, the Danish king was also King of Iceland. In response to the German occupation of Denmark, Britain offered to help Iceland defend itself and encouraged it to join the war alongside Britain. The offer was rejected.

As the Germans advanced through Norway, we began to think how useful bases in Iceland would be and how dangerous it would be if the Germans took over Iceland. Consequently, we decided to prevent any possibility of that by going there ourselves. Thus began Operation Fork. Not our smoothest operation, in the sense that it was thrown together pretty hastily at four days' notice and relied on newly recruited and not yet fully-trained Royal Marines, with a shortage of weapons and very few heavy weapons. Having said that, it worked.

On 8 May 1940, the force departed from the harbour in Greenock on board the cruisers HMS *Berwick* and HMS *Glasgow*, with two destroyers HMS *Fearless* and *Fortune* as escort. Very early on the morning of 10 May, a reconnaissance plane from HMS *Berwick* flew over Reykjavik, waking a number of the inhabitants. Shortly afterwards an Icelandic policeman saw the fleet arriving and raised the alarm, and pretty soon after that about 400 marines from *Berwick*, having transferred to *Fearless* for the landing, arrived in the harbour, where they were met by the British consul and some rather upset locals.

However, there was no resistance and our troops immediately took control of the radio and post office. The Icelandic government issued a strong protest about the occupation, but was eventually persuaded to cooperate. The Germans considered mounting an invasion of Iceland in response to the British invasion, and prepared a plan for Operation Ikarus, but it never happened.

Finally, in July 1941, the US took over responsibility for Iceland from us, with the consent of the Icelandic government.

India

The story of our involvement with this impressive country is a long and fascinating one, but unfortunately we've only got time in this book for a brief version, particularly since our close involvement with India is something almost all Brits are at least aware of and this book is supposed to be exploring the sort of history Brits are less aware of.

The East India Company was chartered in 1600. Somewhat confusingly for modern Britons, this wasn't just interested in India (and not just in the east of India either) since it was also targeting trade in areas further east. By 1613 it had established a trading base at Surat in India; by 1639 it was founding Fort St George at Madras (Chennai); and in 1668 it established a trading post at Bombay (Mumbai). Towards the end of the seventeenth century, the East India Company ran into big trouble with the Mughal authorities. It lost Child's War of 1686–90 after a Mughal fleet attacked the English base in Bombay and forced it to surrender. Then in 1695 an English pirate attacked and seized Mughal ships leading to fury against the East India Company.

Nevertheless, the East India Company began slowly to eclipse other European rivals. The Portuguese and Dutch eventually dropped out of the race to be the major European power operating in India, which left the French to deal with. In the eighteenth century, this rivalry produced a series of bitter wars between Brits and local allies on one side against the French and their local allies on the other side. The First Carnatic War ran fom 1746 to 1748 and saw the French attack and capture Madras, even taking Robert Clive prisoner. Almost before the First Carnatic War had ended, we were into the second one. In this one, from 1749 to 1754, we and the French were heavily involved with local politics. The two European powers backed rival claimants to the throne of Hyderabad and rival claimants to be Nawab of Arcot. In 1751, Clive took Arcot and Muhammad Ali Khan Walajah was recognised as Nawab. Peace came with the Treaty of Pondicherry in 1754. But again it wasn't to last for long. By 1757, the Third Carnatic War had broken out. In Bengal, Clive won a hugely significant victory over the French-backed Nawab of Bengal, Siraj ud Daulah. In 1760, Sir Eyre Coote won an important victory over the French at the Battle of Wandiwash and in 1761 we took the major French base at Pondicherry. They got it back, by the Treaty of Paris in 1763, but they also agreed to stay out of involvement in local politics and not build more fortifications. The French finally ceased to be a threat to us in India during the Napoleonic Wars.

With French influence in India declining, we had more opportunity to challenge local rulers for power. Between 1766 and 1799 we fought four wars against Mysore, which ended finally with a decisive British victory at the Battle of Seringapatam in 1799, in which Tipu Sultan was killed.

In the late eighteenth and early nineteenth century we fought a string of wars against the Maratha Empire. The First Maratha War of 1777–83 was a conflict that saw internal disputes both on the Maratha side and on the British side. We lost the Battle of Wadgaon, but won a subsequent confrontation. The Second Maratha War of 1803–05 saw more tough fighting. Arthur Wellesley (yes him) won the Battle of Assaye and later said that it had been a harder battle than Waterloo. The Third Maratha War of 1817–18 was decisive. We won significant victories at the Battle of Sitapuldi and the Battle of Mahidpur. The war destroyed the Maratha Empire as a rival to British power in India.

By now the East India Company was in control of much of India and over the ensuing decades its power spread even further. For instance, in the 1840s the Sikh Wars saw the spread of British control through what is now the part of Punjab that is within India, as well as the part that today is within Pakistan. In 1854 the company annexed Berar, and in 1856 captured Oudh (Awadh). In 1858 the

Indian Rebellion broke out, leading to a tough conflict and harsh action by the British.

It was after the rebellion that the British government itself took over control of India from the East India Company.

During 1944, the Japanese invaded India and it took bitter fighting to push them out.

In 1947 India became independent.

Indonesia

We took an early interest in what is now Indonesia. Drake, for instance, on a round-the-world voyage came home via Java, Sulawesi and the Moluccas (Maluku Islands). Of the European powers, it was the Portuguese first, and then more extensively and successfully the Dutch, who became deeply involved in this part of the world.

Rivalry between the Dutch and ourselves over this area was at times extremely bitter. In the notorious and murky Amboyna Affair, some East India Company men were executed by a Dutch East India court on the charge of conspiring to seize the Dutch-held fortress at Amboyna, now called Ambon. This became a source of continuing English anger towards Holland and played a part in the wars between England and Holland. In 1654, Cromwell forced the Dutch to pay financial compensation to the victims' descendants and give us Manhattan as well. In 1673, Dryden produced the tragedy *Amboyna; or the Cruelties of the Dutch to the English Merchants*. I've never read the play myself, but judging from the title you would guess that Dryden doesn't make the Dutch look good in it.

We still managed to set up in business at, among other places, Bengkulu on the south-western coast of Sumatra, where we established a trading post in 1685 and built Fort Marlborough in 1714. And in 1793, British naval officer Lieutenant John Hayes endeavoured to establish a settlement near Manokwari, in Irian Jaya.

Inevitably, when we ended up at war with Holland at the end of the eighteenth century, the extensive territories it controlled in what is now Indonesia were an obvious target for us.

Our first invasion started in the last years of the eighteenth century after a pro-French regime had come to power in Holland. We took Malacca, Padang, Ambon and the Bandas without much trouble. Admiral Peter Rainier played a prominent role in these events, and when we captured a Dutch 16-gun brig at Kuyper's Island, Java, on 23 August 1800, its captors took it into service as HMS *Admiral Rainier*. Temate resisted for a while, but finally fell in 1801. There was a slightly messy and confusing battle at Kupang on Timor, which ended with some of our troops dead, a lot of the locals killed, and us bombarding the town. After all that, though, we handed back what we had taken from the Dutch under a peace treaty of 1802.

Then in 1810, as hostilities resumed, we returned. We took Ambon again, despite French reinforcements. Some of the garrison at Temate mutinied and we took that. And then we started working our way through assorted other Dutch posts as Lord Minto (great name) moved to expel the Dutch from Java. The campaign took just forty-five days. We installed Thomas Stamford Raffles as lieutenant-governor. Yes, before he got Singapore, he was our man running a bit of what's now Indonesia for us. Sadly, his wife Olivia died there in 1814. The Anglo-Dutch convention of 1814 again gave territory back the Dutch.

Finally, an 1824 treaty between us and the Dutch separated our spheres of influence, giving us control of what would become Malaysia and the Dutch what would become Indonesia.

With the Second World War we were back in Indonesia. As the Japanese swept through the Dutch East Indies in 1941 and 1942, forces were sent to help the Dutch. These were mainly Australian, but there were also British. For example, the British 79th Light Anti-Aircraft Battery landed in Dutch-controlled West Timor in February 1942. They fought bravely against both Japanese air and ground attacks, but eventually Timor fell to the Japanese, though guerrilla action against them continued.

Then in 1945 we landed again in Indonesia in the face of heavy fighting. After the Japanese surrender there was an explosive situation in Indonesia in which pro-independence Indonesians were trying to prevent the return of Dutch colonial rule. British forces were supposed to restore Dutch control and disarm the Japanese. The Japanese ended up at times both helping the pro-independence Indonesians and fighting them. In this chaotic and dangerous situation, Brigadier Mallaby was killed in Surabaya and in November 1945 we launched an attack on the pro-independence forces there, supported by tanks, air and sea bombardment (including from HMS *Cavalier*). Many Indonesians were killed, and there were a lot of British and Indian casualties as well, before Surabaya fell. Our troops left Indonesia later that month, and after a bitter struggle Holland recognised Indonesian independence in 1949.

Iran

All Brits know we have invaded Iraq, yet many tend to think we haven't invaded Iran. But we have on a number of occasions, something that the average Iranian in contrast to the average Brit probably knows very well.

As with the Gulf States, our early involvement with Iran (Persia, as it was known) is linked to the East India Company's activities and its desire to protect them.

In 1763, the East India Company opened a trading post at Bushehr, a port that was to play a major role in our relations with the country (and still does since the site of Iran's controversial nuclear reactor is nearby).

After that, the East India Company's desire to protect its ships from attack at sea led to a number of operations against targets in what is present-day Iran. Thus, for instance, in 1809, after his attack on Ras al-Khaimah in the current-day United Arab Emirates, Captain Wainwright ordered his flotilla to cross the Persian Gulf and attack the town of Bandar Lengeh in present-day Iran. The locals fled and we burned twenty dhows. Wainwright's forces then moved on to the Iranian Qeshm Island in the Straits of Hormuz. Here Wainwright landed troops, and with the sloop *Fury* firing in support the landing party, despite suffering heavy casualties, eventually managed to capture a fort.

In 1856, full-scale war broke out between us and Persia, and a more serious and extensive invasion got under way. This war started over two major issues. First, the Persians had once controlled Herat in Afghanistan and wanted to retake it. After several attempts in 1856, with Russian encouragement, they succeeded. Second, things had been getting rather complicated diplomatically in Tehran. In this, the British Ambassador had been accused of having improper relations with the wife of a man he wanted to appoint as secretary. To make matters even more complex, the wife happened to be a sister of one of the Shah of Persia's wives. When the Persians arrested the woman, our ambassador demanded she be released and when she wasn't he broke off relations with Persia.

The war was on and Bushehr was our first major target. We landed an army under Major General Stalker at Hallila Bay, 12 miles south of Bushehr, in December 1856, and while that fought its way towards Bushehr, the fleet under Rear Admiral Sir Henry Leeke prepared to attack the town too. There was a potentially problematic incident when ships ran aground due to the tides, but they continued firing while stuck and eventually the combined land and sea attack forced the port to surrender. The Persian flag was cut down and the British colours hoisted.

In 1857, reinforcements arrived in the shape of two divisions from India under the command of General Sir James Outram. In February, he advanced inland from Bushehr and clashed with a Persian force gathered there. After a dramatic cavalry charge of the 3rd Bombay Light Cavalry, the Persians were defeated, losing at least 700 killed, compared to only sixteen men killed on our side.

A subsequent operation involved a flotilla of three steamers making its way up the Karun River as far as the Persian, now Iranian, town of Ahvaz. Captain Rennie landed his 300 troops and with, supporting fire from the gunboats, took the town.

Eventually peace was signed. The Persians withdrew from Herat and we withdrew from Persia.

British influence in Persia increased in the late nineteenth century and competition between Britain and Russia for influence over Persia culminated in the Anglo-Russian Treaty of 1907, which established separate British and Russian spheres of influence in Persia.

During the First World War, our forces were in action in Persia once again. In the south of the country, one Wilhelm Wassmuss, also known as the German Lawrence (of Arabia), tried to rouse local tribes to strike at British interests. But the comparison to Lawrence is a little unfair to Lawrence, since Wasmuss was far less successful. He contributed significantly to Allied operations by losing his German Diplomatic Code Book, which allowed Admiral Hall to read German diplomatic communications for much of the war. In August 1915, we reoccupied Bushehr. Towards the end of the year, Sir Percy Sykes established the South Persia Rifles to protect our interests there, and by December 1916 it had brigades based at Shiraz, Kerman and Bandar-Abbas.

Then in 1918, with Russia after the revolution out of the war against Turkey, British forces advanced into northern Persia and the Caucasus to counter Ottoman advances and Bolshevik influence. At the end of the war, we made sure we were guaranteed access to Persian oil and, for a while, troops under General William Edmund Ironside occupied Northern Persia.

In the Second World War, we invaded again. In 1935, the then Iranian government had asked countries with which it had diplomatic relations to call it Iran instead of Persia, so this time we invaded Iran instead of Persia. Again oil was a vital consideration, as was the desire to transport supplies from the Persian Gulf through Iran to the Soviet Union. There were fears of increasing German influence over Iran and in 1941, in coordination with the Soviets, we invaded. In an echo of the Anglo-Russian treaty of 1907, the plan was for the Soviets to take control of northern Persia, while Britain would take control of the south.

The invasion began on 25 August 1941, with Abadan, site of a major oil refinery, as a prime target. HMS *Shoreham* sank the Iranian ship *Palang*, while Indian troops from Basra crossed the Shatt al Arab and took the town. HMAS *Kanimbla* landed troops at Bandar-e-Shahpur to take the port and petrol terminal there. Indian troops from Basra then advanced towards Ahvaz, which Captain Rennie had taken in 1857. Meanwhile, further north, General William Slim led British and Indian troops across the Iraq/Iran border to capture the Naft-i-Shah oilfield and then pressed on towards Kermanshah. The Soviets advanced from the north. By the time hostilities ceased, assorted Iranian warships were sunk or badly damaged, their planes had been destroyed and hundreds of Iranian military personnel were dead. In September, British and Soviet forces occupied Tehran and Reza Shah was forced off the throne to be replaced by his son, Mohammad Reza Shah Phalavi.

So, over the centuries we have been very busy in Persia/Iran.

Iraq

Unless you have been out of contact with the news for a very long time, it won't come as much of a surprise that we have invaded Iraq. What may come as a surprise, though, is quite how much time we've spent fighting there, even before our recent excursion.

The East India Company took an early interest in the area for strategic reasons. In 1763, for instance, it set up shop in Basra and also set up a camel post from Aleppo to Baghdad – carrying post by camels, not posting camels. Then the company started supplying modern weapons to the authorities in Baghdad and teaching them how to use them. Sounds familiar? And by 1805, with worries about what Napoleon might be up to, if he was given half a chance, Brits were already thinking that maybe it would be useful to control Iraq. Well, after all, Napoleon did invade Egypt, partly with the aim of getting at India.

Having said that, during the Persian War of 1856–57 we went to some lengths to avoid invading what is now Iraq, since, not unreasonably, we didn't want to pick a quarrel with the Ottoman authorities there while also fighting the Persians at the same time. It would be a bit like fighting wars in both Iraq and Iran today. So when we wanted to attack the Persian defences, we sent boats into the Shatt al Arab, but went to some lengths to stay in the Persian bit. Just as when we were in Iraq recently, we had to try to stay in the Iraqi bit of the Shatt al Arab and keep out of the Iranian bit.

But all that went out of the window with the First World War. On 5 November 1914, we declared war on the Ottomans, and by 25 November a British and Indian force had already captured Basra.

In 1915 we pushed north towards Baghdad. By November of that year we were just short of Baghdad and confronted an Ottoman force at the Battle of Ctesiphon. Ctesiphon's a hugely historical place, a sort of crossroads of history. In 363, the Roman Emperor Julian fought the Persians here and that was about as far as the Roman expedition got before turning back. In 1915, we did the same against the Ottomans before turning back.

Unfortunately in terms of historical parallels, we then switched to the Stalingrad parallel, but we were about to end up playing the German role in Stalingrad, not the Russian one. Our retreating army made it as far as Kut al Amara and was then encircled. We subsequently tried to break through to the besieged forces, we tried to supply them by air, we even tried sending a paddle steamer to get through to them. All to no avail. In April 1916, our trapped forces surrendered and over 13,000 soldiers became prisoners. The surrender at Kut al Amara is not something a lot of Brits know about, but it was a huge disaster for us. So you see, we've had miserable times in Iraq before.

After that we picked ourselves up, regrouped and retrained, making Basra into our base and our home in Iraq, just as we were to do during our recent time in the country. By December 1916, we were ready to march north. This time there were no mistakes like those of the previous venture north, and on 11 March 1917 we marched into Baghdad. There weren't any statues of Saddam to pull down yet, but we did issue the proclamation of Baghdad, telling the locals 'our armies do not come into your cities and lands as conquerors or enemies, but as liberators'.

We took it a bit easy on this front for most of 1918, but later that year, with signs of an armistice approaching, we lurched into action to ensure we grabbed as much as possible before the close of play.

After the First World War ended, it was all a bit of a mess for us in the area. We were occupying three separate Ottoman provinces: Mosul in the north, Baghdad in the centre and Basra in the south. There were major cultural and ethnic differences in the make-up of the three provinces. But despite this, the decision was taken to string them together into one political entity – Iraq. In April 1920, we were given the League of Nations Mandate to control the territory. Subsequently, the locals decided that they didn't entirely believe the bit about us coming as liberators instead of conquerors and by June 1920 we had an armed insurgency on our hands which mixed nationalists, religious elements and out-of-work ex-Ottoman army officers. Does any of this sound familiar?

In 1920, in a world without television cameras and which had just come out of an appallingly brutal world war, we used air power and some very tough tactics against the rebels. The tactics did indeed help to bring the military side of the rebellion to an end, but they left a legacy that probably destroyed any chance of the Brits and the Iraqis getting along cheerfully.

Anyway, in 1921 we set up the Kingdoms of Iraq, with a king, Faisal, whom the French had forced out of Syria. It was one of those situations where we had decided that we wanted to remain in control of some of the important aspects of Iraq, and we were going to keep British forces there, but we wanted the Iraqis to run the less important aspects and still get along peacefully with us. Not surprisingly this approach didn't win us many lasting friends among Iraqis and by 1941 we were fighting another war in Iraq and invading it all over again.

By 1939, after assorted political developments, the only forces we had left in Iraq were two RAF bases, one near Basra and one at Habbaniya, between Ramadi and Fallujah, both familiar names from recent events in Iraq. On 1 April 1941, with Germany at one of its strongest points during the Second World War, a nationalist coup d'état led by one Rashid Ali took power in Baghdad after the regent had taken refuge on HMS *Cockchafer* (yes, Cockchafer – named after an insect apparently, not anything else). The new regime looked to the Germans for support against the British.

In response, we rushed in reinforcements to the Basra area and occupied key points in the city, and when the Habbaniya base was surrounded by Iraqi troops and guns, we went on the offensive, bombing them and other military targets further afield. In May, German planes started arriving in Mosul in northern Iraq by way of Vichy French Syria. The German planes were repainted as Iraqi and started attacking us. A British relief force invaded Iraq from Palestine and eventually reached Habbaniya, while additional reinforcements were also airlifted in. This set us up for the Battle of Fallujah. Oh yes, it's not just the Americans who've had one of those, we've had one too. On 19 May, after bombing and shelling Iraqi positions in and around Fallujah, we took the city. An Iraqi counter-attack on 22 May was eventually repulsed after fighting in the streets, and British troops began to advance on Baghdad both from Basra and from Habbaniya. Rashid's regime collapsed, with him fleeing first to Persia and eventually to Germany. We put a pro-British government in power.

That was not, of course, to be our last invasion of Iraq. During the liberation of Kuwait in 1991, British forces were part of a sweeping attack launched through Iraq to outflank Iraqi forces in Kuwait itself. And in 2003 we and the Americans were back again with some of the old names, like Basra and Fallujah, making a comeback on British news.

Ireland

It won't come as any surprise to anybody that we've invaded Ireland. More people, by contrast, will be surprised that quite a lot of the invaders were coming in the opposite direction.

Historical sources suggest there were raids across the sea from Ireland in the fourth century. There is also the famous instance of Patrick being abducted from Britain and taken back to Ireland by raiders. In the post-Roman period, historical and archaeological sources suggest Irish settlers arriving (perhaps to join cultures with existing strong links to Ireland) in a number of places in Britain, including in particular Dyfed and, in what is now Scotland, Dalriada.

No doubt there was already a certain amount of two-way traffic even in this period, and soon the Anglo-Saxons would start taking a serious interest in Irish matters as well. The *Annals of Tigernach* for 629, for example, state that a Saxon prince, Osric, and his retinue were involved in a battle between two Irish forces. And there is a tradition that Saxons were present at the Battle of Mag Rath in County Down in 637. Then in 684, the Northumbrian King Ecgfrith sent an expedition to Ireland that seized slaves and booty.

In 795, the Vikings first raided Ireland and for the next few centuries they were to be the main foreign force in the country.

By the second half of the twelfth century, however, Brits were again a major factor. In 1166, King Dermot MacMurrough of Leinster was forced into exile and he wanted to get back his kingdom. He decided that the best way to do this was by recruiting some foreign help, in this case Norman and Welsh help. It is a classic case of unforeseen consequences. No doubt the English invasion would have come eventually, but that it came then is down to Dermot seeking external assistance in internal conflicts. It is strangely and ironically similar to the way in which Saxons are first supposed to have come to Britain itself, invited by the British King Vortigern to deal with other raiders.

So into Ireland came people like Richard FitzStephen and Richard FitzGilbert de Clare, better known as Strongbow. Strongbow even married Dermot's daughter, Aoife of Leinster, giving him the chance of becoming King of Leinster.

At this point, King Henry II of England decided that things were getting out of hand, with the prospect of a new independent Norman kingdom in Ireland, and he himself now invaded Ireland with an army. This was on a much bigger scale than anything Strongbow had to offer and the result was that the kings of Ireland paid homage to Henry. He in turn made his younger son, John, Lord of Ireland.

John unexpectedly then became king and continued to take an interest in Ireland, visiting it in 1185 and again in 1210.

After that, the English kings lost interest in Ireland until Richard II in the fourteenth century.

In the meantime, other assorted political and military developments were under way. For instance, the Norman forces of John Fitzgerald were defeated by the forces of Finghin MacCarthaigh at the Battle of Callann in 1261. And in 1315, Edward Bruce, brother of the rather more famous Robert, invaded with a Scots army, hoping to open a second front in the war against the English. Some Irish supported him, some opposed him. Eventually, he was killed at the Battle of Fochart in 1318 and the Scots went home. For a while.

By the reign of Richard II, the position of the English in Ireland had become so weak that the Anglo-Irish lords pleaded for the king to intervene. So he took an army of more than 8,000 men to invade Ireland and did a bit of campaigning. It was a success in some sense, but had little long-term effect and the Wars of the Roses were soon to divert English attention elsewhere.

By 1536 there was an open rebellion against Henry VIII and he decided on a policy of bringing Ireland under tight Crown control. Thus began the Tudor invasion of Ireland. The Desmond Rebellions of 1569–73 and 1579–83 in Munster saw tough resistance to the spread of English control, and in 1594 the Nine Years War broke out, with Hugh O'Neil leading resistance in Ulster. He even managed to get Spanish forces to arrive in Ireland in support of him, but the combined forces were defeated at Kinsale. In 1607, in what became known as 'The Flight of the Earls', O'Neil and other local leaders left Ireland, hoping to return with forces to pursue their cause. They never managed to.

In some ways you could argue that the British invasion of Ireland was now complete, but perhaps it's easiest to see some key events in the rest of the seventeenth century as a continuation of what had gone before.

The arrival of Protestant settlers created tensions with locals, and events in Britain were about to have a dramatic impact on Ireland. In 1641 rebellion broke out, but with the English Civil War raging in England, it was not until 1649 that an English army, under Cromwell, was able to confront it. He did so ruthlessly, in a campaign that involved the atrocity of massacring the defenders of Drogheda, and that dragged on until 1653. More land confiscations followed.

In 1688, James II was deposed and replaced by William III. A Jacobite army was raised in Ireland and James, with the support of French troops as well, arrived in Ireland. He met William III and his army at the Battle of the Boyne in 1690. James lost and fled Ireland. By 1691 the Jacobites were defeated and the war was over.

A number of rebellions were to follow. After the Easter Rising of 1916, and the War of Independence against Britain, the Irish Free State came into being in 1922. In 1949 Ireland officially became a republic and left the Commonwealth.

Israel

Brits were probably invading what is now Israel as early as the last years of the eleventh century with the arrival of the First Crusade in the Holy Land. English participation in the First Crusade is fairly minimal and rather controversial, but it does seem reasonable to accept that at least some armed Brits reached the Holy Land with the First Crusade.

It was with the Third Crusade and Richard I that we really got going on invading the Holy Land. In 1190, Richard and his army set out for the region, and after brief stopovers (but violent ones, so not your average getting off the boat to stretch your legs and buy a few souvenirs) in Sicily and Cyprus, by the summer of 1191 he was getting stuck into the Siege of Acre on the coast of what is now northern Israel.

Acre fell in July 1190, and Richard then managed to fall out with both his major allies, Philip of France and Leopold of Austria. It all turned into a diplomatic debacle, with Philip and Leopold deciding that frankly they had had enough and were going home. Richard then executed a large number of prisoners from Acre before moving south.

From Acre he headed towards Jaffa, near present-day Tel Aviv. On the way, Saladin's forces attacked his army at Arsuf in September 1191, and despite Saladin's efforts to break up his forces, Richard managed to hang on and maintain enough cohesion and impetus eventually to secure a victory.

Richard subsequently captured Jaffa and opened negotiations with Saladin. The talks broke down and Richard headed south towards Ashkelon, on the coast of what is now southern Israel, near Gaza and the Egyptian border. He took Ashkelon and set out to refortify it.

In July 1192, though Saladin's army had taken Jaffa back and amid political chaos and conflict on the Crusader side, Richard began to accept that realistically he could not take and hold Jerusalem. Eventually, in September 1192, he signed a peace deal with Saladin and went home. Eventually. We've all had journeys home that we would like to forget and this would definitely be in that category for Richard. He had made himself some very powerful enemies and it was pay-back time. Weather forced his ship into Corfu, which unfortunately was run by the Byzantine emperor, whom Richard had upset by taking Cyprus. He fled from there in disguise, only to end up being captured by Leopold of Austria (see above), who was keen to discuss assorted insults Richard had paid him. After being released by Leopold, he was captured by the Holy Roman Emperor, Henry, who was keen to discuss assorted wrongs he reckoned Richard and the Plantagenets had done him. Richard only got back to his own lands after a huge ransom was paid. There's nothing like a swift, easy journey home, and this indeed was nothing like a swift, easy journey home.

There were assorted other Crusades with assorted British involvement. Take Richard of Cornwall, for example, who was already back in Ashkelon refortifying it in the 1240s, but for more major English involvement the Third Crusade was the main one.

After the Crusades we took a break from invading the area, but with the arrival of the Napeolonic Wars we were back. After invading Egypt, Napoleon had decided to have a go at what is now Israel, advancing along the coast from Egypt and taking Gaza and Jaffa, in a sort of reverse move to what Richard I had been trying. In 1799, Napoleon laid siege to the now Ottoman-held city of Acre. And we went to help. To help the Ottoman defenders that is. A Royal Navy flotilla commanded by Commodore William Sidney Smith arrived and played a key role in combating the French forces. British guns and British sailors helped with the defence of Acre and we also attacked French supply lines both on land and sea. Eventually, Napoleon gave up and went back to Egypt, and shortly after that back to France. He had a somewhat easier journey than Richard.

By 1840 we were back on the attack in the area again and, you guessed it, once again Acre was the location. We've done so much fighting there that it seems appropriate that it has such an apparently British name as Acre, though it's not really named after a British Imperial unit of land measurement, since its local name has always been something like Akko or Akka.

Anyway, all that aside, this time we were attacking Acre again. It was held by Egyptian troops who had come up the same way as Napoleon and we wanted it back in the hands of Ottoman troops to maintain the power balance in the Middle East. So an allied squadron containing British, Austrian and Turkish ships bombarded the defences of the city. Heavily. After two hours of firing, the defenders' grand magazine blew up, and it is reported that every living creature within an area of 60,000 square yards (how many acres is that?) ceased to exist. Two regiments were apparently wiped out, along with fifty donkeys, thirty camels, twelve cows and some horses. The city fell and Sir Charles Smith took temporary command of the garrison. Eventually the Egyptians were pushed back into Egypt.

In the First World War we returned, with some of the old sites reappearing. This time we were fighting the Ottomans instead of helping them. In 1915, the Turks attacked Egypt, but by 1917 British Empire troops had pushed the Turks back and we were attempting to move forward towards Israel. We were held up by fighting around Gaza in spring 1917, and a new commander was brought in, one General Allenby, given the mission of taking Jerusalem in time for Christmas. In October 1917, with a dramatic cavalry charge, Australian cavalry took Beersheva to the south and shortly afterwards Gaza fell. On 9 November 1917, Ashkelon fell to us, yet again, and on 16 November Jaffa fell. Jerusalem fell on 9 December 1917, and Allenby was able to visit Bethlehem itself on Christmas Day 1917. After a pause in early 1918, necessitated by some of Allenby's forces being rushed to Europe to counter the German Spring Offensive, Allenby's troops began to push further north through Israel. In autumn 1918, they won a decisive victory over the Turks at the Battle of Megiddo (sometimes known in English as the Battle of Armageddon, since the word Armageddon may come from the Hebrew for Har Megiddo, the Hill of Megiddo) and on 23 September 1918, just a few days before the Turks signed the Armistice of Mudros, Acre fell to us. Yet again.

After the war we kept control of Israel as the Palestine Mandate. In 1948 we withdrew from the area and the current State of Israel was established.

Italy

Most Brits will know that the first invasion of Britain that we are aware of from a historical point of view came about because of a bunch of Italians (and others) led by one Julius Caesar. Caesar was fortunate in terms of his reputation in writing his own history. People's idea of his invasion of Britain is largely based on what he himself wrote. Imagine if all history was like that, relying on the verdict of the generals and politicians involved. The fact is that he didn't achieve that much over here, despite what he wrote, and eventually, after two stabs at us, he disappeared back over the Channel never to return (though the Romans did, almost 100 years later).

Over the centuries we've got our own back on the Italians and, in fact, we started to do so even before the end of the Roman Empire. Constantine launched his bid for imperial power from Britain and in 312 was marching towards Rome. Ahead lay a sort of Northern Europe versus Mediterranean confrontation, which, on this occasion, Northern Europe was to win decisively. According to Zosimus, with a force drawn from Britain, plus assorted Germans, Celts and others, Constantine smashed Maxentius' larger force consisting of Romans, Italians, Tuscans, Sicilians and Carthaginians, at the Battle of the Milvian Bridge, and subsequently took Rome and transformed the empire and the world by making Christianity the official religion of the empire.

Towards the end of the fourth century, Magnus Maximus tried the same thing. He wasn't anything like as successful as Constantine, as it turned out, but he did set off from Britain and make it as far as northern Italy. He didn't end up with happy memories of an Italian holiday, since he was defeated and executed. At least he's remembered in Welsh legend as Macsen Wledig.

Constantine III tried the same thing at the beginning of the fifth century. He had the same name as Constantine and made his bid almost exactly a century after the first Constantine, so he may have thought he was in for the same kind of success. He wasn't. He made it to Liguria before withdrawing to Gaul. By 411 he was dead, and back in Britain we had rebelled and resigned from the Roman Empire permanently.

After that we left Italy alone for a while. Well, we had quite a lot of other things to think about back home. In the late eleventh century the Normans took control of Sicily, but you couldn't really call it a British invasion since it was more like a parallel invasion to the Norman invasion of England, just in a different direction.

In September 1190, Richard the Lionheart turned up in Sicily with his army. He wasn't in a good mood, since his sister Joanna was in prison there. She had been married to King William II of Sicily, but when he died, his cousin Tancred (not Tankard, even though he may have liked a drink or two) had taken over and imprisoned Joan. Tancred wasn't very happy about Richard turning up and neither were the locals. In October there was trouble in Messina. Richard attacked Messina, captured it, did a bit of looting and burning, and established his base there. Finally, in March 1191, a deal was done with Tancred, and Richard could set off for the main event, for which he had ventured into the Mediterranean, the Third Crusade.

British knights spent a fair amount of time fighting in Italy later in the Middle Ages as mercenaries. Some of the best-known mercenary units and commanders in medieval Italy were English, like, for instance, John Hawkwood and his company.

As British sea power in the Mediterranean expanded through the eighteenth century, we found ourselves frequently in Italian waters and on Italian soil. In 1718, a British fleet under Sir George Byng attempted to force the Spanish out of Sicily and our victory at the Battle of Cape Passaro and subsequent blockade of Sicilian ports played a significant role in achieving that goal. At least temporarily. In 1742, Captain William Martin arrived off Naples with a squadron and demanded that Charles IV, king of the Two Sicilies (it's a long story as to why there were Two Sicilies, to do with containing a bit of southern Italy as well as Sicily, and to do with at one stage there being two different kingdoms both claiming Sicily), get out of a war that we didn't want him in, within half an hour. Charles found Martin's arguments, or at least his guns, highly compelling and accordingly did so.

By the end of the eighteenth century and beginning of the nineteenth century, we were spending a lot of time in the area. Nelson himself was a regular there, and not just because our ambassador to the King of Naples, one William Hamilton, had a rather attractive and very friendly wife called Emma. In the 1790s, Nelson and other Brits also spent a fair amount of time in the seas to the west of Italy. We won the Battle of Genoa in 1797. We were, however, unable to prevent the French advancing overland, and were reduced to doing things like blockading cities after the French had taken them. Something about stable doors, horses and bolting comes to mind

Interestingly, considering we don't normally think of Russians fighting in the Western Med, we did conduct a number of these operations in coordination with Russian forces. Nelson worked alongside Admiral Ushakov to reconquer Naples in 1799. And who could forget the Anglo-Russian Invasion of Naples in 1805?

But all that wasn't the end of operations in Italy by any means. In 1806, for example, we landed a force over 5,000 strong in Calabria under Major General John Stuart to help a local insurrection against the French and to protect our strategic interests in Sicily. On 4 July 1806, a similar-sized French force met them at Maida in Calabria. The French advanced, the British shot them and then bayoneted them, and it was pretty much all over in about a quarter of an hour. After that, Stuart marched around Calabria for a bit, mopping up French garrisons. The campaign didn't have any long-term strategic consequences, but the victory at Maida was jolly popular in Britain, and if you're thinking at this stage that the name sounds familiar, it does. The victory was so popular that a pub and then the Maida Vale area of London were named after it.

And it wasn't just Italy's western side we were interested in. We did a lot of fighting on its eastern side as well. In 1808, HMS *Unite* started lurking in Venetian waters looking for French targets and other British ships were to follow shortly after. Fairly soon we were raiding coastal towns and sending landing parties ashore to destroy fortifications. Eventually, it reached the stage where we were roaming up and down the Adriatic attacking targets pretty freely; HMS *Bacchante* raided Apulia; HMS *Eagle* blockaded Ancona; and a British squadron under Rear Admiral Fremantle attacked

Fiume, destroying ships and stores and fighting in its streets. Later, Fremantle attacked Trieste and helped our Austrian allies capture it.

After the end of the Napoleonic Wars we gave it a rest for bit, but then in 1860 we helped the Italians themselves invade Italy. This is in the sense that the British Navy lent a certain amount of quiet assistance to Garibaldi in his attempts to liberate Italy from foreign dominance and unite it. Our navy, for instance, helped organise an armistice to end the fighting in Palermo and leave Garibaldi in charge there.

In the First World War we were once again back in Italy helping the Italians invade their own country. At the beginning of the war, big chunks of what is now northern Italy were under the control of the Austro-Hungarian Empire. The Italians fought to free these areas and we sent troops to help. In October 1917, the Italians suffered a severe defeat at Caporetto and British forces were rushed out to Italy to help save the situation. British troops played a brave role in the Battle of Asiago in 1918. Edward, brother of author Vera Brittain, was killed here. And they played a significant part in the final decisive victory at Vittorio Veneto in October 1918. Three of the fifty-seven divisions in the victorious force were British.

Early on in the Second World War we found ourselves on the other side from the Italians, after Mussolini declared war on us on 10 June 1940. We were soon, however, hitting back at Italian territory itself. On the night of 11/12 November, in Operation Judgement, Swordfish biplanes from HMS *Illustrious* launched a devastating attack on the Italian battle fleet in the Italian port of Taranto. Other actions, including the Battle of Cape Spartivento, off Sardinia, followed, and then by 1943 we were ready for the final invasion of Italy.

Operation Husky was the invasion of Sicily in July 1943. In just over a month British, Canadian and American troops took the island from the German and Italian defenders. Then it was on to the mainland. A detailed account of the grim fighting that followed as British and other Allied troops battled their way through Italy is beyond the remit of this book and has been covered in great depth elsewhere. Basically, our Eighth Army crossed the straits of Messina on 3 September 1943. The Italian armistice with us was announced on 8 September. On 9 September British forces were back in Taranto, landing there in Operation Slapstick, while the Americans landed at Salerno. Bitter fighting against the Germans followed, including the

1. Richard Coeur de Lion in front of the Houses of Parliament. The sword and democracy, an interesting shot that focuses on two very different aspects of what Britain has brought to assorted parts of the world. Two edges, you might say. Like Richard's sword.

2. The cost of war. The *Burghers of Calais* by Rodin. Six burghers of Calais expecting to be executed by Edward III. It's a tragic and moving story, probably somewhat undermined for some today by a confusion between burghers with an 'h' and burgers without an 'h'.

3. Clive of India, located near the Foreign Office. Probably not the sort of figure they would choose to inspire our present Foreign Office staff if they were putting up a statue today.

4. Captain Cook. A man who helped open up the world for humanity in general, but also for us so that we could go and take over bits of it.

5. Nelson in (rather static) action at the Battle of St Vincent, 1797.

6. Nelson in (equally static) action at the Battle of Copenhagen.

7. Nelson (again rather statically, but at least in this case, that's fair enough) dying at the Battle of Trafalgar, 1805.

8. Wellington surrounded by his men. Though fortunately for us (and unfortunately for Napoleon) he had more than just the four of them when he was on campaign.

9. The cost of war. The memorial to those soldiers of the Brigade of Guards killed in the Crimean War, 1853–56.

CHARLES JAMES NAPIER

GENERAL

BORN

MDCCLXXXII

DIED

MDCCCLIII

ERECTED BY PUBLIC SUBSCRIPTION

THE MOST NUMEROUS CONTRIBUTORS

BEING PRIVATE SOLDIERS

10. General Sir Charles James Napier, who spent quite a lot of time roaming India, fighting and killing people, and who took control of Sindh.

11. Field Marshal John Fox Burgoyne. One of those Victorian soldiers who had a career that included fighting under Wellington in Spain, fighting in America in the war of 1812 and commanding assorted things in the Crimean War. Not a figure today who most people are going to remember. Still he's got himself a statue.

12. Field Marshal Sir George Stuart White. Another Victorian soldier with a long career that included fighting in Afghanistan, Burma and South Africa. He even got the Victoria Cross for bravery in Afghanistan.

13. Colin Campbell, Field Marshal Lord Clyde. Yes, yet another Victorian field marshal. We had quite a few of them in those days. This one's CV featured lots of wars, including crushing the 1823 Demerara slave rebellion and defeating the Indian rebellion. Today his statue has a base that's peppered with indentations from a bomb and doesn't include a death date. I think we can assume he has died, so that has gone missing somewhere over the years.

14. The world according to the Albert Memorial – Africa.

15. The world according to the Albert Memorial – Asia.

16. The world according to the Albert Memorial – The Americas.

17. The world according to the Albert Memorial – Europe.

18. Robert Napier, Lord Napier of Magdala, who brought elephants from India (as well as a large, well-equipped army) to invade Ethiopia.

19. Gordon of Khartoum. He looks pensive. Considering how it was all going to end for him at Khartoum, maybe that's fair enough.

20. Britannia looking out over London and the world.

JELLICOE
1859-1935

21. With a considerably less grand spot than Nelson in Trafalgar Square, but still commemorating the might of British sea power into the twentieth century, a bust of Jellicoe.

22. Like the units themselves, memorials to units from the First World War come in many forms and sizes. The Imperial Camel Corps ride forward.

23. Field Marshal Harold Alexander, 1st Earl Alexander of Tunis, named after the scene of his greatest triumph.

24. The cost of war. The Guards Memorial, by Horse Guards Parade, London.

grim struggle for Monte Cassino and the landings at Anzio. Rome fell in June 1944, and by spring 1945 British forces were fighting in northern Italy.

Ivory Coast

Ivory Coast has Liberia to its west and Ghana to its east. For a long time, the French controlled the territory that is now Ivory Coast (we controlled the territory that is now Ghana and signed a treaty with the French) and it's not an area we have had that much to do with.

In the late nineteenth century, an interesting figure people should know more about, Samori Ture, created the Wassoulou Empire that incorporated an area in the north of what is now Ivory Coast. In January 1885, as part of his attempts to resist the French, he offered to put the empire under British protection. We decided not to take up his kind offer, but we did sell him lots of modern repeating rifles, which Ture then promptly used against the French.

In 2004, in what became known as Operation Phillis, with civil war gripping the Ivory Coast, a company of Gurkhas was flown into the capital Abidjan to evacuate British citizens, and deployed along routes to the airport, while HMS *Albion* was ordered to head for the area as extra support.

Jamaica

In 1494, Columbus was the first European to reach Jamaica and he named it Santiago. In 1523 the Spanish founded Santiago de la Vega as capital of the island. When we finally took over the island we, not very imaginatively, called it Spanish Town. We can't have thought long and hard about that one.

This being the Caribbean, an area where we tended to attack a lot of things, it's hardly surprising that during the period of Spanish control, we attacked the island on a number of occasions. In about 1596, English Admiral Sir Anthony Shirley attacked and burned the capital. In 1635, one Colonel Jackson had another go. After a fierce battle at Passage Fort, he defeated the garrison and entered Santiago de le Vega and pillaged the town. Finally, in 1655, a major expedition under Venables and Penn arrived. They had failed in an attack on Santo Domingo and decided to take Jamaica as a consolation prize. Penn and Venables invaded and captured the island, and we kept it, despite two Spanish attempts to retake it. It didn't save Penn and Venables, as they ended up in the Tower of London when they got back to England.

Jamaica soon became a major destination to which slaves were transported.

There were fears of invasion by the French and Spanish during the American War of Independence, but Rodney and Hood's victory off Dominica prevented that. And, similarly, Admiral Duckworth prevented an invasion in 1806 during the Napoleonic Wars.

Jamaica became independent in 1962.

Japan

Japan is one of those countries where you know we've fought them across South East Asia, but aren't so aware we've actually been there in their own water and on their own soil. But we have.

After a brief flirtation in the late sixteenth and early seventeenth century when English traders first visited Japan and a trading post was briefly established on the island of Hirado, the British and the Japanese largely left each other alone for the next couple of centuries or so, until Japan started opening up to the West in the mid-nineteenth century. But it was an uneasy opening-up, with misunderstandings and apprehension on both sides. In 1862, a party of Britons on the road through the village of Namamugi were deemed to have shown insufficient respect to the regent of the Satsuma region of Japan and his bodyguards. The subsequent assault on the British party led to the delightfully named Satsuma War. Tragically, this has nothing to do with small orange citrus fruit, and everything to do with large cannons on both sides.

Britain demanded reparations for the assault, but the Satsuma region refused. So after a year of fruitless (no joy, no citrus) negotiations, we sent a Royal Navy squadron to Kagoshima to put just the right amount of pressure on Satsuma (too much pressure and there would have been Satsuma juice everywhere). When the arrival of the squadron wasn't sufficient to get our money, we decided to increase the pressure by seizing three Satsuma vessels in Kagoshima harbour. Ultimately, perhaps, this was a little too much pressure, because the Satsuma forts then somewhat surprised the British squadron by opening fire on it. Our boys retaliated and the end result was five killed on the Satsuma side and eleven killed on our side, but we caused a lot of damage to the town and the result was a British win on points, with Satsuma paying £25,000 compensation and entering into a treaty with us.

After a number of other hiccups, including the 1864 Bombardment of Shimonoseki by us, the French, the Americans and the Dutch, we eventually started to get along very well with the Japanese. In fact, by 1902 we were good buddies, happily signing the Anglo-Japanese alliance, and in the First World War the Japanese fought on our side (pinching a bit of German-held territory in China). By the Second World War that had all slightly changed.

I have touched elsewhere in this book on the titanic struggle between the British Empire and Allies on one side and the Japanese Empire on the other, and most of the action between Britons and Japanese took place a long, long way from Japan.

In the last few months of the Second World War in the East, however, we were preparing for a fighting invasion of Japan. As the tide of battle moved closer to the Japanese home islands, feverish planning started for Operation Downfall, the Allied invasion of Japan. It would have been on a scale that would have dwarfed D-Day and, though it was mainly a US operation, British forces were intending to make a major contribution with, for instance, British ground troops destined for Operation Coronet, the invasion of Honshu, and British naval forces planned to play a major role in Operation Olympic, the invasion of Kyushu. As we all know now, the nuclear bombing of Japan and the country's surrender made the fighting invasion unnecessary.

So when British forces did finally march into Japan, it was as part of the British Commonwealth Occupation Force. This contained, among others, numerous Australians and the British 5th Infantry Brigade. BCOF's role ended in 1952, but already by 1951 we were getting distracted by events elsewhere in the region, in this instance how our forces and their enemies were doing in the Korean Peninsula.

Jordan

When you think of British military operations in Jordan, you tend to think of T.E. Lawrence, Lawrence of Arabia. Hard not to, really, with the powerful image of Lawrence standing in swirling white robes staring out over the desert sands – particularly after the film.

It has to be said that Lawrence was by no means the only Allied officer engaged in working with the Arab rebels against the Ottoman Empire and, even more importantly, it has to be pointed out that without the Arab rebels and the Arab leaders there wouldn't have been much of an Arab rebellion for Lawrence and other Brits to work with. Nonetheless, it's still a great story and one that is comparatively well known, so I'm not going to deal with it in great detail here. Also, some of the key events, such as those after the capture of Damascus, happened outside the borders of what is now Jordan.

Lawrence arrived in the area in autumn 1916 to work with the Hashemite forces in the Hejaz and to help them to attack the crucial strategic Hejaz railway that ran from Damascus to Mecca, linking Ottoman forces in Arabia with those in Syria. In July 1917, Lawrence, with Arab forces and with the support of British Navy vessels, managed to take Aqaba, now in Jordan. This was long before Aqaba became a holiday destination, but it was an important victory both strategically, in allowing British (and French) supplies and support through to the Arabs, and psychologically as well. In January 1918, Arab forces with Lawrence beat the Ottomans at the Battle of Tafileh, and in April 1918 Arab forces clashed with Ottoman units at Ma'an in what is now Jordan.

After the war, in one of our more disastrous and morally unappealing decisions, we carved up the Middle East with the French according to the Sykes-Picot Agreement. The effect of this can still be seen in the political conflicts of the region today. This process, however, meant that when it first emerged, the Emirate of Transjordan was under British Mandate.

Gradually, the emirate acquired more independence and it eventually became fully independent and a kingdom in 1946. But in 1956, at a time when the King of Jordan feared trouble from a coup or from Syria and/or Iraq, we rushed troops back to Jordan for a temporary stay, in the suitably steadfastly named Operation Fortitude.

6

KAZAKHSTAN TO LUXEMBOURG

Kazakhstan

Kazakhstan is a huge country. By the mid-nineteenth century it was part of the Russian Empire and out of our reach, both geographically and politically.

However, Kazakhstan does have a coastline on the Caspian Sea and in the period around the end of the First World War the Royal Navy was in action there, so yes, our forces have been there.

On 21 May 1919, the *Emile Nobel*, an ex-Russian ship and one of a flotilla of British ships on the Caspian, was reconnoitring Fort Shevchenko (now Alexandrovsk in Kazakhstan) when Bolshevik gunners fired a shell at her, killing eleven of her crew. In response, the *Emile Nobel* opened up with her 4-inch guns. The flotilla then destroyed nine boats in the port and later RAF attacks forced the Bolsheviks to take the rest of their vessels from the harbour there.

Kenya

Not one of our most dramatic invasions.

In the late nineteenth century, we were competing with Germany for control over territory in East Africa, and in 1886 Germany signed a treaty setting out who could operate in which territory. We were given an area that included Kenya, and the Imperial British East Africa Company (IBEA), was sent in to make British control a reality by signing treaties and setting up trading ventures. In 1887, they leased coastal territory from the Sultan of Zanzibar. However,

IBEA Co. was not a huge success. It ran into huge and expensive difficulties in Uganda and, in 1895, the British government took over and created the British East African Protectorate of which today's Kenya was part.

There was fighting in what is now Kenya during the campaign against Lettow-Vorbeck in the First World War (see Mozambique).

In 1963, some years after the Mau Mau rising, Kenya became independent.

Kiribati

Kiribati is an island nation in the middle of the Pacific Ocean comprising thirty-three atolls dispersed over millions of square kilometres. Although the islands aren't large, Kiribati has a total population of over 100,000.

And if you've ever wondered where the name Kiribati comes from, it's the local version of Gilberts. Yes, because we used to call these islands the Gilbert Islands, after the British captain Thomas Gilbert, who sighted the islands back in 1788. Although, we didn't start calling them that until the late nineteenth century. It was a Russian and a French captain who started the fashion.

British settlers seem to have arrived in 1837. By 1892, we were worried about the possibility of German and American influence spreading in the Gilbert Islands and Captain Davis, on board HMS *Royalist*, toured the atolls establishing a British Protectorate and helping sort out assorted local disputes.

There were bitter battles here in the Second World War between the Japanese and Americans, in particular the Battle of Tarawa.

Kiribati became independent in 1979.

Korea, The Democratic People's Republic of

This is the country we usually call North Korea.

Our main military involvement with North Korea has, of course, been the Korean War. This bitter war, though deserving of a lot more attention than it usually gets, is very well known and very well documented in other books, and with a vast subject like *All the Countries*

We've Ever Invaded, I'm sorry to say that space is limited so I can't go into much detail here.

Basically, after the Second World War, Korea, freed from Japanese occupation, ended up divided along the 38th Parallel between a Soviet-backed regime in the north and an American-backed regime in the south. After increasing border tensions, North Korea invaded South Korea on 25 June 1950. The United Nations called for forces to resist the North Korean advance, but the North Koreans pushed deep into South Korea. However, the North Koreans were prevented from taking the key strategic port of Pusan and in September 1950 General MacArthur landed two divisions at Inchon in the North Korean rear, forcing the North Koreans to retreat rapidly as our side pursued them deep into their territory. At this point the Chinese came into the war and it was the UN forces' turn to retreat, eventually to a line well south of Seoul. Gradually, UN forces pushed the enemy back again until the fighting ground to a halt in something of a stalemate in the area of the 38th Parallel.

British forces fought bravely in many locations during the Korean War, including the stage where UN forces pushed deep inside North Korea.

Korea, The Republic of

This is the country we usually call South Korea.

Pretty much everyone has heard of the Korean War, but did you also know that we occupied a bit of South Korea in the late nineteenth century and set up a naval base there?

Port Hamilton, or Geomun-do, is a group of islands off the southern coast of the Korean Peninsula. Sir Edward Belcher (great name) dropped in on board HMS *Samarang* in 1845 and named the place Port Hamilton after the then secretary of the admiralty. By the late nineteenth century, we were worried about expanding Russian influence in the area, so we decided to do a bit of expanding ourselves, and in April 1885 (in what for fairly obvious reasons became known as the Port Hamilton Incident), three British warships arrived to establish a base on one of the islands here as a counterbalance to Vladivostok on the Russian coast. There are still British graves here, including two sailors from HMS *Albatross* who were killed in 1886 by their gun exploding. In 1887 we demolished the base and abandoned it.

As with the push into North Korea during the Korean War, British forces played a key role in the fighting in South Korea. The 27th British Commonwealth Brigade, for instance, helped defend the Pusan bridgehead and joined in the subsequent push north from there to meet up with the forces put ashore in the Inchon landings.

Kosovo

Kosovo is recognised as a country by the UK and many other nations, but not by Serbia and Russia, among others, and it is not a member state of the United Nations.

Most readers will remember the Kosovo War, so I won't go into great detail here. The RAF was involved in sorties against targets inside Kosovo and elsewhere in 1999. When Slobodan Milosevic finally agreed to withdraw his forces from Kosovo, British forces played a key role in the UN Kosovo Peace Implementation Force (KFOR) as it moved into the territory in June 1999. KFOR itself was based around the Allied Rapid Reaction Corps Headquarters, with British Lieutenant General Mike Jackson in command, and it included a British brigade composed of elements from the 4th Armoured Brigade and 5th Airborne Brigade.

Kuwait

As with other Gulf States, we started off by signing a maritime treaty with Kuwait. In 1841, they agreed not to attack local sheikhs at sea and to allow us to sort out disputes. Then we got into a battle for influence in the area with the Ottomans and, in this case, the Germans.

Kuwait had been pencilled in as the terminus of the proposed Berlin–Baghdad railway. We decided we would rather not have a direct line from Berlin to the Gulf, so in 1899 we entered into a treaty with Kuwait whereby we took control of Kuwait's foreign policy and in return we protected Kuwait and gave it an annual subsidy.

In 1913 we were even given a monopoly on oil exploration and exploitation. We, however, missed out here in a fairly large way, since commercial exploitation of Kuwaiti oil didn't really start until towards the end of our time in the country.

On 20 June 1961, Kuwait became fully independent. Not wasting much time, on 25 June 1961, the then president of Iraq, President Qasim, declared that Kuwait was part of Iraq and he was going to annexe it. Amid fears that the Iraqis might send an armoured brigade into Kuwait, we went straight back. We rushed in troops, with forward units advancing to the strategically vital Mutla Ridge, only 5 miles from the Iraqi border. Eventually, the immediate crisis passed and as Arab League forces moved in to protect Kuwait, British forces pulled out, with the withdrawal complete by 19 October.

Then in the 1990s we were back when another Iraqi leader went a lot further down the path than Qasim. This time, on 2 August 1990, the Iraqi army did invade Kuwait. A coalition was formed to expel the Iraqis, with Britain playing a major part. We sent loads of armoured vehicles and about 43,000 ground forces personnel. We sent frigates and destroyers to the Gulf and we sent RAF squadrons. And we sent the SAS.

The air bombardment campaign started on 17 January 1991, and the ground assault began on 23 February. Coalition forces advanced rapidly to liberate Kuwait and 100 hours after the start of the ground campaign, a ceasefire was declared.

Kyrgyzstan

We've never really invaded Kyrgyzstan, though we have had the chance to get involved here.

A territory called the Khanate of Khokand, which incorporated parts of what is now Kyrgyzstan, lay sandwiched between expanding spheres of Russian and British influence during the so-called Great Game of the nineteenth century.

In 1864, the Russians made their first move on the region, seizing a bit of the Khan's northern territories. The Khan begged us for military assistance, but we decided we weren't interested at that stage. By 1876, even if we had been interested, it was too late. The Khanate of Khokand had been abolished and the area absorbed into the Russian Empire.

Laos

And the capital of Laos is? Vientiane. It's one of those questions you might get asked in a quiz. The fact is that Laos, of the three states that used to make up French Indo-China, is the one which Brits, as a whole, are probably least aware of. We've all heard of Vietnam and Cambodia and the wars there, but far fewer know much about Laos and its similar history of post-colonial conflict. Most people can name the Viet Cong and the Khmer Rouge, but what about the Pathet Lao?

Like Vietnam and Cambodia, Laos saw its own British invasion long before the Americans were in any way involved.

For most of the Second World War, Vichy French authorities ran Laos, with Japanese forces free to move in and around the area. In March 1945, with the war in Europe almost finished, the Japanese took full control of the country and encouraged the people of Laos to regard themselves as independent from the French. When it was Japan's turn to surrender, it was our turn to occupy a big chunk of Laos. In September 1945, with Laos north of the 16th parallel under Chinese control, the area south of the 16th parallel came under the control of British and Indian troops.

We stayed here until 1946, helping, among other things, the French to regain power, using British planes to fly French troops into southern Laos. Having said that, it wasn't long until French control of Laos would end forever.

Latvia

Latvia is the middle one of the Baltic trio, sandwiched between Lithuania and Estonia. Obviously, with L and T playing a big part in the names Lithuania and Latvia, there could be some confusion over cars that you may see. For clarification, LT is Lithuania, LV is Latvia. I've no idea why it's that way round. It just is.

As with Estonia, a lot of our history of military involvement with Latvia is tied up with Russia. In the Napoleonic Wars we spent some time fighting Russia, but by the summer of 1812 we were fighting France alongside the Russians as Napoleon's armies marched through Russia. Riga, the capital of Latvia (and then under Russian control), was being besieged by the French. The suburbs were burnt, but the arrival of English and Russian gunboats saved the city itself and lifted the siege.

With the Crimean War we returned, but this time not to save Riga. Instead we bombarded it and generally roamed Latvian waters irritating the Russians. For instance, on 30 July 1855, HMS *Archer* and HMS *Conflict* attacked the town of Windau, now Ventspils, in Latvia, scattering troops and destroying public buildings.

With the Russian Revolution we returned to Latvian waters. In December 1918, with Red Russian forces only 25 miles away and advancing, Royal Navy shore patrols landed in Riga and marched through town to arrange the evacuation of Allied citizens and the Latvian government itself. HMS *Ceres* ended up firing on the barracks of a Latvian regiment that had mutinied. And we were in Riga again the following year, this time to help save it from the Germans and the Russians. In the autumn of 1919, HMS *Dragon*, a light cruiser, was part of a British and French fleet dispatched to Riga to aid Latvian troops in a counter-attack. During the action, *Dragon* was hit by fire from the shore and nine crew members were killed and four wounded.

Ultimately, we played a small but significant role in helping Latvia gain independence.

Lebanon

Lebanon's a country that has seen more than a bit of conflict and, as you would expect, bearing in mind all the other places we've invaded, we've made our own major contribution to it.

In 1839–40 we fought the confusingly named Syrian War there (also known, to add to the confusion, as the Second Syrian War, or Egyptian-Ottoman War, or Second Egyptian-Ottoman War). Egypt and Turkey were competing for control of the region and the area of present-day Lebanon which, unfortunately for it, was stuck in the middle. Not for the first time, mind you. Egypt, for example, used to fight over this area with assorted powers from Asia, like the Hittites, and Babylonians long ago.

This time, Mehmet Ali, the Pasha of Egypt, had destroyed a Turkish army in Syria at the Battle of Nezib. Shortly after, at a most inconvenient time and in a most inconsiderate manner, the Turkish Sultan Mahmud II died, leaving a 16-year-old to run the Ottoman Empire.

Fearing chaos in the Middle East, as we often do, we sent Commodore Charles Napier and a small naval squadron into action. In August, he promptly arrived off Beirut and demanded that Mehmet Ali's troops withdraw. They promptly ignored him since Napier only had a small force. But when reinforcements arrived for Napier in September, the situation changed dramatically. We bombarded Beirut and put ashore a landing force at Jounieh to the north.

Napier then set off for Sidon, bombarded it and landed to take the city itself. Meanwhile, to the north, the Egyptians abandoned Beirut. The focus then moved to Egypt, where Napier arrived with his ships and negotiated a peace treaty with Mehmet Ali.

By the early twentieth century, Egypt was firmly within our sphere of influence, while to the north and east the Ottoman Empire tottered on. In the First World War, we were on the other side from the Turks, and by autumn 1918 General Allenby's army was pushing the Turks back through the same territory we had helped them regain in the Syrian War, as the 3rd Indian Division advanced towards Beirut.

Under the Sykes-Picot Agreement, the French rapidly took over Lebanon from us. And so it was that after Hitler invaded France, Lebanon came under the influence of the Vichy government, which in turn meant that we had to invade Lebanon yet again.

There were fears that Germany could use Lebanon and Syria as a base to destabilise Iraq, so in 1941 Operation Exporter was launched. What it was exporting was a large Commonwealth force under the command of two British generals, General Henry Maitland Wilson in the Mandate of Palestine and Lieutenant General Sir Edward Quinan in Iraq. The campaign was launched on 8 June 1941 and involved some surprisingly (considering that not many Brits today know much about it) heavy fighting, both in the air and on the ground, including in the advance to Beirut the Battle of the Litani (involving Australian forces and 11 Commando), the Battle of Jezzine and the Battle of Damour. Eventually, the Vichy position became untenable and with the Australian 21st Brigade about to enter Beirut, General Henri Dentz, the Vichy commander, sought an armistice.

Moshe Dayan, later Chief of Staff of the Israeli Defence Forces and known for the black eye patch he wore, lost his eye in this campaign while working with an Australian unit. And the writer Roald Dahl, then a fighter pilot, flew in the campaign here.

In February 1983, we returned to Lebanon with BRITFORLEB, the British force in Lebanon, to assist with multinational efforts to deal with the then crisis here and to evacuate civilians.

Lesotho

Basutoland is one of those names that you might remember if you ever collected stamps. It's also the name by which Lesotho used to be known.

People think of Lesotho as a small country, but there are over 2 million people living here and it has had plenty of interesting history, including being invaded by us.

King Moshoeshoe I came to power in the 1830s. For a considerable time he repulsed both overly keen Brits and overly keen Boers. But by 1868 Moshoeshoe was feeling the pressure from the Boers and eventually agreed to Basutoland becoming a British protectorate. Moshoeshoe died in 1870 and in 1871 we moved in and annexed the country to Cape Colony. In the early years, this meant little change in Basutoland, but by the late 1870s the situation was getting a lot more tense. Governor Henry Bartle Frere wanted to reserve some of the territory for settlement. He also wanted the locals' guns under the 1879 Peace Protection Act. The result was the Basutoland Gun War. Obviously all modern wars have guns in them, but this was about guns as well, so that's why it got the name. It would get a bit boring and hugely confusing naming every war that just involved guns, the Gun War.

It didn't go very well for us. When Basotho chiefs started a rebellion, we sent in a force from Cape Colony to crush it. Which didn't happen. Instead our troops found themselves in some difficulties, with, for instance, an ambush of a mounted column at Qalabani in October 1880 inflicting heavy casualties. Eventually we decided it was time to talk and in 1881 a peace treaty was signed giving the Basotho much of what they had wanted, including the right to keep their guns. In 1884, Basutoland was made a Crown colony and given more self-government.

Lesotho became independent in 1966.

Liberia

Not an area of huge British activity. We seem to have built trading posts in the territory in 1663, but the Dutch objected and rapidly destroyed them.

Unsurprisingly, though, armed British ships have spent some time in action in Liberian waters. For example, in 1721 the Welsh (or British) pirate Bartholomew Roberts captured the frigate *Onslow* at Cestos Point, on the River Cess in Liberia. And in the nineteenth century, British anti-slaving patrols operated in the waters of present-day Liberia.

In the 1820s, the American Colonization Society began sending to the area freed slaves from America, a move that created the foundations of the state of Liberia. Shortly after that the new Liberian government tried to impose duties on goods imported into its territory. We didn't like this too much so we seized the revenue schooner *John Seyes* at Edina, in Liberia, and confiscated it.

Libya

Well, with the memory of our recent air campaign fresh in everybody's mind, it will certainly come as no surprise to anybody that we have been inside Libya's airspace. But our involvement with Libya goes back a long way before that.

Tripoli was one of the North African bases of what we then called the Barbary Corsairs, so that being the case, armed Brits have visited it on a number of occasions over the centuries.

Admiral Robert Blake, with an English fleet, dropped in on Tripoli in 1655 and helped arrange the release of some English prisoners.

Later in the seventeenth century, with a treaty under threat, English ships blockaded Tripoli. Then on 14 January 1676, in a daring raid, Lieutenant Cloudesley Shovell led a boat attack into Tripoli harbour and burned four ships here, with no English losses recorded. This was followed up by Sir John Narborough destroying four more of the Dey of Tripoli's ships in the open sea, and eventually the Dey got the message and signed a peace treaty in March 1676.

In 1816, Lord Exmouth turned up with a British fleet to emphasise that we would not tolerate attacks on our ships.

Our main military incursions into Libya took place in the Second World War. By this stage Italy controlled Libya. On 10 June 1940, Italy declared war on us. The 11th Hussars were ordered into action and by 14 June British forces had invaded Libya and captured Fort Capuzzo. They also captured Generale di Corpo Lastrucci, who was the Italian tenth Army's engineer-in-chief, plus his staff car, his staff officer, two lady friends and important maps.

In September 1940, with the Battle of Britain still raging and us fearing imminent invasion from the German armies gathered just across the Channel, Mussolini decided he would take advantage of the situation to invade Egypt. This proved to be a spectacular miscalculation, one of many in Benito's life.

The Italian forces advanced from Libya into Egypt and stopped at Sidi Barrani to establish defensive positions as a base for a further advance. They made the mistake of arranging their positions at such long distances from each other that it was difficult for their fortified camps to give each other assistance.

In December, we hit back with Operation Compass, which was supposed to be a limited five-day attack against the Italian positions. However, unexpected success and the crumbling of the Italian defences meant that the limited attack became a full-scale counter-offensive.

By 15 December we were back inside Libya and Fort Capuzzo was once again in our hands. Tobruk fell on 22 January 1941. Meanwhile, in the south of Libya, the Long Range Desert Group operating with Free French Forces from Chad attacked the Italian garrison at Murzuq. On 9 February 1941, our forces, having overrun Cyrenaica, reached El Agheila and Churchill ordered the advance to be stopped so that troops could be sent to defend Greece. By this stage, the Italian Tenth Army had ceased to exist and about 130,000 prisoners of war had been taken.

This is where Rommel appears on the scene, having been sent with the Afrika Korps to bolster the Italians. In March he attacked at El Agheila and drove our forces back across the Egyptian border and by mid-April the front line was as far back as Sallum (though we still held Tobruk in Libya, now besieged). In June 1941 we struck back with Operation Battleaxe, but this turned into a costly failure, although we took Fort Capuzzo in Libya. Yet again. Before being forced to withdraw from it. Yet again.

After this, Wavell was replaced by Auchinleck as Commander-in-Chief Middle East Command and our forces were reorganised and given the famous name, the Eighth Army. In November 1941, we launched Operation Crusader. Despite successes for both sides, Rommel was forced to withdraw and in early December he ordered his troops back to the Gazala line, and eventually they withdrew as far as El Agheila again. Tobruk was relieved. Mightily relieved.

But it wasn't to last. Rommel was resupplied and pushed the Allied forces back to Gazala. In the Battle of Gazala in May and June 1942, the Eighth Army was forced to withdraw and Tobruk fell. Rommel pursued them into Egypt, but his heavy losses of tanks at the Battle of Gazala meant he was unable to secure a decisive victory and his advance was stopped at the First Battle of El Alamein in July. This is the point at which Montgomery comes into the fighting.

In October 1942, Montgomery and the Eighth Army went onto the offensive, and at the Second Battle of El Alamein at the end of October and beginning of November 1942, Rommel's forces suffered a stunning defeat. Yet again they were forced back to El Agheila in Libya. But there was to be no recovery for them this time.

In December, Montgomery forced Rommel back from El Agheila. The Eighth Army reached Sirte, Gaddafi's home town, on 25 December (he had been born there just a few months previously in June 1942). Eventually, Tripoli fell to the Eighth Army on 23 January. Shortly after that the front line moved out of Libya and into Tunisia.

From 1943 to 1951, we controlled Cyrenaica and Tripolitania, while the French were in control of Fezzan in the south. Then in 1951 Libya became independent under King Idris.

In 1969, Gaddafi staged a successful coup against King Idris. In 2011, British planes played a huge role in the events that led to the end of Gaddafi's regime and his death.

Liechtenstein

Liechtenstein is a tiny principality sandwiched between Germany and Switzerland. A lot of Britons couldn't easily find it on a map, so perhaps it's not surprising that, as far as I know, we've never invaded it.

In the First Word War, because of Liechtenstein's extremely close relationship with Austria, we weren't quite sure what to do about it.

So in the end we decided that while we weren't actually at war with it, we were going to apply an economic embargo on it anyway.

Lithuania

Lithuania is the southernmost of the Baltic trio, lying just to the south of Latvia. But unlike the situation with Latvia and Estonia, we had been in action in Lithuania long before our navy took to roaming the Baltic. Lithuania is also different from the other two countries in the sense that while its inland part has been controlled for lengthy periods by Russia, its coastal part has also seen controlled for significant amounts of time by Prussia and Germany.

Before King Henry IV was King Henry IV, he was just plain (well admittedly he was a major aristrocrat, but plain compared to a king) Henry Bolinbroke. However, broke was one thing he wasn't. Because, at the end of the fourteenth century he was forking out thousands of pounds, when thousands of pounds wasn't just a lot of money, but really a *lot* of money, to send himself and hundreds of knights on crusade in Lithuania. You didn't get the sun, sea and sand of a journey to the Holy Land, but there was still plenty of kudos in it. Unfortunately, from Henry's point of view there wasn't much victory in it either. He spent 1390 with 300 English knights, plus all their hangers-on, assisting the Teutonic Knights in the siege of Vilnius. (The symbol of the Teutonic Knights was a black cross later adopted by Germany. Hence all the fiddly black crosses kids used to try to stick on German aircraft kits after they had hastily glued them together.) Then he was there again in 1392. But all this proved rather pointless. Vilnius didn't fall and Henry went on pilgrimage to the Holy Land instead, where he apparently decided that one day he would lead a crusade to take Jerusalem. That didn't happen either.

After that the English left the Lithuanians alone for a while. In fact, rather than invading the country we got quite fond of parts of it, particularly the port of Memel (in German), or Klaipéda (in Lithuanian). Instead of invading with navy ships, by the second half of the eighteenth century we were going to Memel to get wood to build those navy ships.

Like I said, the Lithuanian coast had closer links for a long time to Prussia than Russia, so it managed to escape our attentions during, for example, the Crimean War, but we did return after the First World War. In the turmoil that gripped the area, both Germany and Russia, and eventually Poland, competed for control of parts of Lithuania. Eventually, most of Lithuania gained independence, but the key port of Memel/ Klaipéda was still outside their control, with it and the area around it having been made a Mandate of the League of Nations after the First World War. Some of the Lithuanian population of the area rose in revolt, with assistance from Lithuanians in the independent part, demanding unification with Lithuania. So along with the French we sent in the navy. Not in a big way, exactly, but we sent them in anyway. On 17–18 January 1923 our cruiser HMS *Caledon* arrived in Memel together with two French torpedo boats. A French cruiser was also on the way. The French firmly demanded that things were put back the way they were. We were a little more reticent, or at least as reticent as you can be when sending in a cruiser. Eventually, a deal was done and everybody went home comparatively happy.

Luxembourg

Another small country that we haven't really invaded very much.

As you can see from looking at the sections on Belgium, Germany and France, we have had lots of armies near to Luxembourg over the centuries, but I can't find evidence of any that actually crossed the border. Though, of course, if you do know of any, please let me know.

Marlborough and his army were certainly very close at one point to occupying Trier, just across the border from Luxembourg, in present-day Germany. He then advanced southwards along the east bank of the Moselle River, with Luxembourg on the other bank, as far as Sierck.

But Brits have fought and died in Luxembourg, including Flight Lieutnenant D.A. Cameron, killed in action on 10 May 1940 near Diekirch and now buried there.

In September 1944, Luxembourg was liberated from German occupation by the Americans. But there was at least one officer in the British Army who played a hugely significant role in Luxembourg's liberation. Jean, the Grand Duke of Luxembourg himself

(Luxembourg's a Grand Duchy, not a kingdom, so Grand Duke is as high as it gets here), volunteered for the Irish Guards in 1942. He participated in the battle to liberate Caen and the liberation of Brussels. He was here on 10 September 1944 for the liberation of Luxembourg, and after that he was part of the invasion of Germany.

7

MACEDONIA TO NORWAY

Macedonia, Former Yugoslav Republic of

In 1918, British and Greek forces were faced by the Bulgarians in bitter fighting at the Battle of Doiran, now on the Greek border with the Former Yugoslav Republic of Macedonia. This was one of the toughest battles fought by Britain in the First World War, yet today very few people have heard of it.

The Bulgarians were well dug in at Doiran and we had made several attempts in previous years to capture the defences here. In September 1918 we tried again. Both British and Greek units advanced with great bravery and some of the Bulgarian trenches were taken, but after bitter counter-attacks and heavy artillery and machine-gun fire, both British and Greek forces were pushed back. Combined British and Greek losses were over 7,000 men.

Fearful of being outflanked by Allied forces advancing on their flank, the Bulgarians were eventually forced to retreat and in the ensuing week we pursued them back to the Strumica Valley. By the time hostilities with Bulgaria ceased on 30 September, the 27th Division was in the region of Kosturino, Rabrovo and Cestovo.

In August 2001, British troops returned to Macedonia on a more peaceful mission, this time as part of a NATO team to help disarm Albanian rebels and calm a tense situation.

Madagascar

Madagascar is the fourth largest island in the world. Its capital is Antananarivo. And, yes, we've invaded it a bit.

A couple of early settlements in the seventeenth century did not do very well. British pirates had rather more success. Well-known Scottish pirate or privateer William Kidd (not to be confused with American frontier outlaw Billy the Kid) visited Madagascar, as did plenty of other pirates from Britain. In fact, with its strategic position on trade routes, Madagascar became such a good location for pirates to operate from that rumours even started of a pirate state here. And English piracy in the area even became a diplomatic problem. In 1695, Henry Avery, one of the English pirates who frequented Madagascar, seized a ship owned by the Emperor of India, the Great Mughal. The English East India Company was forced to escort Mughal shipping in order to get its trading privileges restored.

Gradually, Madagscar became an area of rivalry between France and Britain. In 1811, for instance, we fought the Battle of Tamatave. The French fleet paused to capture the port of Tamatave on Madagacsar from the malaria-weakened British garrison here and then battle was joined. It was one of those sea battles where both sides occasionally found themselves sitting round not doing very much due to the fact that there wasn't any wind to get them where they wanted to go. It turned into a messy engagement in which both sides suffered damage and, fortunately from our point of view, the French suffered rather more. The French ships fled and eventually we cornered the French ship *Néréide* at Tamatave and captured both it and the port. The ship was taken into British service, and imaginatively called HMS *Madagascar*.

Subsequently, we saw a chance of spreading British influence by working with a powerful ruler on the island, Radama I. Under the Anglo-Merina Treaty of Friendship of 1817 we agreed to train and support his army, and in the end he united two-thirds of the island under his rule. Radama's successor was his wife Ranavalona I. She may have been his wife, but she didn't agree with him on Britain at all. In fact, she ended the treaty of friendship with Britain and wasn't too keen on some other Europeans either. She did, though, unite us and the French in wanting her gone. In 1845, British and French ships were in Tamatave again, this time attacking Ranavalona's

rule. HM frigate *Conway* and two French ships positioned themselves off Tamatave and demanded Ranavalona agree to stop some
of the actions she was taking against European traders. A British
and French landing party attacked the fort at Tamatave, but
cooperation between the two parties wasn't exactly perfect, with
British and French wrestling over control of a captured banner. A
fair bit of the town was destroyed, and eventually we and the French
departed taking assorted property and ships with us.

Ranavalona died in 1861, and with us concentrating our attentions elsewhere, it was the French, rather than us, who took control
of Madagascar. By 1942 we were seriously worried about that,
because Madagascar was loyal to the Vichy French government and
there were fears that the Japanese could be given naval bases on the
island and threaten our operations throughout the Indian Ocean.
So we decided it was time to invade Madagascar again in an epic
operation, Ironclad, which is somehow unknown to most people
today. It was to be our first amphibious assault since the disastrous
Gallipoli operation, so we decided not to take too many chances
and sent a major fleet, with the flag battleship *Ramillies*, the aircraft
carriers *Indomitable* and *Illustrious*, the cruisers *Devonshire* and
Hermione, plus eleven destroyers, six minesweepers, six corvettes
and auxiliaries.

On 5 May 1942, our 29th Infantry Brigade and 5 Commando
landed, with Royal Marines and two other brigades from the
5th Infantry Division. The landings were made near the port of
Diego Suarez (now called Antsiranana) in northern Madagascar.
Determined Vichy defenders held the invaders off until, in a dramatic, daring and extremely risky operation, the destroyer HMS
Anthony managed to slip past the Vichy coastal artillery in the dark
and land a Royal Marines force in the heart of the port itself. Luckily
the plan worked and Diego Suarez surrendered on 7 May.

Then the Japanese got in on the act shortly after, in one of their
most westerly operations, sending midget submarines into Diego
Suarez harbour and seriously damaging *Ramillies*. Two of the
Japanese midget submarine crew escaped onto the island and conducted a firefight with the Royal Marines, in which the Japanese
were eventually killed.

In the following months British forces gradually pushed forward. We made another amphibious landing at Majunga on

10 September and finally, on 5 November, Annet (the Vichy French commander) surrendered.

We handed control of the island over to Free French forces in 1943.

Malawi

Malawi's capital is Lilongwe. This fact is not only useful for pub quizzes, but it's also a name that rolls off the tongue. Try it.

In 1859, David Livingstone turned up at Lake Malawi, which was then called Lake Nyasa. By 1888 the African Lakes Company had set itself up in the area. But it had competition. Big competition. The Portuguese aspired to link the territory they controlled on the east coast of Africa to the territory they controlled on the west coast and the area of present-day Malawi was in the middle of the projected Portuguese coast-to-coast zone of control.

Despite all this, and despite the Portuguese being our long-term friends, we decided we still really wanted the territory for ourselves. In 1889, Cecil Rhodes helped fund the local British consul in Mozambique, Harry Johnston, in a PR campaign to sign local chiefs up to treaties with Britain before the Portuguese could really get moving. The Anglo-Portuguese crisis of 1889–90 (yes, there was one) led to an ultimatum from us on 11 January 1890, and when the Portuguese eventually backed down, it led to the Treaty of London in August 1890 defining the borders of Angola and Mozambique. It didn't make us at all popular with the Portuguese, but it did help us to secure the land we wanted.

Nyasaland (as Malawi was then known) was formally declared a British Protectorate in 1891.

In 1964 Nyasaland became independent and became Malawi.

Malaysia

It's a part of the world we've long had an interest in.

Already by 1592 Sir James Lancaster was turning up on Penang with his ship the *Edward Bonaventure* for a few months of looting vessels.

In 1786 we established our first major presence here with the British East India Company leasing Penang from the Sultan of

Kedah. On 11 August, Captain Francis Light raised the British flag and changed the name of the island (for a while at least) to Prince of Wales Island. Presumably the Prince of Wales was at least mildly chuffed. It's always nice to have an island named after you. We liked it so much we decided to lease another chunk of land opposite Penang, which we grandly called Province Wellesley (not that Wellesley, the Duke of Wellington, a different Wellesley, Richard Wellesley, who was Governor of Madras and Governor-general of Bengal) and which is now Seberang Perai.

That was just the start of it. During the Napoleonic Wars we took over control of Malacca from the Dutch, so the French didn't get their hands on it (though we gave it back to the Dutch in 1815 when the war was over) and we eventually swapped another bit of territory with the Dutch and took long-term control of it.

And so we went on through the nineteenth century adding little bits and pieces here and there (like an acquisitive squirrel gathering tasty nuts – admittedly like a very large imperial squirrel gathering tasty nuts, but like one nonetheless). In the 1840s began the fascinating episode of the so-called White Rajahs of Sarawak. One Brit called James Brooke, after helping out the Sultan of Brunei when he was in a tight spot, was made Rajah of Sarawak. He and his descendants ruled Sarawak as Rajahs all the way until 1946.

In 1846, we picked up Labuan as well. And in 1878 we leased Sabah from the Sultanate of Sulu. In 1909, we pinched a bunch of states off Siam and added them to the territories we controlled in what is now Malaysia. And where we weren't actually taking control, we took sort of control by assigning British 'advisers' to local rulers. By the First World War we had direct or indirect control throughout the region.

During the Second World War, the Japanese invaded and took over the whole area. We tried to get it back. One thing we did was to support the Malayan People's Anti-Japanese Army, a resistance force that had a strong element of ethnic Chinese in its ranks. People from our Force 136 landed to make contact with the resistance fighters, and by the end of the war we were sending in supplies by air.

By the summer of 1945 we were preparing to launch Operation Zipper to commence the liberation of Malaya and Singapore. The Japanese surrender meant the full implementation of the plan was unnecessary, and instead we moved in forces to implement the surrender, disarm the Japanese and return Malaya to British rule. On 28 August 1945, Task Force 11, which included the battleship HMS *Nelson*, two escort carriers and assorted other vessels, arrived in Penang.

But there was trouble ahead. The Malayan People's Anti-Japanese Army had ceased to have the Japanese to fight, and as the world descended into the Cold War, Malaya descended into the so-called Malayan Emergency, in which we fought the guerrillas of the Malayan Peoples' Liberation Army from 1948 to 1960. Eventually, we won the war against the guerrillas, but our time in control of the area was coming to an end.

In 1963 Malaysia became independent.

Maldives

A stunningly beautiful country. When we chucked the Dutch out of Sri Lanka, or Ceylon as it then was, we took over from them the influence they had had over The Maldives. In 1887 we signed an agreement with the Sultan by which we had control of the external relations and defence affairs of The Maldives.

During the Second World War we began to take more of an interest in the area from a military point of view. In 1941, engineers landed from HMS *Guardian* to build an airbase on Gan Island. There were also facilities for ships, jetties for flying boats, and coastal and air defence systems. In March 1944, there was action here when U*183* torpedoed the tanker *British Loyalty*.

The Maldives became fully independent from us in 1965, but the last Brtitish troops didn't leave Gan Island until 1976.

Mali

Mali is a huge country in West Africa that was well within the French sphere of influence during the late nineteenth and early twentieth century, so we haven't really invaded it much. However, Britons have had some dramatic times there.

And you'll have heard of one of its major cities, Timbuktu. The town grew rich on trans-Saharan trade and in the seventeenth and eighteenth centuries it became a sort of African El Dorado for Europeans, a legendary but unlocated golden city full of wealth. Consequently we set out to find it.

In 1805, a Scot named Mungo Park led an expedition including thirty soldiers and assorted officers along the Niger River towards Timbuktu, deep into what is now Mali. He had already been into the region back in 1796, when he had reached the Niger at Segou and followed its course until he ran out of supplies.

His 1805 expedition was both more successful, in the sense that he got a lot further, and less successful, in the sense that he (and lots of others) died. After resting for two months at Sansanding, in present-day Mali, he pressed on. Though his journals eventually made it home, dispatched by Park before his death, Park himself never did, and an investigation to find out what happened to him and his fellow men found only Park's munitions belt. In 1824, a French geographical society offered a reward of 10,000 francs for the first non-Muslim to reach Timbuktu and return safely to tell about it. Another Scotsman, Gordon Laing, made it to Timbuktu in 1826, but didn't have much time to celebrate since he ended up being killed there. As a result it was a Frenchman who finally picked up the ten grand in 1828 and set the scene for French, rather than British, expansion into the area.

Later, we had a chance to add a chunk of Mali to the British Empire, but we turned it down. In the late nineteenth century, Samori Ture created an empire that incorporated quite a bit of Mali. In January 1885, as part of his attempts to resist the French, he offered to put the empire under British protection, but we decided not to pick a quarrel with the French about the area.

The country came under Vichy French control during the Second World War and only switched sides after the Allied invasion of Algeria in 1942. Consequently, the only Brits arriving in Timbuktu in that period were prisoners. John Turnbull Graham and William Souter from the SS *Allende* are buried in war graves there.

Malta

Malta is, of course, now a popular tourist destination. Older readers in particular will also know of Malta's heroic defiance against German attacks during the Second World War and, of course, most people will be aware that Britain has strong connections with this little island nation. Not quite so many, however, will know how those connections came about.

Malta was already well known to us long before we took control here. There were, for example, Knights of Malta from Britain, like English Hospitaller Nicholas Upton, who was commander of the sea defences of Malta in July 1551 when he managed to fight off a surprise attack, only to collapse and die at the end of a long day's fighting. And in the seventeenth century Admiral Sir John Narborough, leading a squadron in the area for operations against the Barbary Corsairs, decided that he would only salute the knights at Valetta if they would salute him back with their guns. The Knights refused and the Grand Master apparently questioned Narborough's rank, but eventually the potential conflict was solved in a friendly fashion and Narborough based his squadron in Malta for a while from the middle of 1675.

Indeed our invasion of Malta, if you can call it that, was to be a rather friendly one as well – friendly that is to the Maltese, although considerably less friendly to the French.

In 1798, Napoleon dropped by Malta on his way to attack Egypt. By this time the Knights of Malta seem to have outstayed their welcome with the local Maltese, some of whom petitioned Napoleon to remove power from them. This Napoleon did, and left a French garrison there when he departed. Fairly rapidly, the French became deeply unpopular too and a rebellion started. Which is where we come in again.

We installed a naval blockade of the islands to prevent supplies and reinforcements reaching the French and we sent help to the rebels. In October 1798, Nelson turned up and in the same month the French surrendered the citadel of Gozo. In December 1798, Nelson sent Captain Alexander Ball to assist the rebels and he proved so popular with the locals that he was elected president of the Assembly in February 1799. Much better than just a polite 'thank you' or box of chocolates.

Then, in September 1799, 800 British troops under General Thomas Graham arrived, and in June 1800 another 800 British troops under Major General Henry Pigot landed. In September 1800, the French finally decided that they had had enough and surrendered. Under the Treaty of Amiens in 1802 we were supposed to evacuate the island, but we didn't want to. War broke out again in 1803 and we stayed, with Ball returning as our representative. He died here in 1809 and is buried here, and in 1810 the Maltese built a memorial in his memory. There was plenty of support among the Maltese for British control, which in many ways was fortunate because the Treaty of Paris in 1814 confirmed British control.

Malta became independent on 21 September 1964.

Marshall Islands

The Marshall Islands are situated in the Pacific, a little north of the equator and a long way north of New Zealand.

A lot of nations have been involved with the Marshall Islands, although they are named after a Brit.

The Spanish were probably the first Europeans to reach the islands. Then Captain John Marshall turned up. In 1788 he was captain of the British Navy ship *Scarborough*, a ship of the First Fleet taking convicts to Botany Bay. On the return journey from Australia, he dropped in on the islands. He originally called them Lord Mulgrove's Range. Fortunately, they eventually became known as the Marshall Islands. Otherwise the UN would now have a member country called Lord Mulgrove's Range, which, since it sounds more like a kitchen feature in a large country house, would seem strange.

Eventually, the Spanish took control. In 1884, they sold the islands to the Germans, who lost them in the First World War to the Japanese who were then fighting on our side. And they, when not fighting on our side, lost them in the Second World War to the Americans. The Americans then used them for, among other things, nuclear tests. Bikini Atoll, part of the Marshall Islands, has given its name to the swimwear, but there were also some big, big explosions there in the post-war period.

Finally, the people of the Marshall Islands got to run their own country again.

Mauritania

Some Brits when they hear the word Mauritania will think of an enormous and rather impressive ocean liner built in the early twentieth century, the RMS *Mauretania*, sister ship of the unlucky RMS *Lusitania* sunk by a U-boat in 1915. But that's Mauretania with an 'e' from the Roman North African province. This is Mauritania with an 'i', the enormous country in north-west Africa, with a long and varied history.

Part of that long history includes invasion by us, perhaps inevitably bearing in mind its long coastline and its position not a huge distance, in global terms, south of these islands. One of the main things we were after there was gum (not chewing gum, but gum arabic). And we weren't the only ones. Competition from other European powers was enthusiastic, and at times more than just enthusiastic. It was, frankly, violent.

In 1445, Prince Henry the Navigator set up a Portuguese colony on the island of Arguin, the main aim of this venture being gum arabic and slaves. In 1633 the Dutch pinched Arguin. Then we got hold of it in 1665. Then the French had it again. Then the Brandenburg/Prussians got in on the act. Then France. Then the Dutch. Then the French. Locals must have wondered whose flag they would see when they glanced up next.

And these gum wars weren't fought just at Arguin. There was another gum arabic trading port on the Mauritanian coast at Portendic. In 1834, this was reckoned to be a British port, to the apparent irritation of the nearby French governor of Senegal who sent two warships to the port and ordered two British merchant ships waiting to load gum arabic to get out of there. When they refused to do so, the French opened fire on the locals and the gum they were waiting to load, and continued even though a British flag had been placed on the gum. There was much debate in Parliament over this gum crisis with the French, and the Royal Navy was accordingly sent out to protect our ships.

Mauritius

Mauritius lies in the Indian Ocean about 560 miles east of Madagascar. Since it's stuck in the middle of an ocean, you are probably already by now thinking that it's unlikely we never invaded it. And, of course, we have.

It was famously home to the Dodo. But an invasion of hungry European sailors soon saw to that.

Mauritius is named after Maurice. Not any Maurice, but one Maurice in particular, Prince Maurice of Nassau, stadtholder of the Dutch Republic, at the time that a Dutch admiral arrived on the island in 1598. English pirates seem to have taken an early interest in Mauritius. And the Dutch attempted to settle the island, but eventually gave up, allowing the French to move in and rename Mauritius Île de France, Island of France, a fairly clear message to the world who was boss here.

Not surprisingly, bearing in mind our long series of wars with the French, we didn't take the hint.

In 1747–48, Rear Admiral Edward Boscawen attempted an invasion that turned into what must be one of our least successful long-distance military ventures. He set off from Britain in 1747 with six warships and a landing force. He attempted to invade Mauritius, only to be deterred by heavy surf, so he diverted to attack Pondicherry in India, only to run into trouble with the monsoon there and then peace was declared anyway.

As the Napoleonic Wars ground on, French naval forces based in Mauritius were increasingly making themselves a nuisance for Britain by preying on our trade routes to India, so in August 1810, a squadron of four British frigates arrived to blockade Grand Port. Once there we duly sent a landing party to capture the small, strategic, fortified island of Île de la Passe, and when a French squadron turned up shortly after we got ready for battle. Unfortunately for us, it didn't quite go to plan. The French knew the waters rather better than us and we ended up with two ships captured and two others grounded and burnt to avoid French capture. It was the worst naval defeat we had suffered for a time and our hopes of capturing Mauritius seemed dead as, well, as a dodo. Later in 1810, when we had recovered our strength, we returned to Mauritius. This time we were determined to end French control of Mauritius once and for all.

On 29 November the landing started at Grand Baie. By the evening the vanguard and naval brigades were ashore and by mid-day on 30 November the entire force had landed as the advance guard pushed rapidly forward pursuing the retreating enemy. On 1 December the French forces made a stand outside Port Napoleon, but were overwhelmed by the British assault. By 2 December it was all over.

We dumped the name Île de France and, not surprisingly under the circumstances, we dumped the name Port Napoleon as well.

Mauritius eventually became independent from Britain in 1968.

Mexico

As you would expect, Mexico got a fair amount of early attention from British buccaneers and privateers.

In 1568, for instance, Francis Drake was almost killed in a battle near San Juan de Ulua.

Sir Christopher Myngs, English admiral and pirate, mercilessly sacked San Francsico de Campeche so brutally in 1663 that Charles II was prompted to suspend such attacks for a while.

British raiding in the area continued in the eighteenth century. In 1743, Commodore Anson, on his lengthy and challenging jaunt around the world, intercepted Spain's yearly Manila galleon from the Philippines off Cape Espiritu Santo and seized more than 1 million gold coins. He must have been a happy man.

And in the nineteenth century, when the President of Mexico suspended interest payments to foreign countries, we sent in the ships again, this time in alliance with the French and Spanish. The Royal Navy arrived in Vera Cruz in 1861 and helped put troops ashore there. However, we soon realised that the French were in for rather more long-term aims than just getting their money. So we left the French to get stuck into a lengthy and messy civil war, while we got out.

Micronesia

What we are talking about here is the Federated States of Micronesia, because Micronesia itself is a much bigger region, with loads and loads of islands. Most of them small islands. The clue is in the name Micro-nesia from Greek *mikros* for 'small' and *nesia*, 'island'.

There are four states in the Federated States – Yap, Chuuk, Pohnpei and Kosrae – and the country's flag has four stars on it.

Generally speaking, our armed forces haven't had that much to do with the area, but they have been there. HMS *Rosario* operated in the area in the 1870s, and in September 1878 Captain Dupuis and HMS *Rosario* turned up on Kosrae hunting for the notorious pirate Bully Hayes. In the Second World War, Chuuk Lagoon, or Truk Lagoon as it was then known to us, became a major Japanese naval base. The main Allied effort against Truk/Chuuk was conducted by the United States, but our forces were involved too. In June 1945, a British Pacific Fleet carrier task force bombarded Truk with naval gunfire and launched air raids against it.

Moldova

It's fair to say that this country hasn't seen a lot armed Brits through its territory. But it has seen at least a few.

In the First World War, the Royal Naval Air Service (RNAS) also ran armoured cars, and in 1916 a bunch of them, plus other Brits including transport and nursing units, found themselves trying to assist the Russians to hold back the German General von Mackensen's advance through Romania towards Russia. There is a sharp pointy bit of what is present-day Moldova that reaches down to the Danube in the vicinity of where these operations took place, with Romania on one side of it and what is now the Ukraine on the other side. We have a record of some of the RNAS armoured cars at one time at Braila on the Romanian side of the pointy bit of Moldova, and at another time a few miles away at Reni on the Ukrainian side. We know that they brought cars up the Danube by barge, so that could have taken them through Moldovan waters. Equally, if any of the units used the main railway line from Russia to reach Braila, then that too would have taken them through

Moldovan territory. Obviously, at the time, the men and women of these units had much more important things to think about (matters of life and death) than whether they were passing through something that would one day be Moldova, but it's an intriguing minor historical mystery nonetheless.

Anyway, whatever happened near the front, at least some RNAS armoured cars did definitely make it into Moldova, because they were sent to be repaired and refitted at Tiraspol, the second largest city in the country.

Monaco, Principality of

An interesting case this. Tiny Monaco is one of the very few countries we may not basically have invaded. And yet it's also one of the relatively few countries that *have* sort of invaded us. Amazing. Charles Grimaldi of the ruling dynasty of Monaco took part with his ships in the sack of Southampton in 1338.

And in another bizarre twist in the Southampton/Monaco relationship, it is HMS *Southampton* that has one of the better British claims to having been in action in Monaco, or at least in what are now its territorial water. HMS *Southampton* is recorded as capturing the ship *Corso* off Monaco on 2 December 1796. It's also worth noting here that Nelson found himself patrolling the area off Monaco. Though having said that, it doesn't seem to have been one of his most exciting experiences. He noted with some disgust at one point that there were no significant vessels in any bay from Monaco to Vado.

We came close to invading Monaco on land in the Second World War, but didn't in the end. In 1944, British paratroopers, having parachuted into southern France as part of Operation Dragoon, fought their way along the coast as far as Grasse and Cannes, only a few short miles outside Monaco, before being ordered to embark at Cannes on 26 August and sail to Naples. Monaco itself was liberated by US paratroopers on 3 September. It's possible that some Britons were involved in the liberation of Monaco on some level, but I don't have the evidence of that right now. If you do, let me know.

Mongolia

Mongolia is one of the few countries in the world where not only have we not invaded, but we don't seem to have done anything military with it at all. In 1918, during the Allied intervention in Russia after the revolution there, we had a British military mission at Irkutsk, a mere 50 miles north of the Mongolian border, but so far I haven't found any evidence that we got any closer than that.

This was probably the time we had most influence in Mongolia. We briefly offered support to Grigory Semyonov, who at one stage was operating along the Mongolian border. He was a warlord partly of Buryat descent and spoke fluent Buryat and Mongolian and had served in Mongolia. And Major Dockray, a retired British Army officer, was responsible for the new radio tower in Urga (the former name of the capital Ulan Bator).

Montenegro

Montenegro, if you think about it (or even when you don't), means 'black mountain' in Italian. The Montenegrins call it Crna Gora which, unsurprisingly, means 'black mountain' in their language.

Montenegro has a long and beautiful coast, so it has received occasional visits from us. During the Napoleonic Wars, for example, a Royal Navy detachment under Captain William Hoste of HMS *Bacchante* took Kotor from the French garrison. He worked with local forces to haul ships' gun to positions above the fortress there and started bombarding it. After ten days, on 5 January 1814, the French gave up and surrendered.

During the First Balkan War we helped assorted other nations blockade the port of Bar in Monetenegro. Bar was barred, in fact.

In the First World War, Kotor was a big enemy submarine base and the focus of assorted actions by the Allies.

There was a certain amount of British involvement in Montenegro in the Second World War. In 1941, for example, when the Italians took Kotor, a Royal Navy submarine, HMS *Regent*, was dispatched to Kotor to try to evacuate British and Allied personnel. In 1944, with the Partisan Second Division in Montenegro under particular pressure, we helped organise an emergency landing strip near the village of Brezna, in which waves of British and American Dakotas protected by Spitfires and Mustangs rescued more than 900 of the wounded. German forces were only about 5 miles away when the last plane took off and they reached Brezna itself soon after.

Morocco

Loads of Brits now head to Morocco for their holidays, most of whom won't be aware of our long and fascinating history of involvement with the country. To be fair, a lot of that history has been about peaceful collaboration, but there has been military action as well, and it's such an interesting and little-known story, I've got to give it all a quick mention here.

When Brits think of Queen Elizabeth I, they don't tend to think of Morocco, but the fact is that she got on rather well with the Sultan of Morocco, Ahmad al-Mansur, apart from anything else because both of them feared and disliked Philip II of Spain. There was plenty of trade and even discussions of possible joint attacks on Spain. It was all rather warm and cosy.

And to some extent this spirit of friendship and cooperation continued under their successors. In 1632, for instance, English and Moroccan forces cooperated to capture the city of Salé in Morocco from pirates.

However, things were to get a little less friendly towards the end of the seventeenth century. That was when we took over Tangier. Charles II was given it as a wedding present from the Portuguese when he married Catherine of Braganza. Some people give fondue sets (which are very nice, I love a fondue). The Portuguese, however, were thinking on a rather bigger scale and gave Tangier instead. So, in a sort of peaceful invasion, we actually occupied and ran Tangier from 1661 to 1684. Yes, temporarily we controlled a little bit of Morocco. We thought it would make an excellent naval base and spent a lot of time and money building a mole there, of the harbour kind obviously, not some kind of large imitation of a small, furry tunnelling creature. However, not all the locals were very enthusiastic about our presence. In 1664 they killed the second English governor there, Lord Teviot. The Sultan decided he wanted us out as well, and as it became clear that our base in Tangier was more of a liability than an asset, we decided to leave. Before we did so, we demolished bits of the town, including our expensive mole, which we blew up.

So ended our occupation of Moroccan soil rather ingloriously. At least friendly relations with Morocco were gradually restored during the eighteenth century.

When Operation Torch, the Allied Invasion of Algeria and Morocco, took place in November 1942, the invasion of Morocco was basically an American mission, but British forces did play a minor supporting role; the escort carrier HMS *Archer* arrived in Casablanca on 18 November bringing US personnel and aircraft.

Mozambique

Mozambique was controlled by the Portuguese for a long time and, of course, Portugal has been a friend for a long time, so up until the twentieth century we hadn't invaded it very much.

Our time came in the First World War. The local German commander Lettow-Vorbeck was leading a column wending its way around East Africa, keeping German hopes in the area alive. We were trying to catch him and defeat him. By November 1917 Lettow-Vorbeck was very short of supplies. In an extraordinary and little-known episode of the war, the Germans sent an airship to try to re-supply him. The naval airship *L59* had made it all the way south to a position near Khartoum before the mission was called off.

Then, in late November 1917, Lettow-Vorbeck crossed into what is now Mozambique in search of supplies. We followed. British troops landed at Porto Amelia/Pemba and along with other British units moving south overland, pursued Lettow-Vorbeck not very successfully to the territory around the port of Quelimane. Further British troops were landed in the summer of 1918. On 3 July 1918, Lettow-Vorbeck attacked the railway station of Nhamacurra, defeating a British and Portuguese force. Many of those who died on our side did so because while trying to escape they drowned or were killed by crocodiles in the Nhamacurra River. Fighting in France and Belgium was mostly a hugely grim experience, but at least there weren't that many crocodiles around. Eventually, Lettow-Vorbeck eluded the main forces pursuing him by turning north and moving out of what is now Mozambique. We followed. Again.

Namibia

Namibia is on the west coast of Africa, just north of South Africa.

We took an early interest in the area. In the late eighteenth century, HMS *Nautilus* was sent to Das Voltas Bay looking for a place for a penal colony. But it was decided to opt for New South Wales instead. Shortly after that we 'took possession' of a length of what is now Namibian coastline, which was news to the Portuguese who had claimed some of the same coastline about 300 years earlier. Anyway, it was all sorted out in 1815 and 1817 with us giving up claims north of Cape Fria in Namibia.

Having taking an initial interest in the area, we were unusually slow (by our standards) in trying to take genuine control. Eventually, we lost out to the Germans who, having started a lot later in building an empire, were in something of a hurry.

We only managed to hang on to two bits of present-day Namibia. Admittedly, they were very useful bits. We kept Walvis Bay, with its natural deepwater harbour. And we kept the Penguin Islands with their natural penguins (presumably) and, better still in commercial terms, their natural guano supplies. Both these became part of the Cape Colony.

In 1914, with the outbreak of war with Germany, we asked the South African government to invade what was then German South-West Africa. The Royal Navy transported South African troops north to take the port of Lüderitz in September 1914. Meanwhile, the Germans, in return, took the vulnerable Walvis Bay Enclave. So it was goodbye to our natural deepwater harbour for a bit.

On 25 September 1914, an attempt to invade from the south came to a disastrous end at the Battle of Sandfontein. The Germans struck back by briefly invading South Africa before being stopped at the Battle of Kakamas on 4 February 1915.

In March, General Louis Botha started advancing inland from the coast and Namibia's capital Windhoek was captured on 5 May 1915. Other South African columns attacked from other directions and by July the remnants of the German forces that had retreated north surrendered.

In 1920, control of Namibia was given to South Africa as a League of Nations Mandate. In 1990, after a guerrilla war fought by SWAPO, Namibia became independent, with British troops helping in the United Nations Transition Assistance Group. In 1994, Namibia even got Walvis Bay and the Penguin Islands back from South Africa.

Nauru

Nauru is the world's smallest republic, with an area of just 8.1 square miles. It's an island country in the Pacific, sort of north of New Zealand, a bit over to the west, and east of East Timor.

Nauru's quite a long way from most places and it wasn't until 1798 that a European turned up. In this case it was a Brit, the sea captain and whaler John Fearn. He called the island Pleasant Island, so unless he had a strange sense of humour, we can assume he liked it.

In 1888, it was the Germans who (as already noted) having started late were in a hurry to catch up with the empire-building of their European competitors and added it to their empire.

Phosphate reserves were discovered on the island in 1900 and those huge phosphate resources have played an enormous role in Nauru's history.

The First World War came to Nauru on 9 September 1914, when a radio station was destroyed by the warship HMAS *Melbourne*. The island wasn't immediately occupied, but British phosphate miners here wanted the Germans out and on 6 November 1914, Australian troops took control of the island. At the end of the First World War, with Nauru's financial worth estimated as several hundred million pounds, Britain, Australia and New Zealand vied for control. Eventually, control of the phosphate mining and the island was split between the three.

Even Nauru, despite being a very, very long way from Germany, didn't escape unscathed from Hitler's forces during the Second World War. In December 1940, the German auxiliary cruiser *Komet* shelled mining areas and oil depots. Then on 26 August 1942, it was the turn of the Japanese to arrive on Nauru. They surrendered to the Australians on 13 September 1945 and Nauru was made a UN trusteeship again under Britain, Australia and New Zealand.

Nauru became independent in 1968.

Nepal

Ever wondered what the origins of the Gurkha regiments in the British Army are? Well as you might suspect, it's all down to our invasion of Nepal.

We had already sent men on a mission into Nepal in 1767 under Captain Kinloch. It hadn't been a success.

By 1814, with a border dispute between us and Nepal festering, we decided to try again. We planned an attack on two fronts, with two columns in each front. Three of the columns failed to make much headway in the face of tough terrain and tough opposition. But the last column under Major General Ochterlony managed to defeat Nepalese General Thapa on 9 May 1815. In 1816, Ochterlony was back with more men and more artillery, and made a bold move through a rarely used pass, which put the Nepalese defenders at a disadvantage. We were victorious in the fighting at Makwanpur in February and eventually the Nepalese were forced to agree to peace terms.

We took away a lot of their territory, but then later gave some back. In the progress of the war, we had been so impressed by the fighting spirit of the locals that in the period after the war we started recruiting locals into Gurkha units in the British army. And we still do today.

Netherlands, The

These days, the Netherlands is a partner with us both in the EU and in NATO, and many Brits don't really think of the Netherlands as being an area we have invaded much. But, of course, we have. A lot. Sometimes to help the Dutch, but sometimes to fight them.

Mind you, some of our early military ventures into the area weren't about either fighting against the Dutch or even alongside them. Like at Battle of Sluys in 1340, it was the French we beat, destroying most of their fleet.

In the late sixteenth century, the Netherlands was an area of major strategic interest for us. After the Treaty of Nonsuch gave England a serious say in Dutch affairs (and also paved the way for the dispatch of the Spanish Armada against us), in 1585 and 1586 Elizabeth sent two armies under Robert Dudley, 1st Earl of Leicester, to fight in the Netherlands in support of the locals against the Spanish. The poet and soldier Sir Philip Sidney (who also happened to be a relative of Dudley's) briefly ended up as governor of Flushing (one of a number of Dutch towns that had English garrisons) and in July 1586 he successfully attacked Spanish forces near Axel, before eventually getting shot at the Battle of Zutphen and dying shortly afterwards at Arnhem, a place that is particularly special in British history because of events there during a much more recent war.

By the middle of the seventeenth century, things were getting a little less friendly between us and the Dutch. In fact, a lot less friendly.

The First Anglo-Dutch war of 1652–54 saw naval actions both in English and Dutch waters.

Then we (sort of) lost the Second Anglo-Dutch war of 1665–67.

Subsequently, in the Third Anglo-Dutch War of 1672–74 we tried to get our own back with a planned invasion of the Netherlands, working with the French. It was all a bit messy (and not very successful), and included assorted naval actions in Dutch waters, like two Battles of the Schooneveld and the Battle of Texel. During this war, the Duke of Monmouth led a brigade of troops accompanying the French invasion of the Netherlands, and they were present at the Siege of Maastricht in 1673.

Then, in 1688, William III left the Netherlands to become king over here, which obviously changed relations between us and the Netherlands. For most of the eighteenth century we tended to be on the same side as the Netherlands in assorted wars. For instance, in the War of the Spanish Succession, Marlborough commanded Dutch troops as well as English. And we were on the same side again in the War of the Austrian Succession, even though it wasn't an entirely successful war from our point of view. A British force under the Duke of Cumberland, along with our Dutch allies, was defeated near the borders of what is now the Netherlands, just outside Maastricht, in 1747 at the Battle of Laufeld.

Eventually, the love affair between us and the Dutch wore off. In 1780–84 we fought another war against the Dutch, instead of alongside them, and blockaded the Dutch coast and temporarily occupied a fair number of the territories they controlled in the East.

During much of the French Revolutionary Wars and Napoleonic Wars, the Netherlands was firmly on the side of the French. This led to some invasions by us, ones that few Brits have ever heard of.

How many Brits know about the British and Russian expedition to Holland in 1799? Yep, there was one. An expeditionary force of Russian and British troops landed on the North Holland Peninsula and won assorted engagements, including the Battle of Callantsoog and the Battle of Krabbendam, before being forced to withdraw.

Then in 1809 there was the Walcheren Campaign. This was a bit of a disaster. In fact, a lot of a disaster. The idea was to open another front against France. Indeed in July 1809 we took something like 40,000 troops accompanied by thousands of horses and loads of artillery across the sea to invade the Dutch island of Walcheren. The campaign accomplished a few things, like, for, example, taking Flushing in August, but large numbers died from disease and generally the brief invasion was a huge and costly failure.

After the Napoleonic Wars, things settled down between us and the Dutch, and it wasn't until the Second World War that we invaded the Netherlands again, this time to help free the Dutch. After assorted military activity in the Netherlands during the war, including sending support for Dutch resistance groups, in the second half of 1944 British forces along with other Allied units were advancing towards the Netherlands.

In September 1944, Operation Market Garden was launched and the bravery of the Allied troops involved liberated significant parts of the Netherlands, but left a lot of the country under German control after the tragic events at Arnhem. In October 1944, there was heavy fighting around Overloon. At the end of October and beginning of November, British forces, including troops from the British Special Service Brigade, were once again invading the island of Walcheren, this time along with Canadian troops. The last German forces in the Netherlands did not surrender until May 1945.

New Zealand

Almost everybody in Britain knows of our close relationship over the years with New Zealand, so I'm not going to focus in too much depth on the country in this book.

The British presence on the islands all started off quite peacefully, but then it all got a bit messy.

In 1642, the Dutchman Abel Tasman (of Tasmania fame) turned up and was the first European to discover the islands. Subsequently, they were named New Zealand. Slightly confusingly, because today Zealand is a Danish island, whereas we now call the Dutch place they were originally named after 'Zeeland'. Oh well.

Then in 1769, our James Cook turned up and mapped most of the coastline of the islands. By the 1830s, Britain and France were both interested in taking control of the islands and eventually in 1840 our Captain William Hobson negotiated the Treaty of Waitangi with Maori chiefs and declared British sovereignty.

Soon after the treaty, disputes, particularly over land, started between the Maoris and settlers, and rapidly the situation ended up in war, or, in fact, a series of wars.

From 1845–46 there was the Flagstaff War, so named because a local Maori leader and the local British leadership went through a bizarre contest whereby the flagstaff flying the British flag was chopped down, then replaced, then chopped down again, then replaced again and so on until it all ended in bloodshed. We won eventually, but only after some bitter fighting and significant losses.

There was a string of other campaigns and wars. There was, for example, the First Taranaki War of 1860–61, which we sort of won, but not hugely convincingly. This was followed by the Invasion of Waikato in 1863–64 and the Second Taranaki War of 1863–66. In Te Kooti's War, 1868–72, the prominent Maori leader Te Kooti waged a long guerrilla battle. Then there was Titokowaru's War. And finally, in the 1890s, there was the Dog Tax War, which was over, you guessed it, dog tax.

It's an extraordinary story of conflict and hardship, particularly for the Maoris, that deserves far more space than can be given in a small book like this.

New Zealand became independent from Britain through a series of steps that gradually gave it more and more control over its affairs.

Nicaragua

People who lived through the Cold War will also remember the war in Nicaragua in which the Americans backed the Contra guerrillas fighting to overthrow the Sandinista government.

But many people who are aware of that war, aren't aware that we have fought our own wars in the country's territory as well.

Nicaragua lies on the wide bit of the Central American isthmus, with Honduras to the north and Costa Rica to the south. If you've been reading this book in alphabetical order you'll probably already have worked out by now that lying in a tempting, handy-for-the-ocean, not-far-from-the-Caribbean-and-South-America location like this, and having been controlled by the Spanish for a long time, the country is extremely unlikely to have escaped the attention of British pirates and, of course, it didn't.

Granada, on Lake Nicaragua, was a major target because it was a wealthy town and control of it and of Lake Nicaragua pretty much gave control across the isthmus from Pacific to Caribbean. Granada is one of those slightly confusing names, because there seem to be a lot of Granadas and/or Grenadas. This Granada is not to be confused with the Caribbean Island, the place in Spain, the TV company, or the car made by a well-known company.

In 1665, pirates including Henry Morgan ventured up the San Juan river to Lake Nicaragua and proceeded to sack Granada. To protect the San Juan River, the Spanish built the Fortress of the Immaculate Conception. This didn't stop William Dampier in 1685 landing on Nicaragua's Pacific coast and burning down the colony on 8 September.

As the years wore on, we formed an alliance with the local indigenous Miskito Kingdom and with a society that developed in the coastal regions of Nicaragua and Honduras that involved both Miskitos and ex-slaves. Together Brits and their local allies would raid the Spanish-held areas.

In 1740, we concluded a Formal Treaty of Friendship and Alliance with the Miskito Kingdom, or Mosquito Kingdom as we tended to know it. Under the terms of this treaty, the Miskito King, Edward I, accepted King George II's overlordship in return for military protection. In 1762, during the Seven Years War, a combined expedition attacked the Fortress of the Immaculate Conception, but was held off in a heroic defence led by 19-year-old Rafaela Herrera, daughter of the recently deceased garrison commander.

In 1780, Nelson himself was involved in yet another British expedition to try to capture Granada. In March, forces including elements from both the army and navy set off up the San Juan River, with the intention, once again, of making it to Lake Nicaragua. Nelson saw hand-to-hand combat, capturing a Spanish battery on Bartola Island. At the end of April they had managed to capture Fort San Juan (5 miles upstream), but by the time of the surrender, Nelson had fallen ill and been taken back down the river. He was not the first to fall ill, or the last. By the time we were forced to withdraw from the fort in November hundreds had died.

Under the 1786 Convention of London we pulled out our settlers from the area, but we continued to claim it was our protectorate. In the early nineteenth century, Spanish imperial control in the region ended, and we were still interested. Particularly in the region's mahogany. In 1841, we helped the Miskitos occupy San Juan del Norte and in 1848 we occupied it ourselves, calling it Greytown after Jamaica's then governor.

Eventually, in 1860, we signed the Treaty of Managua with Nicaragua and gradually British influence in the area waned as Nicaraguan and American influence rose.

But still today English is spoken by some groups in Nicaragua.

Niger

Not a country we've had that much to do with militarily really.

In 1805 Mungo Park (see Mali) set off to explore the Niger River and what was left of his expedition passed through what is now Niger in a canoe that he had named the 'HM Schooner *Joliba*'. Unfortunately for him, what was left of his expedition wasn't left very much longer, because they all died further down the river.

During the First World War there was a major Touareg rebellion against French rule in Niger, allegedly encouraged by pro-German elements. About 1,000 Touareg warriors attacked the town of Zinder, in Niger, just north of the Nigerian border. In response, we sent troops from Nigeria to help the French suppress the rebellion.

Nigeria

As with many areas in Africa, a lot our early interaction with the territory that is now Nigeria was involved with the slave trade. As early as the seventeenth century, Brits were trading in slaves here, but we didn't take great interest in seizing land at this stage. Finally, in the early nineteenth century, we abolished the slave trade and attempted to bring an end to it by preventing others from carrying it on. Our West Africa squadron conducted extensive operations with this in mind, with its 3rd Division responsible for covering the Bights of Benin and Biafra.

By the middle of the nineteenth century, we were ready to start expanding influence over big chunks of territory. Our first target was Lagos, now the capital of Nigeria, and during the slave trading years a major slave port. In 1851, we bombarded Lagos in order to replace the local ruler with someone we preferred, and in 1861 we sailed and seized it for ourselves.

As the nineteenth century wore on, we proceeded to expand our control of territory, usually by signing treaties with local leaders. It became a race for control against the French, and then against the Germans as well. In 1882 Edward Hewett, the British Consul in the area, ventured up the Niger on board HMS *Flirt* (great name), attacking those whom he felt were resisting British rule, and signalling firmly to the French that this was a British area of influence – a fairly heavy-handed form of flirting then.

In 1886, the Royal Niger Company was chartered to run the area and the game of expansion by a mixture of treaty and force continued. Our expansion did not come without resistance. For instance, the Brassmen's rebellion – a local revolt by the king and people of Brass against the Royal Niger Company – caused a fair amount of destruction and slaughter, and came as a big shock to us. But it did not stop us.

In 1895, we faced down the French when they attempted to expand their area of influence into what is now Nigeria and attempted to establish their right to sail down the Niger.

Then in 1896, with the Kingdom of Benin reluctant to acquiesce to our plans for it, an expedition under James Phillips headed for Benin in a badly planned attempt to deal with this issue. The expedition was ambushed and pretty much wiped out. In February 1897, a punitive expedition under Rear Admiral Henry Rawson invaded Benin. After ten days of heavy fighting, our troops reached Benin City, looted it and burned part of it. This is how many impressive Benin Bronzes came to be in Britain.

In 1900, the Royal Niger Company transferred control of its territories to the British Crown and the expansion accelerated.

Then there was the war in which we smashed the Aro Confederacy. The campaign started in November 1901 and by 28 December we had captured Arochukwu, though resistance dragged on into 1903.

In 1903, Frederick Lugard attacked Kano and then he attacked Sokoto as well. In 1906 an expedition was sent to destroy the Satiru rebellion.

Other wars dragged on, like the Ekumeku War, and all in all our invasion of what is now Nigeria could be described as long, messy and violent.

Nigeria became independent in 1960.

Norway

We have had plenty of Norwegian Vikings roaming the British Isles, and Norwegian waters and soil have seen plenty of armed Brits as well.

For instance, in 1665, there was the rather unfortunate (from the British point of view) Battle of Bergen. It's an unsavoury tale of inefficient treachery. The Danes (who then ran Norway) were friendly with the Dutch. We weren't since we were fighting them at the time. But King Frederick III in Copenhagen had let it be known to us that he had switched sides as and when there was a big rich Dutch East Indies convoy in one of his ports, so that we and he could pinch the boats and share the loot. When we learnt that just such a convoy was in Bergen, in Norway, Rear Admiral Thomas Teddeman set off with a force to capture it. Unfortunately, Frederick's orders on switching sides hadn't actually arrived in Bergen, so the Danes there and Commodore Pieter de Bitter instead defended the convoy vigorously and it was all a bit of a diplomatic and military disaster for us. The Commodore might have been de Bitter, but probably not half as much as Rear Admiral Teddeman was at the end of it all.

During the Napoleonic Wars we invaded Norwegian waters again, fighting a number of actions against the Danes and Norwegians during the so-called Gunboat War. It wasn't all plain sailing for us, but we did put in some good performances.

For example, on 23 July 1810, we fought the Battle of Silda in which HMS *Belvidera* and HMS *Nemesis* saw off four enemy vessels while attacking the pilot's station on the Norwegian island of Silda. On 6 July 1812, a small group of British warships fought a small group of Danish warships in the Battle of Lyngør. When we'd finished lingering at Lyngør, we'd sort of won, having destroyed one of their frigates and captured two of their ships (at least briefly – we abandoned them when they grounded).

And in the early part of the Second World War we spent a lot of time in Norwegian waters and some time on Norwegian soil as well.

In February 1940, there was the *Altmark* Incident. At this time, with Norway still neutral, a German tanker, the *Altmark*, was returning to Germany through Norwegian waters. On board were 299 British merchant seamen captured from ships sunk by the German raider *Graf Spee*. We then sent in the destroyer HMS *Cossack* and Churchill gave orders that unless the Norwegians stopped the ship *Cossack* would. The Norwegians refused, the *Altmark* ended up running aground and after a short fight with the Germans on board we freed the prisoners.

Rather less successful, in fact quite a lot less successful, was the Narvik operation. Some people might think there wasn't much going on in Western Europe between the start of the Second World War and the invasion of France. Well one of the things that was going on was Narvik. The port of Narvik in northern Norway was of key importance to the German war machine, because through it much Swedish iron ore was transported to Germany. It was also an area that had been of interest to both us and the Germans for broader strategic reasons and both sides had long been discussing plans for the area. In early April 1940, the Germans occupied Narvik with a force of ten destroyers and we sent ships to Narvik too. In the ensuing fighting we destroyed the German naval force. Major General Pierse Joseph Mackesy was then sent with troops to take Narvik itself, and by the end of May an Allied force of British, French, Norwegian and Polish forces had taken the place. By that time the German invasion of France was under way and French and British priorities lay elsewhere. In June, the Allied forces were withdrawn by sea from Narvik and Norway was overrun by German forces shortly afterwards.

The Second World War also saw some notable British raids on Norwegian territory, including assorted commando landings on Norwegian islands. I'll mention here just the raid on the Lofoten

Islands in March 1941. Partly because it was the first, partly because the Lofoten Islands sound rather exotic in a Scandinavian kind of way, partly because the name of the raid, Operation Claymore, sounds suitably fierce, and mainly because during the raid, in addition to destroying a lot of shipping and the fish oil and glycerine factories that were the targets, we also captured Enigma cipher rotor wheels that were of great importance.

There were also, of course, daring attempts by both sea and air to sink the *Tirpitz* in a Norwegian fjord, which we finally did, and assorted attacks on the Norwegian heavy water industry.

Then, in a little-known, but in some ways quite dramatic operation in late 1944 and on into 1945, in cooperation with Soviet forces in the area we helped exiled Norwegian forces land in and operate in northern Norway to help liberate the area.

Finally, in May 1945 in Operation Doomsday, the British 1st Airborne Division landed at Oslo and Stavanger to deal with the German surrender in Norway. There were fears of German resistance, but in the end things went quite smoothly and peacefully, and Major General Urquhart was there to greet Crown Prince Olaf and Norwegian government ministers when they arrived.

8

OMAN TO PORTUGAL

Oman

Our forces have spent time in Oman. In 1798, serious British involvement with the area began when the Sultan signed a treaty with the British East India Company.

Then in 1883, HMS *Philomel* helped with its guns to defend besieged Muscat. And in 1915, troops rushed from India helped to repel another attack on Muscat.

More recently, in the 1950s, British forces assisted the Sultan's forces in the Jebel Akhdar War. And in the 1960s and 1970s, Brits again assisted the Sultan's forces in the fighting in Dhofar.

Pakistan

Pakistan is a fascinating country with a wealth of culture and tradition. In terms of the British Empire, though, it's also the location of the famous North-West Frontier, where Brits battled locals for a very, very long time in a very, very long series of military encounters.

Because it's such a long, complex story, and because many Brits already know something about our military involvement with Pakistan, and because this book is supposed to focus on the lesser-known events, this will be only a brief summary of what happened.

Britain gradually gained control of the different sections of territory that now make up Pakistan. For instance, in 1843, Sir Charles Napier invaded and took over Sindh after victory at the Battle of Miani.

The First Sikh War ran from 1845–46 and saw bitter fighting between East India Company forces and the forces of the Sikh Empire. The result was a victory for the company, but only after a series of tough encounters. Then in 1848 the Second Sikh War broke out. In November, Sikh forces won something of a victory at the Battle of Ramnagar. The Battle of Chillianwala in January 1849 was a bitter encounter that led to heavy losses on both sides, but ended in something of a draw. Finally, things began to go the way of the British forces. The Battle of Gujrat was fought in February and by the end of March the war was over and the Punjab was annexed.

In the north-west, a series of engagements, conflicts and rebellions ran pretty much continuously from when we started pushing into the area after the annexation of the Punjab and began taking chunks of territory that had previously been Afghan, until the time we left. There are so many of these military confrontations that it's impossible to list them all here, so some examples will have to do to give a taste of what went on in Britain's almost unending attempts to subdue the area.

In 1863, for example, the Umbeyla Campaign targeted Pashtuns and Bunerwals. After the initial attack got bogged down against local resistance, reinforcements were sent in and the force made it through to Malka and burned it.

Or there was the Hazara Expedition of 1888, which ended with the village of Pokal being destroyed.

Or there was our conquest of Hunza and Nagar in 1891.

Or the Chitral Expedition of 1895, which was dispatched to relieve British forces surrounded and besieged in a fort in Chitral.

Or in 1897, the Malakand Campaign, launched as a result of local hostility to the line we had decided to draw between Afghanistan and British-controlled territory. Winston Churchill himself was present at the Siege of Malakand.

The same year there was the Tirah Campaign.

Or what about the operation in the Tochi region in 1914–15? Or the assorted campaigns in Waziristan that followed the Third Afghan War of 1919? Or Pink's War of 1925 in which we bombed Waziri tribesman? Or the fighting again in Waziristan in 1936–39?

Pakistan became independent in 1947.

Palau

Palau is an island nation lying about 500 miles east of the Philippines and a long, long way south of Japan.

Here is an interesting story about our early involvement with the Palau Islands. No invasion, in this case, for a change. Englishman Henry Wilson, captain of the East India Company vessel *Antelope*, was shipwrecked off Ulong in 1783. Wilson and about fifty men survived and became friendly with the King of Palau, assisting in fighting his wars, and the king's son accompanied Wilson back to Britain in 1784. Soon after arriving, the son died from smallpox. He was buried in St Mary's Churchyard, Rotherhithe, and the East India Company built a memorial.

At the end of the eighteenth century, a Brit named McCluer laid a foundation stone for a fort on Palau that was to be called Fort Abercrombie, but it never got any further than that.

In the nineteenth century, different European powers competed for control of the islands and we inevitably got involved in the area. In January 1881 HMS *Lily* arrived to try to impose a settlement in a dispute involving a looted wreck, and in 1883 HMS *Espiegle* tried to end a local war.

In 1885, the then Pope, Leo XIII, was dragged into the dispute, being asked to adjudicate between Britain, Spain and Germany. The Pope accepted the Spanish claim to the islands, but gave us and the Germans economic concessions. In 1898, Spain lost the Philippines in the Spanish-American War and decided to sell the islands to the Germans anyway.

Not that Germany managed to hang on to them for long. They lost them to Japanese control in the First World War. And then Japan lost its control of the islands in the Second World War.

Panama

Panama has a long coastline on both sides, and used to be controlled by Spain, so not surprisingly we have invaded it a number of times.

To begin with, being in the part of the world where it is, assorted British raiders, pirates and privateers have done a certain amount of damage here.

Panama, for obvious reasons, had long been a place connecting the Pacific and Atlantic. Francis Drake, for instance, dropped in to try to capture the town of Nombre de Dios early in his career because this was where gold and silver from Peru was put onto ships from Spain. He got into the town, but his forces withdrew when he was wounded. Drake ended his career off Panama as well, being buried at sea off Portobelo when he died of dysentery in 1596.

Henry Morgan, under an official commission to attack Spanish interests, invaded Panama in 1670. In December he captured the fortress of San Lorenzo on Panama's Caribbean coast and then headed across the peninsula with about 1,400 men towards Panama City. When he and his men arrived, in January 1671, he defeated the Spanish garrison and sacked the town. Much of it went up in flames and a new settlement of Panama would eventually be built a few miles away. Apparently unknown to Morgan, by the time he attacked, Spain and England had signed a peace treaty. This was all slightly embarrassing and Morgan ended up being dragged back to England under arrest. However, he convinced the authorities that he really hadn't known about the treaty and by 1675 he was in Jamaica, knighted and now lieutenant-governor of the island.

At the end of the seventeenth century, an event took place in Panama that may have changed the face of Britain rather more than it did Panama. A Scot called William Paterson had helped found the Bank of England and a lot of people would view that as enough to put on their CV as a lifetime achievement. But Paterson wanted to do more. He decided that what the world and particularly Scotland needed was a settlement in Panama that would facilitate trade across the isthmus, a sort of Panama Canal, in a sense, without actually building a canal. So Paterson set up the so-called Darien Scheme to establish such a settlement. Thousands of Scots invested, thousands volunteered to be settlers. The English parliament, fearing a threat to English trade, forced English investors to withdraw from the scheme.

When the settlers arrived in what they called New Caledonia, the scheme rapidly turned into a disaster. There were two expeditions, but large numbers of the settlers died from disease and malnutrition, and the Spanish sent forces to attack the Scots. By the time the scheme had collapsed and the remaining settlers had struggled home, more than 2,000 had died and Scotland was faced with large financial losses from the enterprise. Some have argued that the impact of Darien contributed to acceptance of the Act of Union with England in 1707.

Later in the eighteenth century, it was the British Navy's turn to have a go at invading Panama, in an attack that would leave an interesting legacy today. This time the target was Portobelo, a major Spanish naval base on Panama's Caribbean coast. Yes, we were at war with Spain yet again, this time in the War of Jenkins' Ear. So, in a rather dashing attack, with only six ships, Vice Admiral Edward Vernon arrived in the harbour (surprising the Spanish defenders somewhat), British sailors and marines scaled the fort walls and the Spanish surrendered. We stayed in Portobelo for three weeks, generally wrecking important parts of it. British losses were light and Brits everywhere were very pleased with Vernon and started naming things after his victory. Hence the Portobello Road in London and the Portobello area of Edinburgh as well.

Papua New Guinea

So do you know where New Britain and New Ireland are? They have had something of a Germanic flavour in the not too distant past. They used to be called New Pomerania and New Mecklenburg (and they are both still in the Bismarck Archipelago). So now do you know where they are?

OK, the fact that this is the Papua New Guinea section is probably a bit of a giveaway, but otherwise not many Brits would have a clue that they are located off the northern tip of Australia.

The Spanish claimed the archipelago as far back as the sixteenth century, but by the 1870s we had one John Moresby (hence Port Moresby, the capital) surveying the south-east coast of New Guinea and in 1884, while we took the south-east bit, the Germans took over the north-east. This, as you have probably guessed by now, is when New Britain and New Ireland picked up their Germanic alter egos.

In 1914, Australian troops invaded the German-controlled bit and took it over. There was bitter fighting here in the Second World War between Japanese and Australian forces

Papua New Guinea became fully independent in September 1975.

Paraguay

Paraguay is a landlocked country sandwiched between Argentina to the south and Brazil to the north, plus it's got Bolivia to the northwest. A lot of Brits get Paraguay and Uruguay confused.

It's a long way from the sea, but it is linked to the sea by river and, yes, the British Navy has been up there. We have also been in conflict with Paraguay, but not in Paraguayan waters, so as far as I know at the moment we haven't really invaded Paraguay.

In 1845, during the British and French blockade of the Rio de la Plata, Commodore Charles Hotham was operating with a British and French convoy and, despite Argentine attacks, in the *Fulton* he made it all the way to Asuncion, the present-day capital of Paraguay. The aim was to recognise Paraguay, lure the country into the war on our side and sign a treaty. The Paraguyans didn't quite see it our way and we had to make the long return journey, again under Argentine attacks.

Then, in 1859, there was the Canstatt Affair, which led to the Buzzard/Grappler Affair. A lot of affairs. The president of Paraguay had imprisoned a certain Santiago Canstatt among a group of people he had accused of plotting to kill him by shooting him in a theatre. This was some time before Abraham Lincoln took his unfortunate trip to the theatre. Canstatt was a British subject and we weren't very happy about him being chucked in jail. So two ships, *Buzzard* and *Grappler*, were dispatched to seize the *Tacuari*, Paraguay's only warship, when it left Buenos Aires. The attempt failed, but shots were fired and the Paraguyan president reluctantly released Canstatt. The naval events took place outside Paraguayan waters, but it's an interesting story anyway.

During the Paraguayan War of 1864–70, the Royal Navy was back in Paraguayan waters, running the enemy blockade into Paraguay on a number of occasions in attempts to get British citizens out.

Peru

Peru is a long way from these islands. Hidden away on the west coast of South America, the only way marauding British ships could reach it was either by travelling all the way around the Cape of Good Hope past Australia and across the Pacific, or by ships tackling the treacherous and fearsome Cape Horn. In the days before modern safety features and navigational equipment on boats, you might almost think Peru would have been out of harm's way from us. But you would be wrong.

British raiders were already working the Pacific coast of South America by the late sixteenth century. Francis Drake, for example, sacked Callao in 1578, and in 1587 Thomas Cavendish sacked Paita. And in a now almost forgotten but true story, eighteenth-century Britain sent a fleet literally around the world to invade Peru.

The context is one of our better-named, though not better-known, wars. It is the so-called War of Jenkins' Ear conducted against Spain, starting in 1739, and was named after one Robert Jenkins, who arrived in Parliament prior to the war to complain about his rough treatment by Spanish coast guards and, in the days before computer presentations, used his severed ear to illustrate the point rather dramatically.

In 1740, in what must surely be one of the more ambitious military operations ever launched by Britain, Commodore George Anson was given the unenviable assignment of leading six warships, *Centurion*, *Gloucester*, *Severn*, *Pearl*, *Wager* and *Tryal*, across the Atlantic from Britain, around Cape Horn and up the Pacific coast of South America. His mission (and this was just part of it) was to include capturing Callao and the port of Lima in Peru, and then if possible to capture Lima itself and raise a Peruvian rebellion against Spain. He was also supposed to do assorted other things on this extraordinary mission, including capture Panama.

The story of Anson's journey round the world is a bit of a saga, quite a lot of a saga, in fact, so I'll just touch briefly here on the Peruvian aspects of it.

By the time Anson made it to Cape Horn, his force had already had quite a time of it. He had been allotted no soldiers so had been forced to make up his contingent of 500 from invalids at the Chelsea Hospital. The expedition had been hit by dysentery, malaria and other diseases. And they had had to dodge Spanish warships.

Rounding the Cape they were then hit by huge storms and freezing conditions, and the ships were scattered. Still without three of his ships, Anson took a census in September 1741 and found that of the 961 men he had started out with, 626 had already died. Nevertheless he pushed on, and when he received news that the authorities in the port of Paita had been told of his whereabouts, he decided to invade. Paita has one of the best natural harbours on the Peruvian coast.

Anson landed at night in an attempt to capture some treasure stored there for export. The inhabitants of Paita legged it for the hills when they saw Anson's invaders. They had already been raided by Britons in the past, so perhaps they had decided this was the safest bet.

The British stayed in the town for three days, looting valuables and food, before Anson ordered the release of prisoners and the burning of the town, except for two churches. One sailor was killed, possibly accidentally by his own side.

After that, Anson headed north towards Mexico and eventually, after a further long string of dramatic events, back across the Pacific. He returned to Britain and became famous. Only about 500 of the original 1,900 members of Anson's expedition made it back alive. The expedition left a legacy of disputes over the prize money in court. Not a spectacular end to such an expedition, but perhaps not surprising.

British volunteers played an important part in Bolivar's campaign to liberate Peru. On land, many helped win Bolivar's crucial victory at the Battle of Ayacucho in December 1824. At sea, Lord Cochrane, previously a captain in the British Navy, created a Chilean navy that fought in the campaign to free Peru and that had a very significant percentage of experienced British and Irish officers, midshipmen and sailors in it.

There is one last venture of our ships into Peruvian waters that is worth mentioning here, the Battle of Pacocha in 1877. This time, we were facing an opponent from the now independent state of Peru. There was revolution in Peru and the ironclad *Huáscar* was raiding shipping, only to make the mistake of attacking some British ships. We sent Rear Admiral de Horsey after it, and an inconclusive battle ensued. However, the battle is memorable for one thing at least: HMS *Shah* fired the first ever torpedo used in action. It missed.

Philippines

Today we don't tend to think of the Philippines as a country that has seen much British influence, but, yes, we have invaded it and we have even ruled some of it for a bit.

The Philippines are, of course, named after Philip, the Philip in question being Philip II of Spain. Naming whole lands after ruling monarchs always seems slightly strange somehow, a bit like parents who name their children after themselves, though I've no idea whether Philip demanded or secretly suggested the islands be named after him, or whether Ruy Lopez de Villalobos, who named Samar and Leyte as Las Islas Filipinas, thought it would be a short cut to a bit of royal favour. To be fair, we have done the same (as with Carolina and Georgia).

Our links to the Philippines go back a long way. In the late seventeenth century a somewhat reluctant buccaneer, Captain Swan, ended up in Mindanao with his crew before joining the army of the local ruler Rajah Laut. When Swan tried to leave for London, he ended up being speared by the rajah's men. Resignation disputes could get very nasty in those days.

By the eighteenth century we were ready to try something incredibly daring and audacious, and unlike some of the incredibly daring and audacious things we have tried, this one actually worked. Sort of. For a while.

In 1762, a British fleet consisting of seven ships of the line, plus some frigates and store ships, set off from Madras in India with forces on board that even included a couple of hundred French deserters. On 25 September, Colonel William Draper and his troops landed a couple of miles south of the Manila city walls, and on 4 October Draper's men and the fleet opened fire on the defences of Manila, breaching them. The defenders counter-attacked, but were driven back. At dawn on 6 October, Draper's men stormed the breach and broke into the city. To save the city, the defenders of the port and citadel surrendered and agreed to give us 4 million silver dollars to protect the town and its inhabitants.

Taking Manila was pretty much the high point of the whole episode from a British point of view. The destruction and looting that went with it did not endear us to the locals and resistance rapidly grew. In 1763, we agreed to give Manila and Cuba back in return for Florida and Minorca, and British troops left Manila in 1764. For some time afterwards we tried to get the 4 million dollars' ransom, but somehow we never quite managed it. We also, rather cheekily, hung on with a base in the Sulu Islands until 1773.

We were involved in the Philippines area again in the Second World War, though the main Allied forces fighting in the area at that stage were Filipino, American and Australian. HMS *Ariadne*, for instance, along with a larger number of Australian vessels, such as the cruisers HMAS *Australia* and HMAS *Shropshire*, was part of the great armada assembled to invade and liberate the Philippines at Leyte Gulf in 1944.

Poland

Poland is a country that has seen so much war that when you consider everywhere else we have invaded, you feel vaguely confident that British forces must have seen a lot of action on Polish land or sea. Poland has had endless foreign military units moving through it, but very few of them have been ours, although we have had some conducting operations here.

We fought and lost a war against the Hanseatic League in 1470–74 with the Hanseatic port of Danzig (now in present-day Poland) taking a leading role in actions against us.

During the Thirty Years War assorted British troops fighting for foreign rulers roamed parts of what is today Poland. Many of these reached high positions, with the Scot, Major General Sir David Drummond, being made governor of Stettin (now Szczecin in Poland).

During the Napoleonic Wars, we took part in several operations linked to Danzig, then Prussian. In 1807, we sent ships to assist in the defence of Danzig against the French. The British sloop *Falcon* tried to help reinforcements get into the besieged city and the eighteen-gun *Dauntless*, dauntlessly tried to get 150 barrels of gunpowder into it, only, rather unfortunately, to run aground, and even more unfortunately, to do so next to an enemy battery, which not surprisingly shelled the ship until French grenadiers could capture her. Then in 1812, with Danzig occupied by the French, we tried something even more ambitious. Admiral Martin loaded a bunch of soldiers onto British and Russian ships and landed them near Danzig, behind French lines, in a daring manoeuvre.

After the end of the First World War, the Royal Navy was back in Danzig again, while the British Army got involved in its only major operations on Polish soil. Along with units from other Allied nations, our soldiers had the unenviable task of policing assorted plebiscites organised to decide the post-war frontier between Germany and Poland – unenviable because these were regions with mixed German and Polish populations where emotions could run extremely high about which side of the border people would finally be on.

The two major areas where we were involved were Upper Silesia and East Prussia. In East Prussia two British officers found themselves, under an atmosphere of pressure from both sides, in command of the local police. A battalion from the Royal Irish Regiment was also sent to help. When the plebiscite took place on 11 July 1920, most voters opted to be Prussian and the majority of the disputed territory went to Germany.

In Upper Silesia, the situation was even more tense. After a Polish uprising in the area against German control in 1919, an Allied commission including British representatives was sent to the area and a plebiscite took place on 20 March 1920. But the results were mixed and there was disagreement in the Allied camp over how to proceed. In the chaos and confusion, a second Polish uprising took place in August 1920 and a third in 1921. British troops were among the units struggling to bring peace and order to the area, which they eventually achieved. The Allies, however, could still not agree on how to divide the territory, but eventually agreed to hand the decision over to the League of Nations, which decided to hand the majority of Upper Silesia's industrial heartland to Poland.

It's one of the ironies of history that everybody could have saved themselves the effort since the disputed areas were generally going to end up as Polish or Soviet territory after the Second World War anyway.

In the Second World War, the SOE conducted assorted operations in Poland and the RAF flew heroic missions to drop supplies to the fighters of the Warsaw Uprising before the city was crushed by the Germans.

Portugal

In terms of countries, Portugal is supposed to be our oldest friend. That doesn't mean we haven't invaded its territory. We have, on a number of occasions. At least we were often doing it on behalf of the Portuguese, or a faction among them.

As early as 408, a British-born general, Gerontius, leading an army that probably included Britons, invaded Lusitania in what is modern-day Portugal on behalf of Constantine III. To be fair, Gerontius may not have had many local allies in his invasion, but, as the history of British intervention in the area progressed, that was to change.

An early appearance of British forces in Portugal on the side of the Portuguese was in the Second Crusade. This Crusade started in response to the fall of Edessa, one of the Crusader kingdoms in the Holy Land created by the First Crusade. But like other Crusades, the Second Crusade had a slight tendency to spread beyond its original remit. In 1147, a detachment of Crusaders set off from Dartmouth by ship. They were aiming for the Holy Land, but due to weather they had to take a break in Portugal. Here they were duly recruited to the campaign of King Afonso I to take Lisbon from the Moors, and after four months of siege, with the help of Briton's Crusaders, Lisbon fell to Afonso.

In 1384, English troops were rushed to Portugal to help the Portuguese in the vital battles of Trancoso and Aljubarrota against the Castilians.

Then, with the arrival of the Spanish in Portugal, things became temporarily more complicated. For instance, we all know that the Spanish Armada was a famous disaster for the Spanish, but what doesn't get such wide publicity in Britain is that our own version, the English Armada, which set sail for the shores of Portugal and Spain just after the Spanish one, was not a great success either. Spain had occupied Portugal, and the Portuguese clergy and aristocracy had accepted Philip of Spain as their king at the Cortes of Tomar in 1581. The British idea was that we would arrive in Lisbon with a fleet and the Portuguese would rise up, shower us with flowers and plentiful supplies of fortified wine, and throw out the Spanish. The reality was rather different. Sir Francis Drake as admiral and Sir John Norreys as general led a fleet of almost 150 ships along the northern Spanish coast, failed to take Corunna and landed finally at Lisbon. Unfortunately for them, instead of finding welcoming Portuguese, they found determined Spanish defenders and no sign of a mass Portuguese insurrection. Eventually, after burning the Lisbon granaries, but not achieving much else, they had to give up and try their secondary mission of establishing a base in the Azores.

When that failed too, they were left with little other option but to limp home. Drake managed to plunder Porto Santo in Madeira as part of a series of minor plundering and ship-seizing operations, but all along Britain's armada had been steadily losing ships, men and hope. Many ships didn't make it home and nor did a lot of men.

In the seventeenth century, after the English Civil War, in a little-known but interesting saga, Prince Rupert, nephew of Charles I, commanded a Royalist squadron that refused to give up even after the execution of the king in 1649. By 1650 it had been forced out of its former base in Kinsale and had taken refuge in Lisbon harbour. An English fleet under Robert Blake arrived off the Tagus and block-aded Rupert inside, while molesting Portuguese shipping. After unsuccessful attempts to escape, Rupert finally managed to get his ships out and into the Mediterranean, only to lose most of them to Blake near Cartagena. Eventually, Rupert made his way across the Atlantic to the West Indies looking for a safe haven, before heading back to France. Rather a long way round, really.

Assorted other examples of military involvement with Portugal followed. During the Seven Years War we were back to rushing British reinforcements to help Portugal against the Spanish, and a combined British and Portuguese force under John Burgoyne and Charles Lee retook the Portuguese town of Vila Velha in a battle in October 1762.

There were other naval operations in Portuguese waters, including in 1780, when we defeated a Spanish squadron at the Battle of Cape St Vincent.

During Napoleon's assorted rampages across Europe we returned to Portugal once again, this time to help kick out the French. After a period moving to and fro across Portugal's frontier with Spain, much of the action in the Peninsular War took place in Spain, so we will look at it in more detail in the Spanish section. It is worth briefly mentioning two incidents: the unfortunate Convention of Cintra, in which, rather embarrassingly, we agreed for the Royal Navy to transport a trapped French army with all its equipment out of Portugal, causing a massive political scandal in Britain; and the Lines of Torres Vedras. When things were a bit problematic with the French, Arthur Wellesley, later Duke of Wellington, decided to secure his base in Lisbon by constructing a massive, intricate system of defensive fortifications protecting the Lisbon Peninsula.

The French arrived, the British sat back all cosy behind the lines, and eventually the French were forced to retreat to Spain.

Again there were more naval actions, including another victory for us over another Spanish (they were allied with the French at the time) fleet at another Battle of Cape St Vincent in 1797.

It was also during the Napoleonic Wars that we ended up occupying Portuguese territory for a time. Twice. Madeira was important to us, partly because of the wine, of course, and the English community on the island associated with it, but also because it had become a place where merchant ships were collected into convoy to go through the Channel. We occupied it briefly from 1801–02 when it seemed like Portugal might be turned against us. Then in December 1807, with Portugal under severe pressure from the French, we returned. A force of eight warships and fifteen transports under Rear Admiral Samuel Hood sailed in with over 3,500 troops. We annexed the island for four months, during which time it was a Crown colony, before un-annexing it once we were sure the Portuguese were really on our side. Four months – some Brits go on holiday to Madeira for longer than that today. It was a friendly occupation and we returned Madeira to the Portuguese safely in 1814.

Later in the nineteenth century we tried intervening in Portuguese politics again. This time we became involved in the delightfully named Liberal Wars. Nothing to do with David Steel or Nick Clegg, but an argument over the rights of the Portuguese crown and who should be wearing it. We took the Liberal side and dispatched a naval detachment. After a disappointing start, in which a squadron under Commander Glasscock positioned itself in the Douro and managed the unenviable achievement of being shelled by both sides, we made ourselves useful escorting Liberal forces to that place beloved of today's Britons, Faro on the Algarve. Then, while we destroyed the other side's navy, at the (yet another) Battle of Cape St Vincent, the Liberals took Lisbon. Finally, after a few more plot twists and turns, peace was declared and our side had won.

That was almost the end of it, in terms of us conducting military operations in Portuguese waters and on Portuguese soil, but it's worth mentioning one more incident in the history of Britain and Portugal, one that, though it didn't end in invasion, shows that even with this old friend there was still a potential for a serious disagreement. In 1889–90, in the Anglo-Portuguese Crisis, things got slightly heated between us when what the Portuguese called a 'Portuguese scientific expedition' and what we called a 'Portuguese potential invasion force' strayed out of Portuguese-controlled territory in West Africa and into what we regarded as our sphere of control. We responded with a naval show of strength, including sending a British squadron to Gibraltar, just along the coast from Portugal, and made assorted other threats, so that eventually the Portuguese withdrew their scientists and soldiers.

Anyway, when all's said and done, British tourists who splash in the waters off Portugal today are only following a tradition established centuries ago.

9

QATAR TO RWANDA

Qatar

There was once a time when all that many Brits knew about Qatar was that it is the only country with a name in English that begins with 'Q'. But the nation has, of course, been steadily growing as a massive economic and increasingly very significant political power.

The Persian Gulf was an area of great trading interest for us in the nineteenth century and we made frequent efforts to ensure things in the region were run the way we wanted. Thus in 1820, the East India Company ship *Vestal* ended up bombarding Doha in Qatar in 1821, destroying much of the town and forcing hundreds to flee.

In 1841 we were back shelling Doha again. Then in 1868 we imposed a settlement on Bahrain and Qatar after conflict in the area, which became an important point in establishing Qatar as an entity separate from Bahrain.

After that, Ottoman influence became significant in Qatar and it wasn't until 1916, during the First World War, that British troops marched into Qatar. In November of that year Qatar, signed a treaty giving us control over its foreign affairs in return for our protection of the state.

Qatar became fully free of our control in 1971.

Romania

Didn't Romania used to be Rumania or Roumania to us? Well, it seems to be Romania now, and however you spell it, we have spent time fighting here.

Captain John Smith, he of Pocohantas fame, rather less famously at one stage may have ended up with other English mercenaries and volunteers fighting in Transylvania (no vampire jokes here please), though the historical facts are a little unclear.

In the Crimean War, the Royal Navy blockaded the Danube, and a landing party attacked the small Romanian town of Sulina, drove out its Russian garrison and set light to it. The town not the garrison.

In the First World War, in a now almost entirely forgotten episode (see also Moldova) that deserves to be more widely known, the Royal Naval Air Service's armoured cars were dispatched into Romania to help the Russians fight the army of the advancing German General Mackensen. There used to be a joke that RNAS stood for 'Really Not A Sailor'. The armoured car unit didn't operate as airman either. Also in the area were nurses of the Scottish Women's Hospital and a unit of the British Red Cross Society.

Amid the chaos of fleeing refugees and appalling road conditions, the armoured car crews carried out their duties bravely and some of them were commended for their courage by the Russians. The fighting at Viziru ended in defeat for the Russian forces, but at least the RNAS armoured cars had performed well.

Russia

Many Brits who grew up in the Cold War spent some time worrying about the possibility of Russian tank divisions advancing up Whitehall. That didn't happen, but British invasions of Russian soil and Russian water have happened.

In 1807, after signing the Treaty of Tilsit with France, Russia was forced by Napoleon to declare war on us. We promptly responded by seizing the payroll of a Russian Mediterranean flotilla, which happened to be sitting handily in Portsmouth harbour, and then we sent Vice Admiral Sir James Saumarez to the Baltic with a fleet. Saumarez subsequently proceeded to annoy and harry the Russians in the area, getting involved in a number of actions and also attempting to blockade the Russian naval base at Kronstadt (outside St Petersburg).

Not content with operating only in the Baltic, we ventured as far as the Barents Sea and White Sea. HMS *Nyaden*, which we had originally nicked off the Danes at the Battle of Copenhagen in 1807, launched a number of successful raids in the area in the summer of 1809, capturing assorted vessels and launching a night raid on a Russian garrison on Kildin Island. We also briefly took control of Catherine Harbour in the Kola region and seized assorted stores there.

Eventually, after Napoleon invaded Russia, the Russians, for fairly obvious reasons, made peace with us.

In the 1850s, we were back. The Crimean War is, not unreasonably, known as the Crimean War because a lot of it took place in the Crimea. The region is now part of Ukraine, so we'll look at that part of the war in the Ukraine section. What is not so well known is that there was plenty of action going on outside the Crimea as well.

Once again, there was a lot happening in the Baltic region. In 1854, for instance, British and French ships made a couple of attempts against the Russian naval base at Kronstadt. And again there was action in the Kola region. On 23 July 1854, our ships *Miranda* and *Brisk* attacked the town of Novitksa. Then, on 23 August, the *Miranda* anchored off the town of Kola, demanding its surrender. When no surrender was forthcoming, the ship opened fire on the shore batteries and sent a landing party which captured the guns and put the garrison to flight. Government stores and buildings went up in flames.

But this time our operations also extended much further. In the south, along with actions in the Crimea, we operated more widely in the Black Sea and Sea of Azov. Several times we attacked the Russian port of Taganrog, the taking of which would have opened the way for us to the important strategic city of Rostov on Don. In the summer of 1855, a British and French squadron arrived off Taganrog and demanded its surrender. When surrender was refused, we bombarded Taganrog and then sent troops ashore to take it. This assault was beaten back by the defenders. The British and French ships retreated, only to return to bombard Taganrog again and make a failed attempt to enter the Don and then to return a third time and make another failed attack on the port.

We even attacked Russia's Pacific coast, with a fairly disastrous (disastrous for us and our French allies, that is) attempt to capture Petropavlovsk in Kamchatka. A British and French squadron bombarded the town and put a landing party ashore to try to take it, but the landing party was ambushed by the Russians and we and the French had to withdraw.

For most of the First World War the Russians were our allies, but the revolution in Russia led to the country quitting the war and set the stage for our next invasions, this time to counter the Bolsheviks.

Our troops operated on a number of different fronts.

Campaigns in the Caucasus and the Caspian region are mainly dealt with elsewhere, but we also attacked territory in the region relevant to this section. For instance, British planes from Petrovsk bombed targets in Grozny and British planes from Baku bombed docks and shipping at Astrakhan.

Unsurprisingly, bearing in mind our past record in conflicts with Russia, the Royal Navy was active once more. In the Baltic, we blockaded the Russian fleet in Kronstadt, yet again, and not only that, a couple of daring raids by British Coastal Motor Boats were launched into Kronstadt Harbour itself, in which a number of Russian ships were sunk or damaged. On 17 June 1919, Augustine Agar set off with two Coastal Motor Boats. One had to turn back, but he pressed on with his boat, making his way through a destroyer screen. He had to stop to repair the boat after the hull had been hit, and he sank the Russian cruiser *Oleg* before escaping under heavy fire. He was awarded the Victoria Cross for his achievement, and a promotion.

In the White Sea region, operations included running a river force on the northern Dvina River.

This war also involved substantial land invasions in both the north and east of Russia as well.

In the north of Russia, in the summer of 1918, a British expeditionary force arrived to take control of Murmansk, and the North Russia Relief Force occupied Archangel. Along with Brits, there were also French and Americans, and a number of other nationalities, fighting the Bolsheviks in this area. Ultimately, though, it was decided that the intervention was not achieving much and the British troops were withdrawn. You can still see a captured British tank in Archangel today.

It was in the east, in Siberia, that perhaps our most spectacular invasion of Russia took place, an intervention which, though again achieving very little, still deserves to be better known, especially for the staggering distance our troops penetrated into Russia. It was an international intervention, including Britons, Americans, Canadians, Italians, Japanese, Poles and French. The 543 men of the 25th Battalion of the Middlesex Regiment landed in July 1918 and, after fighting against Red partisans on the Ussuri, advanced as far as Omsk, positioning garrisons along the railway lines to protect them. In October 1918, the 9th Battalion of the Royal Hampshire Regiment arrived in Vladivostok and headed for Omsk too. It's worth taking a look at a map to see just where Omsk is in Russia. It's a long, long way from Vladivostok. However, as the White forces opposing the Red Army began to crumble, it became increasingly obvious that this intervention wasn't achieving anything much either, and British forces were withdrawn in 1920.

Rwanda

As the European powers carved up Africa, Rwanda's territory eventually went to Germany.

In the First World War, though, the area became a battle zone between the European powers. But while a British force under Brigadier General Crew advanced south to Bukoba (in Tanzania) on the shores of Lake Victoria, it was the Belgians advancing from the then Belgian Congo to the west who occupied the territory of Rwanda and Burundi, taking Kigali on 6 May 1916. After the war, Belgium retained control of the territories as a League of Nations Mandate. The Belgians did briefly cede Gisaka, a part of Rwanda, to us for incorporation into Tanganikya, before it was reattached to Rwanda in 1924. So we have controlled a bit of Rwanda for a short while.

The British Army sent troops to take part in the United Nations Assistance Mission for Rwanda, as it struggled to deal with the aftermath of the horrifying massacres there in 1994.

Rwanda became a member of the Commonwealth in 2009.

10

SAINT KITTS & NEVIS TO TUVALU

Saint Kitts & Nevis

When I started looking at the history of Saint Kitts & Nevis, I began to wonder who Saint Kitts was, since I can't ever remember hearing of a church dedicated to him or her. It turns out that just as Kit is a recognised abbreviation for Christopher, so Saint Kitts is an abbreviation for Saint Christopher, the island's formal name.

The name Nevis has an interesting origin too. You might think it had been named after a Mr Nevis, but apparently not. It seems that when there were clouds on its peak, they reminded the Spanish of the story of Nuestra Señora de las Nieves, or Our Lady of the Snows. So a Caribbean island is called 'snow'.

Saint Kitts was not only the site of the first permanent English colony in the Caribbean, but it was also the site of the first permanent French colony in the Caribbean. Interestingly, here, the English and French worked together. This, though, turned out to be exceedingly bad news for the local Kalinago population.

In 1538, Huguenot refugees from Dieppe briefly established a colony on Saint Kitts, which they imaginatively called Dieppe. But the Spanish were none too thrilled and kicked the French off the island a few months later.

In 1607, John Smith (of Pocahontas fame) popped in for a visit but didn't stay.

Then in 1623, an English captain, Thomas Warner, gave up trying to establish a colony on the South American mainland and decided to try Saint Kitts instead. In 1624, he established the colony of Saint

Christopher. Shortly afterwards, in 1625, a French captain, Pierre Belain d'Esnambuc, turned up, having lost some of his expedition in a clash with the Spanish and, instead of trying to kick the visitors off the island, Warner helped the new arrivals settle in.

Quite possibly the reason for Warner doing this was that he had decided on a European takeover of the whole island from the Kalinago, because in 1626 the English and French cooperated in killing thousands of the Kalinago at the aptly named Bloody Point.

In 1628 Anthony Hilton with eighty settlers colonised Nevis from Saint Kitts.

But there was trouble ahead for the English and the French. In 1629, the Spanish invaded and the English and French fled before managing to return shortly afterwards.

Then as relations between England and France soured, the French overran the entire island and held it from 1665–67 before the English got their half back under the Treaty of Breda.

In 1689, the French overran the island again and Governor Codrington led an invasion of Saint Kitts in response. On 1 July 1690, British ships opened fire on the French defenders. That night Codrington secretly landed 600 men south of the French position and in the morning landed a further 600 in front of the French position, while those who had landed earlier attacked the French from behind. English losses were ten dead and thirty wounded and by 26 July the French surrender of the entire island was complete.

The French attacked Saint Kitts again in 1705, holding it until the Treaty of Utrecht in 1713. And they attacked yet again in 1782, holding the island until 1783 and the Treaty of Paris.

In 1778, the Bath Hotel on Nevis became the first official tourist destination in the Americas.

Saint Kitts and Nevis became independent in 1983.

Saint Lucia

Saint Lucia is a really beautiful island, and for quite a small country it has a dramatic history. In terms of invasions, most of them involve Britain and France. Not much surprise there then.

Spanish, French, Dutch and English all took an early European interest in the island. In 1605, an English ship called the *Olive*

Branch ended up on Saint Lucia by mistake. It had originally been heading for Guyana. The people on board tried to settle on Saint Lucia. It was another mistake. Disease and the local Caribs wiped out a large number of them in weeks and the others departed. In 1638, we were back, but not for long. The Caribs and disease saw to that.

It turned out that the French were to have a little more luck than us. In 1643 the governor of Martinique, one Parquet (nothing to do with flooring), set up a colony on Saint Lucia under one De Rousselan.

In 1664, Thomas Warner arrived to claim Saint Lucia for England, but like our previous efforts on the island, this was a disaster too. Soon the French were back in overall control. And so it went on see-sawing to and fro, with the British and French both competing to be the dominant European power on the island, and with Saint Lucia changing hands many times.

In December 1778, for instance, with the French temporarily in control, a British fleet turned up to do something about it. On 13 December the fleet started landing British troops on the island at the delightfully named Grand Cul de Sac. On 15 December a French fleet attacked the British fleet, but failed to do much damage to the British operation. The French rushed reinforcements onto the island and the Brits and French clashed in the Battle of Morne de la Vierge. We won and by the end of the year Saint Lucia was ours again. For a time.

Finally, with the end of the Napoleonic Wars, the seesaw stopped tipping and we ended up with long-term control of the island.

Saint Lucia became fully independent on 22 February 1979.

Saint Vincent and the Grenadines

This is an island country in the Caribbean with Saint Vincent as the main island and the Grenadines being a chain of islands stretching down to, yes, Grenada.

When Europeans turned up they found Saint Vincent popu-lated by Caribs. And as Europeans began to bring slaves into the Caribbean, the Caribs were joined by escaped slaves.

There was an English claim to control the island, but in the end the French became the first Europeans to establish a permanent settlement there when they founded Barrouallie in 1719. In 1762, after attacking Martinique, General Robert Monckton sent a detachment to take Saint Vincent, which it promptly did and the Treaty of Paris in 1763 confirmed our control of the island.

The locals, though, had other ideas, resulting in the First Carib War. The war ended in a stalemate in 1773, in which we conceded control of a large part of the island to the locals under their leader Joseph Chatoyer.

The French had not given up either. In June 1779, French forces landed, and with help from the locals rapidly took control of the island.

In 1780, it was us who were invading to reclaim the island. This wasn't one of our more successful invasions. Admiral George Brydges Rodney decided from information he had received that the hurricane season had been so bad that the defenders of the island would not be in good shape to resist him. It turned out to be an erroneous interpretation of the situation. Two hundred and fifty British troops under General John Vaughan landed on the island, only to find that they were seriously outnumbered and, after just one day, the invasion was called off and Vaughan's force re-embarked.

We eventually got the French troops off the island through the Treaty of Versailles in 1783. That still left the issue of how Britain would deal with opposition from the locals.

In the Second Carib War, which started in 1795, Chatoyer was joined by another local leader, DuValle, and by French supporters of the French Revolution. Chatoyer, though, was killed at Dorsetshire Hill by Major Alexander Leith and eventually the rebellion was crushed. Mass deportations followed.

Saint Vincent and the Grenadines finally became independent on 27 October 1979.

Samoa

Samoa is one of those places that sounds so peaceful you almost think that surely we can't have invaded it, but we have been involved in at least two wars here. And we didn't even take control of Samoa at the end of them.

In 1722, Dutchman Jacob Roggeveen became the first European to set eyes on the islands. By the late nineteenth century, Britain,

Germany and the US all had trading posts and were locked in a struggle for power here, a struggle which expressed itself by the different Western powers backing different local factions fighting each other.

The First Samoan Civil War took place between about 1886 and 1894. In March 1889, Britain, Germany and the US all sent warships to Apia harbour and there seemed a likelihood of serious trouble until on, 15 March, a massive storm hit and left the crews of the warships with even more serious problems to deal with.

In the Second Samoan Civil War, the Germans were backing the Mataafans. The British and the Americans were backing Prince Tainu. In January 1899, the Mataafans forced Tainu out of Apia and in March we and the Americans landed in Apia. The Cruiser HMS *Porpoise* and the Corvette HMS *Royalist* landed sailors and marines.

While land forces skirmished in Apia, our ships shelled boats and the outskirts of Apia. Eventually, the cruiser HMS *Tauranga* arrived to assist and we advanced south out of Apia to attack and defeat a rebel force there. Finally, after a series of battles at Vailele, hostilities were brought to an end and the Samoa Tripartite Convention was signed which split the islands between Germany and the US. In return for Britain giving up our claims to Samoa, the Germans gave us control of territory elsewhere.

It probably wasn't the best of bargains for the Germans in the sense that, in August 1914, a New Zealand expeditionary force captured the German-controlled part of Samoa without a fight. The German cruisers *Gneisenau* and *Scharnhorst* (confusingly, Germany in the Second World War also had major ships called *Gneisenau* and *Scharnhorst*, but they were different ones) turned up shortly afterwards and could, no doubt, have recaptured the islands, but Admiral Von Spee decided he wouldn't be able to hold them if he did take them then. He didn't get much of a chance later because by the end of 1914 he was dead and the First World War versions of the *Gneisenau* and *Scharnhorst* had been sunk at the Battle of the Falkland Islands (yes, there's been one of those before as well).

New Zealand then administered the territory until it became independent in 1962.

San Marino

San Marino is one of those countries that some people don't think exists, except when it makes a brief appearance in international football. Did it cease to exist at about the time of the Borgias, or does it only exist to issue stamps? Neither. It is tiny, admittedly, but it is a proper country nevertheless, nestling on the eastern side of the Apennines, surrounded by Italy. Its official name is the rather charming 'Most Serene Republic of San Marino'. Impressively, its official foundation date is AD301, the point at which Saint Marinus himself is said to have left the (now) Croatian island of Ran and established a small church in what is now San Marino.

There was little serene about the situation in the republic as war raged around it in 1944. Until that year, San Marino had remained neutral in a world in flames. There had, it's true, been a slight misunderstanding in 1940, when it was reported to have declared war on Britain and then had to deny it, but apart from that things had been pretty peaceful, that is, until September 1944 when the war reached the Most Serene Republic's doorstep. Perhaps it was just as well for San Marino that things had been peaceful up until then, since its army (with the Crossbow Corps established in 1295) was unlikely to play any decisive role in a world of tanks, heavy bombers and vast armies. Germans, retreating in the face of the Allied troops who were advancing up the Italian peninsula, occupied the country, in spite of helpful large signs at the border stressing the country's neutrality. And then we went in to liberate it.

After bitter fighting the Cameron Highlanders finally took San Marino city on 20 September 1944.

São Tomé and Principe

The country of São Tomé and Principe consists, perhaps not surprisingly, of one island called São Tomé and one island called Principe. They are located in the Gulf of Guinea, about 150 miles off the coast of Gabon. Both islands used to be run by the Portuguese, and with Portugal having long been friends with us, we haven't really invaded São Tomé and Principe. Though, on occasions, the Royal Navy has used the islands as a base.

However, one lot of Brits did launch their own unofficial invasion of Principe.

Captain Howell Davis was a Welsh pirate. He had succeeded in deceiving the commander of a Royal African Company fort in the Gambia into thinking he was a privateer and, as a result, he was able to capture the commander at dinner and demand a ransom.

Encouraged by this, in 1719 Howell decided to try a similar plan to kidnap the Portuguese governor of Principe. So, with this in mind, he sailed into the harbour flying the flags of a British man-of-war. Howell must have thought his plan was working because he was invited to the fort for a drink. But instead of a drink, Howell, much to his (brief, since he didn't survive the day) disappointment, was ambushed and killed.

The pirates then elected another Welsh pirate, Bartholomew Roberts, as their leader and he subsequently launched a revenge raid on Principe, looting and killing.

Saudi Arabia

With Saudi Arabia we are back to the great Arab Revolt (see Jordan) and, of course, along with the Arab participants, T.E. Lawrence and a cast of assorted Brits.

Lawrence arrived in the area in the autumn of 1916 and already by December he had brought ships of the Royal Navy's Red Sea Patrol to help fend off an Ottoman attack on the port of Yanbu, now in Saudi Arabia. In January 1917, the Royal Navy again helped Arab forces, this time in their capture of Wejh, with assistance that included a Royal Navy landing party. And 1917 also saw Lawrence and other British officers help with the Arab campaign against the strategically vital Damascus–Mecca Hejaz railway.

By 1918, the British and the French were stepping up support for the Arab rebels with more advisers being sent, plus substantial amounts of weaponry, including some heavy weapons. In the period after the Turkish defeat in the First World War, Hussein became established as the King of the Hejaz, a region bordering the Red Sea. Subsequently, Ibn Saud took control from Hussein and became king. In 1927, we signed the Treaty of Jeddah, recognising him as ruler of the Hejaz and Nejd, and in 1932 Ibn Saud declared the Kingdom of Saudi Arabia, with himself as king.

Senegal

From the point of view of British and French history, the history of Senegal is closely linked to that of the Gambia in the sense that in the competition for power between the two European powers in this region, the French-controlled region became Senegal and the British-controlled region became the Gambia. Just as we and other Europeans, particularly the French, fought for control of the Gambia, so we fought for control of Senegal and for control of trade there – the slave trade being one of the major elements.

The island of Gorée in Senegal was a particularly hotly contested area. The Portuguese had settled it as early as 1444. We came along and took it from the Dutch in 1664. The French took it and then we took it and eventually the French gained long-term control of it. St Louis was another place that had a similarly varied history and that we held on assorted occasions.

In 1758, a British expedition of two warships and 200 troops, with a plan devised by American merchant Thomas Cumming, took Senegal in a surprise attack. We joined it with the land we already controlled in the Gambia to form British Senegambia. It doesn't look like they thought too long and hard about that name. In 1779, the French were back and in 1783 the Treaty of Versailles once again separated out British and French-controlled areas in the region.

In the Napoleonic Wars we were back, yet again, taking Gorée in 1803 and St Louis in 1809. In the end, we gave them back to the French in 1816 after Napoleon's unlamented (by us) final departure from power.

As the nineteenth century proceeded, things between us and the French settled down in the region, but still there was another invasion of Senegal to come in the twentieth century, or at least an attempted invasion. In September 1940, a British and Free French task force, including the carrier HMS *Ark Royal* and the battleships HMS *Barham* and HMS *Resolution*, arrived at Dakar with orders to try to persuade the French forces there to switch from Vichy to the Free French. The French in Dakar refused to come over to De Gaulle and fighting broke out, with the coastal forts and British ships exchanging fire, and with Free French troops trying to get ashore south-east of Dakar. Fighting between the fleet and Vichy forces continued for some time until eventually the attempt to persuade Senegal to switch to the Free French was abandoned.

Vichy was to hang on to control of Dakar for quite a while longer.

Serbia

In one of those episodes of the First World War that deserves to be much better known, a British naval mission under Rear Admiral Troubridge in the early months of the war advanced into Serbia to help the Serbs resist the Austro-Hungarians. They took with them batteries of guns, a mining section and a torpedo section to help defend the Danube, and they took a picket boat from Malta to Salonika and then put it on the railway to Belgrade.

The mission then proceeded to fight a little war on the Danube against bigger Austro-Hungarian boats. It became affectionately known as the Terror of the Danube – affectionately known by us, that is. No doubt the Austro-Hungarians had other less affectionate terms.

On 22 April 1915 the picket boat, in a daring raid, sank the monitor *Kersh* with a torpedo, for which Lieutenant Commander Kerr was awarded a DSO and each of the crew received a DSM. Eventually, the Austro-Hungarians attacked in force and after bravely defending Belgrade, the survivors of the British naval mission retreated south with the Serbian army on an epic march under appalling conditions.

During the Second World War, Brits, including Fitzroy Maclean, were involved with assorted resistance operations in Serbia. Maclean helped to organise attacks on the Salonika–Belgrade railway to hinder the retreating Germans, and he was present when the Russians and partisans liberated Belgrade from the Germans.

On 24 March 1999, in response to Slobodan Milosevic's actions in Kosovo, NATO launched a bombing campaign against targets in Serbia and in Kosovo. It lasted until 10 June 1999. RAF units played an important role in the campaign and the Royal Navy also fired cruise missiles.

Seychelles

These days the islands of the Seychelles are mostly known by Brits as a gorgeous place to go on holiday. So it's perhaps appropriate that we have invaded them in a comparatively gentle and rather leisurely way.

The French were the first European power to focus on the Seychelles. In the eighteenth century, the French intendant of nearby Mauritius took an interest in the idea of growing spices here. The intendant's name was, strange but true, Pierre Poivre or 'Peter Pepper'.

In 1794, irritated by French raids on our shipping, we turned up in force. Commodore Henry Newcome arrived with three ships and gave the locals an hour to surrender. Which they duly did. That accomplished, in a rather leisurely manner, we didn't do much more to impose our rule.

In 1801, a French frigate carrying prisoners sent into exile by Napoleon turned up, and then HMS *Sybille* arrived and captured it. After brief negotiations with the locals, things were smoothed over and the modus vivendi continued. Later that year, there was a battle between the French ship *La Flêche* and the British ship *Victor*, which the *Victor* won – appropriately, having a name like that. And still the Seychelles' semi-capitulated status continued.

Finally, in April 1811, after the capture of Mauritius, one Captain Beaver arrived at the islands on board HMS *Nisus* to solemnify British rule. He left behind Royal Marine Lieutenant Bartholomew Sullivan, who tried to combat slave trading with varying degrees of success. And British rule was more extensively imposed.

The Seychelles became independent in 1976.

Sierra Leone

Many readers will be aware of recent British military operations in Sierra Leone. By contrast, many readers won't be aware that the origins of the modern state, as with neighbouring Liberia, are to be found in freed slaves settling in the area. While it was American freed slaves who laid the foundations of Liberia, it was British freed slaves who laid the foundations of the nation of Sierra Leone.

We had been actively involved in the slave trade in the area, setting up trading posts at Bunce and York Islands in the seventeenth century. In 1787, things took a different turn. In that year, the Province of Freedom was established, with Granville Town, which is now Cline Town in Sierra Leone.

The new inhabitants of Granville Town (named after Granville Sharp, the British anti-slavery activist who played a major part in establishing the settlement) included many black loyalists from America, who had been given their freedom by the British Army in return for service with the army during the American Revolution, and Londoners.

The settlement was not a huge success. Disease took a toll and in 1789 the local Temne people burned the settlement down.

Shortly afterwards another attempt was made, this time much more successfully. The venture included freed black slaves who had originally settled in Nova Scotia, before making for the much warmer climate of Sierra Leone. In 1792 they founded Freetown, the capital of Sierra Leone. Then in 1794 the French came along and burned Freetown, but the settlers rebuilt it and in 1800 hundreds of Jamaicans also arrived in Sierra Leone. In 1807 we abolished slavery and in 1808 we established a naval base in Freetown for anti-slaving operations. When the Royal Navy captured slaving vessels and freed the slaves, often they would take them to Sierra Leone to settle.

The locals did not always view the expansion of British control with enthusiasm. In 1898, opposition to a Hut Tax led, you guessed it, to the brief but violent Hut Tax War.

In 1961 Sierra Leone became independent.

In 2000, in Operation Palliser, British forces intervened in what had become a terrible civil war in Sierra Leone. Originally, the mission was aimed at safeguarding foreign nationals, but it expanded into an operation that helped defeat the rebels and end the civil war.

Singapore

Not much of an invasion to begin with. Brits and the Dutch were competing for influence in the region at the time. So Stamford Raffles persuaded the local ruler to allow the East India Company to establish a base at Singapore in 1819 and soon there was a settlement there with soldiers and so on. In 1826, Singapore was incorporated in the Straits Settlement Colony when it was established.

By 1941, Singapore had grown to be a hugely important commercial and strategic military base. Its rapid fall to the Japanese that year was a disaster for Britain of staggeringly large proportions.

During the war we conducted assorted incursions into Singapore. In the highly successful Operation Jaywick, British and Australian commandos aboard a Japanese fishing boat, renamed the *Krait*, made their way to Singapore and a team then paddled into the harbour to sink seven ships with limpet mines. The *Krait* and its crew returned safely. Which was sadly not the result of the follow-up attack, Operation Rimau, in which three ships were sunk in Singapore Harbour, but at a terrible cost in terms of team members killed in battle or executed afterwards by the Japanese.

In 1945, we launched Operation Tiderace to retake control of Singapore.

Japan formally surrendered on 15 August. On 31 August, Allied troops set sail from Trincomalee and Rangoon. On 5 September, British warships disembarked British and Commonwealth troops who were cheered with wild enthusiasm by Singaporeans as they marched through the city. A week later, Admiral Lord Louis Mountbatten accepted the surrender of the Japanese military command in Singapore at Singapore City Hall.

Singapore joined Malaysia in 1963 and became independent in 1965.

Slovakia

Slovakia has not been an area where armed Britons have spent much time.

On 29 August 1944, though, in an episode that deserves to be better known in Britain, the Slovak army rose against Slovakia's pro-Nazi government. Thus began the Slovak National Uprising. It was brutally crushed by the Nazis, but before that happened teams from both SOE and the American OSS (US intelligence operations) were flown into the area.

The SOE team, led by Major John Sehmer, parachuted in on 18 September. It was supposed to be on its way to Hungary, but once it arrived it worked with the leadership of the Slovak uprising.

In October, the German counter-offensive began and the SOE team and Slovak fighters were forced back into the mountains. The SOE team, with local help, managed to evade capture and meet up with the OSS team on 6 December. Tragically, on Christmas Day, both groups were surrounded. None of the SOE and OSS teams survived. Some were killed immediately. Others were executed in Mauthausen concentration camp.

Slovenia

A country we have come perilously close to not invading at all. We have done so, though.

As early as the fourth century, Magnus Maximus, who was later to enter Welsh legend as Macsen Wledig, led an army from Britain into mainland Europe to seize the imperial throne. He specifically recruited more Brits for an attempted invasion of Italy and some of his forces ended up in action in what is now Slovenia, losing to the forces of Theodosius.

And we did just scrape across the border from Italy at the end of the Second World War.

In a confused situation in which Tito's victorious Yugoslav partisans were taking back Yugoslav territory previously annexed by Italy, and even pushing on into territory that forms part of present-day Italy, passions were running high and the tensions that were to lead to the Cold War were already evident on the ground.

In this chaos, the disputed territory known as the Julian March was divided in two in June 1945 by the Morgan Line. Most of the area came under Yugoslav administration, but a thin western strip, including, for example, the present-day Slovenian town of Sezana, came under joint British-American control.

In 1947, at the Paris Peace Conference, the areas of Slovenia held by Britain and America were handed to Tito.

Solomon Islands

Among early British visitors to the area were Lieutenant Shortland and Captain Manning in the late eighteenth century.

In the 1870s, HMS *Rosario* clashed with islanders on Nukapu, leading to the ship landing a party here and destroying a local village.

Then, in the late nineteenth century, there was the familiar competition among European powers to take control. In 1893, we declared a protectorate over the southern islands, including Guadalcanal, and in 1899 we took over control from the Germans of the northern islands. In return, we recognised their control over Western Samoa.

During the Second World War the Japanese invaded, followed by the Americans, leading to the crucial actions at Guadalcanal and Tulagi. Members of the British Solomon Islands Protectorate Defence Force also played a brave and important role at this time.

The Solomon Islands became independent in 1978.

Somalia

This is a country that, to put it mildly, has been through difficult times recently and is still, in many ways, going through them at the time of writing.

As you would expect by now, we have played a large part in conflict in Somalia, at times. At quite a lot of times, in fact.

We started taking a serious interest in the area in the late nineteenth century, and by 1888 we had established a protectorate over what became known as British Somaliland. It wasn't a part of the empire that was hugely valued by Britain, and in the early twentieth century we began to realise that some of the locals weren't too enthusiastic about us either. In particular, there was one Somali clan leader, Mohammed Abdullah Hassan, who was very unenthusiastic. In fact, he was so unenthusiastic that he led a long war of resistance attempting to drive us out and build a state.

Hassan started his campaign in 1899 and we soon clashed with him and his forces. We fought him in assorted actions up until 1905, with very mixed fortunes. In 1903 at Gumburu, for instance, his forces overran a reconnaissance force of ours after all their ammunition was expended and almost 200 of our men were killed. At Erego in 1902, Hassan's men ambushed a British column and bitter fighting followed. Finally, on 9 January 1904, we won what seemed a decisive victory at Jidballi in which thousands on the other side were killed. And in 1905 a peace treaty was signed.

But by 1907, fighting had broken out again. In 1913, in the Battle of Dul Madoba, our Somaliland Camel Constabulary suffered badly; thirty-six members died, including the commander Colonel Richard Corfield.

Conflict continued and Hassan was still around, so in 1920 we prepared for another offensive. This time, instead of relying on ground forces, a major role was allotted to the new RAF. Planes were being used against men who had never seen an aircraft before. The air and ground forces developed techniques of cooperation in which aircraft would bomb a fort, and ground forces would then attack with aerial support. After just three weeks, Hassan's main fort at Taleh was taken and he himself fled into the Ogaden. He died later the same year.

To the south of British Somaliland was an area called Italian Somaliland. For a time, this wasn't a problem from our point of view, but in the Second World War it became a problem. A big problem. In August 1940, the Italians invaded British Somaliland with an overwhelming advantage in terms of troops, artillery and tanks. It could only end one way and we managed to evacuate almost all of our troops by sea to Aden.

But Italy wasn't to hold on to British Somaliland for long. By 1941, it was time for us to invade Somalia again. We started with Italian Somaliland. In January, Cunningham's forces advanced north from Kenya into the territory. His troops moved rapidly, taking the port of Kismayu on 14 February and reaching Mogadishu itself on 25 February.

Then in March, Operation Appearance, the first successful Allied assault on an enemy-held beach of the war, went into action, with British and Commonwealth forces from Aden landing on both sides of Berbera and eventually linking up with Cunningham's forces. The whole of British Somaliland was soon back under British control.

British Somaliland became independent from Britain in 1960 and shortly afterwards joined with former Italian Somaliland to become Somalia.

Our naval forces recently returned to the area to counter pirates.

South Africa

Almost everybody knows we have had a lot to do with South Africa so I won't go into it in detail in this book, except to cover some of the basics.

The Portuguese were the first Europeans to spend time in the area of what is now South Africa, but they didn't try to settle. Unlike the Dutch, who settled here later, along with Germans, some Scandinavians and so on.

As with a lot of other Dutch-controlled territory, we got our hands on the Cape during the Napoleonic Wars, when it seemed likely that the French might make use of Dutch-controlled territories against us. We took it in 1795, gave it back to the Dutch for a bit after a temporary peace in 1803, then took it again in 1806 and kept it at the Congress of Vienna in 1815.

In 1820 we brought in settlers to the East Cape, which established a large British civilian population in the area.

Gradually we began to extend our area of control. We fought a long and bitter series of wars against the Xhosa people that extended right up until 1879 as our forces gradually pushed the Xhosa back and eventually took control of their territory. This involved much suffering for the Xhosa and large numbers of casualties.

We weren't the only ones extending our area of control in the region in the early nineteenth century. Shaka, chief of the Zulus, built a massive kingdom through military might as well. In 1879, we invaded it. On 22 January 1879, a British force was defeated by the Zulus at the Battle of Insandlwana, but in a subsequent action, the Zulus failed to take Rorke's Drift, which was stoutly defended by our hugely outnumbered forces in an epic action that led to the award of no less than eleven Victoria Crosses and, of course, the 1960s film *Zulu*. Eventually, the forces of the Zulu King Cetshwayo were decisively defeated at the Battle of Ulundi.

Meanwhile, many of the settlers of Dutch descent, the Boers, had become frustrated with British rule and moved further inland in search of fresh territory beyond British control. New Boer states emerged: Natal, the Transvaal and the Orange Free State. In 1842 we took Natal and annexed it in 1845.

In 1869 diamonds were found near what was to become Kimberley. The diamond fields were in territory claimed by Nicholas

Waterboer, leader of the Griqua people, and also by Boers. In 1871 we annexed the area anyway.

In April 1877, even though the Boers protested, we moved in to take over the Transvaal. This didn't last long because in 1880, the Boers of the Transvaal rose against us and in the First Boer War defeated British forces at the Battle of Majuba Hill on 27 February 1881. Transvaal became independent again and in 1883 Paul Kruger became its president.

In 1886, geology and politics once again caused an explosive combination. In 1886, gold was found at Witwatersrand, Johannesburg was founded, and large numbers of non-Boers moved in to mine the gold. In 1895, one Captain Leander Starr Jameson launched the so-called Jameson Raid in a failed attempt to set off an uprising and seize the area. In 1899, however, non-Boers at Witwatersrand petitioned Queen Victoria, asking her to intervene on their behalf on assorted political and economic issues, and it all ended with Kruger leading the Transvaal and Orange Free State into a war against us.

This was the Second Boer War. Key events like the sieges of Kimberley, Ladysmith and Mafeking are well known, as are setbacks for us at Magersfrontein, Colenso and Spion Kop. Our forces suffered, but in the end we ground down Boer resistance. In June 1900, Pretoria was taken and in October we won a major victory at Bergendal. The Boers continued a guerrilla war for another two years and we responded with harsh tactics, such as the rounding up of Boer civilians into concentration camps. These weren't extermination camps. They were camps where people were concentrated, but they were still terrible places where large numbers died from disease. In 1902, the Treaty of Vereeniging was signed and the Boer republics finally came under our control.

South Africa became independent from Britain through a series of steps.

South Sudan

As with Sudan, we became involved with South Sudan via Egypt, which had taken control of the area in the nineteenth century. For instance, with British involvement and a British governor, the

Egyptians set up the province of Equatoria in the south of South Sudan in 1870.

As with Sudan, South Sudan saw the rebellion of Muhammad Ahmed. And in 1887, an expedition from Britain was sent up the Congo River to rescue Emin Pasha, Charles George Gordon's successor as governor of the Province of Equatoria, from the rebels. After a long and difficult journey, the relief force, known as the 'Advance' reached Emin Pasha. They couldn't save his regime, but they did save him and eventually reached the coast with Pasha in 1888.

In 1898, Kitchener's British and Egyptian expedition reconquered the area, with the final decisive battle taking place at Omdurman (see Sudan) on 2 September. By 18 September, Kitchener had advanced into South Sudan and instead of facing the rebels, he found that he was facing the French. Yes, they were there too. In one of those famous 'incidents' that pepper British history of the nineteenth century, in this case the Fashoda Incident, a French force trying to establish French control of the area had set itself up in a fort at, you guessed it, Fashoda, now Kodok. Kitchener arrived with a flotilla and a tense stand-off developed. In the end, on 3 November, the French withdrew.

We recognised Sudan's independence on 1 January 1956 and South Sudan became independent in 2011.

Spain

Brits tend to be well aware of the time in 1588 when the Spanish Armada almost invaded England. But they don't tend to be quite so aware of the frequency with which Brits have invaded Spain.

In the late fourth century, Magnus Maximus led an army including Britons into Europe in pursuit of the imperial crown and held Spain for a while.

And at the beginning of the fifth century, Constantine III led another army from Britain into Europe. This time a British-born general, Gerontius, was sent with an army to take Spain, which he succeeded in doing. However, Spanish troops recruited into his army were later to turn against him in a move that led to his death in an epic siege. He and a few others found themselves surrounded in a house and held off the Spanish troops, killing 300 of them, until they ran out of arrows.

In the period after the end of the Roman Empire, Brits settled in north-western Spain in an area of Galicia that was known for a while as Britonia. By 572, Mailoc, a bishop of Britonia, was present at the Council of Braga. As with the British settlement in Brittany, we don't know how much violence was involved in this settlement, or whether it was entirely peaceful, but the fact is that Brits seem to have taken control of an area of Spain.

During the Middle Ages we were involved with assorted activities in Spain. In 1367, the Black Prince invaded Spain from Aquitaine with an Anglo-Gascon army in support of Peter of Castile in the Castilian Civil War. At the Battle of Nájera, our longbowmen helped win a crushing victory over the opposition. Not that it achieved too much in the long run as Peter and the Black Prince fell out with each other over money.

It was in the sixteenth century, though, that things really started hotting up between us and Spain. We've already mentioned the Spanish Armada, but the same conflict also saw us attack Spanish territory on a number of occasions. Most memorably on 19 April 1587, prior to the Armada, Francis Drake did his 'Singeing the King of Spain's Beard' by taking between thirty and forty English ships into Cadiz harbour and destroying loads of Spanish vessels. The English were back in Cadiz in 1596, with Sir Walter Raleigh and the Earl of Wessex destroying ships in the harbour and taking the town.

And we didn't stop there. There was plenty more to come in the seventeenth century. Though the 1625 Raid on Cadiz (Cadiz, yet again) has to rank as one of England's more disastrous military expeditions. The attacking English troops landed and took a fort they didn't have to. Then, because they didn't have enough provisions with them, the troops 'liberated' some wine vats. With most of the expedition now drunk, some made it back to the ships and the rest were slaughtered, in both senses of the word, when the Spanish defenders attacked them.

Under Cromwell we were attacking Spain again and a fleet was dispatched with Admiral Blake to take the war into their home territory and water. In 1656, the English were back at Cadiz, not drunk this time, and blockading the port. The Battle of Cadiz was a huge defeat for Spain and a huge victory for England. Blake followed it up on 20 April 1657 with victory at the Battle of Santa Cruz de Tenerife, in which he virtually destroyed another Spanish fleet.

The eighteenth century was also going to be a big century for attacking Spain. The War of the Spanish Succession got under way early in the eighteenth century and we soon had troops roaming the country. In October 1705, an allied army under Charles Mordaunt, the Earl of Peterborough, captured Barcelona. James Stanhope followed that up with assorted other victories, including the capture of Minorca, and victories at the Battle of Almenar and Saragossa. However, he rather lost out to the French at Brihuega and eventually had to surrender in December 1710. Still, by the Treaty of Utrecht in 1713, we kept Minorca, and of course Gibraltar.

By contrast, during the War of the Quadruple Alliance, the Spanish managed to set foot in Britain when 300 Spanish marines landed in Scotland to link up with local Highlander forces before being defeated with their local allies at the Battle of Glenshiel in 1719. Late the same year, we were back to invading Spain again, landing at Vigo and taking it, before marching to Pontevedra.

And in the Seven Years War of 1756–63 we were once again fighting in Spanish waters and on Spanish soil. In 1756, we lost Minorca, but by 1762 we had British troops on the ground in mainland Spain fighting alongside our Portuguese allies and defeating the Spanish at the Battle of Valencia de Alcántara. And we got Minorca back at the end of the war anyway. Although we lost it for the last time in 1781 to a combined Spanish and French force.

And then we come to the French Revolutionary and Napoleonic Wars. Most Brits have heard of the Battle of Trafalgar in 1805, but many of them tend to think of Nelson defeating the French there. What they often forget is that there were Spanish ships opposing our ships as well, and that Cape Trafalgar itself is on the Spanish coast, not the French. Mind you, Nelson's attack on Santa Cruze de Tenerife in 1797 hadn't been such a great success. That's where he got the wound that cost him part of his arm.

When we think of Brits invading Spain during the Napoleonic Wars, we usually tend to think of one Arthur Wellesley (later created Duke of Wellington). We had had successes as well as failures in the period before Wellesley's arrival in Spain. Sir John Moore's death at the Battle of Corunna is one of those memorable incidents in British military history. Wellesley led a gritty campaign against the French and their local allies as the tide of battle ebbed and flowed over the Portuguese border, and as the Spanish increasingly rose against the

French, but eventually he managed to push deep into Spain and stay there. In 1812, he captured Badajoz and after victory at the Battle of Salamanca, the French lost control of Madrid. Finally, in 1813 he chased the French out of Spain back across the Pyrenees into France.

Then we come to the First Carlist War. Lots of Brits know about Wellington in Spain, but not so many know about our 10,000-strong British Legion, consisting of English, Scots and Irish, fighting here in the 1830s in support of Queen Isabella and the Liberals against the Carlists. This was a serious military force that faced heavy fighting and made a significant contribution to the side we were supporting in the war. In 1836, Sir George De Lacy Evans was in command of the force at San Sebastián, and the legion held the fort at Mount Urgull de San Sebastián. In 1837, despite defeat at the Battle of Oriamendi, they helped prevent the fall of Madrid.

And, of course, plenty of Brits went to fight bravely on the Republican side during the Spanish Civil War in the 1930s.

Sri Lanka

The Portuguese were the first Europeans to settle in Sri Lanka. And they were followed and supplanted as the leading European power there by the Dutch. Neither Portuguese nor Dutch, however, managed to take total control of the island. Both had been prevented from doing so by fierce resistance.

In 1795, we arrived in force on the island. Due to French influence over the Netherlands back in Europe at that time, we were rather worried about the French controlling parts of Sri Lanka, particularly the strategic port of Trincomalee with its magnificent harbour. The French Admiral Suffern had already taken it from us in 1782 and though we had got it back in 1783, we had made the mistake (as it subsequently turned out) of handing it over to the Dutch.

This time we weren't to make the same error. We took Trincomalee and kept it until Sri Lanka became independent from us. In addition, we took other key places, like Colombo, Jaffa, Batticoloa, Galle and, in fact, nearly all the low-lying areas along the coast.

Before we could control the whole of the island we had the Kingdom of Kandy to deal with. I know that to many Brits the Kingdom of Kandy will sound like something out of a kid's dream about sweets, but in this case it was a powerful kingdom based on the important city of Kandy in the centre of the island.

We didn't find it easy to take control of the kingdom. In fact, we ended up fighting three wars against it.

The first war broke out in 1803 and we advanced boldly into Kandyan territory. A bit too boldly as it turned out. After fierce fighting on the way, we eventually took Kandy and set up our own local rival to the Kandyan ruler. But our advance got bogged down as the Kandy forces switched to guerrilla tactics. Even worse (from our point of view), they counter-attacked and among other successes (from their point of view) retook Kandy and virtually wiped out our forces. Then when the Kandyans advanced out of the mountains we managed to crush them. But when we advanced into the mountains again, we were crushed. A stalemate developed.

By the time of the second war, the situation had changed. By 1815, we had been able to exploit assorted internal disputes to get some key local figures on our side, and when Kandyan troops pursuing a fleeing noble clashed with our forces, we moved once again into Kandyan territory. This time our forces advanced easily and arrived in Kandy on 10 February. The king was exiled to India and we signed the Kandyan Convention with local nobles, effectively securing British control of the kingdom.

Already by 1817, discontent with the situation led to the Uve Rebellion or Third Kandyan War, in which locals, including nobles, rose against us. We reacted rather ferociously and crushed the rebellion. It was all over by 1818.

Sri Lanka became independent in 1948.

Sudan

Sudan is one of those countries that has a fascinating history about which few Brits are aware. We should know more about it. There are periods in it like the empire of Kush and Meroe, which are particularly interesting.

Britain started getting seriously involved in the area in the late nineteenth century, mainly via our involvement in Egypt. Nineteenth-century Egypt fancied expanding south into the Sudan and sent expeditions that gradually conquered the country. So as we became more involved in Egypt, we became more involved in the Sudan as well. So much so, in fact, that it even reached the stage where the Khedive of Egypt was appointing a Brit, one Charles George Gordon, as governor of the Sudan. He did at least try to stamp out slave-trading here.

It's at this point that Muhammad Ahmed comes into the picture. He led a religious and political rebellion against foreign rule and his followers had quite a lot of success against us. For instance, they defeated a British and Egyptian force near Al Ubayyid in 1882 and subsequently besieged and took Al Ubayyid. What happened then is that Gordon got himself stuck in Khartoum surrounded by the rebels and in January 1885 a British relief column reached the city two days after it had fallen and Gordon had been killed. Muhammad Ahmed himself died some six months after Gordon, but his regime lived on and attempted to spread into surrounding areas. Finally, in 1896, Kitchener, at the head of the British and Egyptian Nile Expeditionary Force, set off to invade Sudan. After assorted engagements on the way, Kitchener's army arrived for the decisive battle at Omdurman on 2 September 1898. The massive firepower that Kitchener's force was able to deploy helped to ensure a crushing defeat for the forces opposing him, with thousands of them dying, compared to only a few of the British and Egyptian force.

After that, in 1916 during the First World War, we were afraid that the Sultan of Darfur would assist the Ottomans against us in Egypt, so we invaded Darfur and incorporated it into Sudan.

We recognised Sudan's independence on 1 January 1956.

Suriname

Suriname is on the north coast of South America, surrounded by Guyanas. Well sort of, it's got Brazil to the south, Guyana to the west and French Guiana to the east. There was also once something called Dutch Guiana, which now consists of modern-day Guyana and Suriname itself. In terms of country names, Guyanas are to South America what Guineas are to Africa. There's more than one and you can get confused if you don't know the area. To be fair, it's our fault, not theirs. We should know our world geography better. Suriname's official language today is still Dutch, which many people wouldn't expect of a country in South America where we tend to think of Spanish, Portuguese or local languages being spoken.

In 1630, a bunch of Brits led by one Mr Marshall arrived and set up a colony imaginatively called Marshall's Creek on the Suriname River. Presumably it was on a creek of some sort. During the Second Anglo-Dutch War, the Dutch took control of our parts of Suriname and when it came to peace at the Treaty of Breda in 1667, we let the Dutch keep them and in return we got New Amsterdam, or New York as we had already called it. Fascinating swap. It would be interesting to compare property prices in Manhattan and Suriname today.

Swaziland

Swaziland has got South Africa on three sides and Mozambique on the east.

We were already in contact with the Swazi at the time of Mswati II, when he was looking for help against the Zulus. By 1894, the Swazi had come sort of under the colonial control of the authorities of South Africa, which they weren't too happy about.

Then in 1899 came the Second Boer War and things got very complicated. Many of the Britons here left, and by October a Swaziland Commando led by Commandant C. Botha (raised from Boer settlers in Swaziland) was attacking a British police post at Kwaliweni. King Bhunu decided to add to the chaos by settling scores with some of his opponents, and in December he died and his mother Labotsibeni Mdluli took over as regent.

We worried that supplies to the Boers from Mozambique could pass through Swaziland, but the new Queen Regent was trying to remain neutral in the conflict, and Boers who fled into Swaziland were disarmed. Kitchener reassured the Queen Regent that as long as she remained neutral, no British forces would enter Swaziland unless the Boers invaded.

Eventually, retreating Boer units did cross into Swaziland and in 1901, with the Queen Regent's agreement, British troops of the Imperial Light Horse and Suffolk Regiment crossed into Swaziland in pursuit. Assorted skirmishes followed as the British units gradually mopped up the Boer fighters. By February 1902 it was all over.

From 1902 to 1906 Swaziland was under British control as part of the Transvaal, and then from 1906 onwards it was separated from the Transvaal. Swaziland became independent again from Britain on 6 September 1968.

Sweden

Vikings, including at least some from Sweden, did, of course, spend quite a lot of time pillaging and plundering across Britain. By contrast we haven't done anything similar on Swedish soil. Indeed, Sweden appears in this book as an example of the British Invasion That Never Really Quite Was. It is also a delightful example of The War That Killed Nobody.

Until 1810 Sweden had been happily fighting alongside Britain in the assorted conflicts that swirled across Europe and around Napoleon at the time. Unfortunately things went a bit badly for Sweden in the war and it meant that the country, under the January 1810 Treaty of Paris, was obliged to join a trade embargo of Britain. Since Britain was one of Sweden's major trading partners, this was a problem for Sweden and much trade continued despite the treaty. Inevitably, this upset the French, who in November 1810 threatened to declare war against Sweden if Sweden didn't declare war on Britain.

So the Swedes gave in and declared war. But, and this is the best bit, without actually making war. In fact, throughout the 'war' a British fleet was based at Vinga Sound, just 14 miles from Gothenburg. The men planted vegetable gardens on the small islands around them, and what they didn't grow was discreetly supplied to them from Gothenburg.

No Britons or Swedes were killed by the other side, but it could be argued that the Swedes sort of lost by an own goal. An attempt by the Swedish government to conscript more farmers led to riots in which thirty Swedes were killed by other Swedes.

Finally, the Swedes and French fell out again and Sweden signed the Treaty of Örebro with Britain, thus bringing to an end the long bitter years of bloodshed – sorry my mistake, the short, comparatively amicable years of no bloodshed.

Switzerland

The Swiss have long been neutral and even managed to avoid being invaded in the First and Second World Wars. Plus they are land-locked, so you would think they might not have been invaded by Brits. But if you think that, you would be wrong.

In 1375 British knights, along with French knights, invaded the Swiss plateau in what is known as the English War, or the rather more fun Gugler War. It almost sounds like this is made up, but apparently it actually happened. Even more delightfully, Guglers may mean 'hoodies', because apparently it was winter so the knights wore hoods or cowls, in German a *gugel*, over their helmets to keep themselves warm. A less jolly interpretation of the name is that it came from the pointy helmets some of the knights wore.

At the time there was a lull in the Hundred Years War that left a lot of knights on both sides without gainful employment and without slaughtering and looting to do. As a consequence, when Enguerrand VII de Coucy decided he wanted to put together an army to pursue his inheritance claims, he found no lack of volunteers. In fact, the army he assembled is said to have numbered at least 10,000–16,000 and maybe more. The knights came from both sides of the Hundred Years War, with plenty of Englishmen involved, and seem to have included the fascinating Owain Lawgoch (Owain of the Red Hand). As Welsh as his name (except for being born in Surrey) and descended from Llyweln the Great, Owain was a claimant to the title Prince of Gwynedd as well as of Wales. He spent much of his life in France organising assorted attempts to invade and claim the throne of Wales before being assassinated by a squire, John Lambe. At a time when he wasn't trying to invade Wales, Owain joined the Guglers as they headed for Switzerland. Owain didn't have much luck with invading Wales and, as it turned out, he didn't have much luck invading Switzerland either.

The Guglers plundered Alsace in autumn 1375 before heading south. In December 1375 they crossed the Jura Mountains and headed into Switzerland. You can see why they needed their hoods, as it must have been a distinctly chilly journey. Owain Lawgoch set himself up at the Abbey of Fraubrunnen. But the locals resisted the Guglers. Three hundred knights were killed at Buttisholz on 19 December, a Bernese citizen force killed more Guglers at Ins, and then on 27 December, the Guglers were attacked at Fraubrunnen. Another 800 Guglers were killed here, but Owain himself survived. Finally, the Guglers had had enough of Switzerland and departed, with the Gugler army itself soon to dissolve.

Syria

We've invaded Syria more than once over the centuries.

As early as the First Crusade, armed Englishmen seem to have been roaming Syria. When the army of the First Crusade turned up at the Syrian port of Latakia in 1097, after they had sweatily walked all the way across the Balkans and Turkey, they may have been somewhat surprised, and perhaps a little miffed, that an English fleet seemed to have got there first. Having said that, nobody now seems entirely sure what this English fleet was doing there, or who was in control of it. In a little-known fact of British history, after the Norman invasion of England substantial numbers of Anglo-Saxon exiles seem to have enlisted in the Emperor of Byzantiums' Varangian Guard (a sort of French Foreign Legion of its day, or rather Byzantine Foreign Legion) and it has been argued that this English fleet was part of the force.

In the modern period, you would think our invasions of Syria would start with the Syrian War of 1839–40 in which we played such a large part. And it probably does, just about. Confusingly, the Syrian War (also called the Second Syrian war, or Egyptian-Ottomon War, or Second Egyptian-Ottoman war) saw extensive action on the land and in the waters of present-day Lebanon, Israel and Egypt, but not that much, or at least not that much involving us, in the area of present-day Syria. But since our ships' operations seem to have extended all the way from Alexandria in Egypt to 'Scanderoon', the rather jolly English spelling of present-day Iskenderun in Turkey, it seems reasonable to assume that we were in Syrian waters at least at some point.

There are no such questions over the British invasion of Syria in 1918 though. We were here, and here in force. After Allenby's decisive victory over the Ottoman forces at the Battle of Megiddo (see Israel) on 19–21 September, his forces swept through Syria. Allenby's troops, along with Lawrence and fighters of the Arab Revolt, entered

Damascus at the beginning of October, with Lawrence in an open-top Rolls-Royce. Homs fell on 16 October and Aleppo was taken on 25 October. For a time after the war we maintained troops in Syria.

Eventually, the French were to take control of Syria under a League of Nations Mandate. Which meant that after the German invasion of France in 1940 and the creation of the Vichy French government, Syria in 1941 was a problem for us. Indeed, there were fears that German operations through Syria could undermine our position across the Middle East, particularly in Iraq.

On 8 June 1941, Operation Exporter went into action. British, Commonwealth and assorted other forces invaded Syria from the south, from what was then the Palestine Mandate. British and Commonwealth forces also invaded Syria from Iraq to the east. Despite a setback at Quneitra, and bitter fighting against often determined Vichy defenders, the force attacking from Palestine had taken Damascus by 21 June. Further north, the force attacking from Iraq took the fabulously historical city of Palmyra on 2 July. On 3 July, William 'Bill' Slim won the Battle of Deir ez-Zor and by 8 July, the 10th Indian Division was approaching Aleppo. An armistice was signed on 14 July.

Tajikistan

Lying to the north of Afghanistan, Tajikistan was on the Russian side of the net during the Great Game of the nineteenth century. But there is some evidence that we tried to cause the Russians trouble here when we could.

In the late nineteenth century we were using Afghanistan, which we partly controlled, as our proxy in the area to control Russian expansion southwards. In 1883, allegedly under British influence, the Afghans broke an agreement between us and the Russians of 1873 and invaded part of present-day Tajikistan in the region of Shighnan and Badakhshan. The local Tajiks seem to have preferred Russian rule to Afghan rule and threw the Afghans across the Panja after fighting at Somatash and Yaims.

In the late nineteenth century we helped to ensure that our ally the Emir of Afghanistan got control of a chunk of disputed land in this area to create the so-called Wakhan Corridor, that strange, sticking out, pointy bit at the top right-hand corner of Afghanistan. It's a narrow piece of land that stretches all the way to China and it served an important purpose. It helped ensure that the British Empire and the Russian Empire didn't have to share a border here, and it's there to this day.

Then, after the Russian Revolution, suddenly Russian control of what is now Tajikistan seemed vulnerable. The most effective local opposition to Soviet rule came from local rebels (particularly in the Fergana region of Tajikistan). Some of the Soviets were convinced we must be arming and aiding these rebels.

Tanzania

Tanzania isn't an ancient name. Originally there were two separate entities, Tanganyika and Zanzibar. Tanganyika became independent from Britain in 1961 and Zanzibar became independent from us in 1963. In April of 1964, they joined together to become the United Republic of Tanganyika and Zanzibar, which, let's face it, is quite a mouthful. In October 1964, they abbreviated it all down to the much handier United Republic of Tan-Zania, or Tanzania. I just put the hyphen in to show the join.

Zanzibar and Tanganyika had very different histories for a very long time. The Zanzibar archipelago consists of a group of islands off the East African coast, but the two main ones are Zanzibar itself and Pemba.

Fascinatingly, for a long time Zanzibar wasn't paired with Tanganyika, but with Oman a long way to the north. It wasn't to last. When one particular sultan died, one of his sons became Sultan of Oman and the other became Sultan of Zanzibar.

We took a lot of interest in Zanzibar because it was a huge trading centre dealing in large quantities of British and Indian manufactured goods. On 25 August 1896, a sultan whom we liked died suddenly, and a man we didn't like proclaimed himself sultan. We weren't chuffed and we weren't going to pretend we were. We issued an ultimatum and gathered a task force of cruisers, gunships and marines. Handily, a lot of the Zanzibar army were on our side under British Brigadier General Lloyd Matthews, who happened to be their commander. Not surprisingly, the war was short and indeed tends to be known as the 'shortest war in history', though frankly there have been an awful lot of wars and not all of them had a person with a watch timing them so we'll never really know. Our ultimatum expired at 0900 hours, a suitably businesslike time for an ultimatum to expire. At 0902 we opened fire. The palace was hit several times and by about 0940 it was all over, leaving a lot of the people inside the palace dead, the palace on fire and the man who had proclaimed himself sultan fleeing to the German consulate.

Our involvement with Tanganyika took a very different course. British explorers like Burton, Speke and Livingstone took an early interest in the area, but ultimately it was Germany that won out here in the colonial sweepstakes.

So, in the First World War we decided to invade. It didn't start well for us. Not well at all. In the Battle of Tanga, in November 1914, also known as the Battle of the Bees due to a strange bee intervention in which some of our forces and some of the Germans were attacked by a swarm, we landed troops at the strategic port of Tanga ,only for them to have to re-embark when the defenders defeated us. At the same time we also lost the Battle of Kilimanjaro.

We did have more success on the water, eventually cornering the German light cruiser *Königsberg* on the Rufiji and sinking it. Meanwhile, two British gunboats, HMS *Mimi* and HMS *Toutou*, after being brought overland to Lake Tanganyika, had helped push the Germans off the waters there.

In 1916 the situation on land changed radically. General C. Smuts invaded from three different directions with a large force, including South Africans, other Africans, Brits, and Indian troops, and the rest of the war turned into a bitter and brutal game of chase as our side pursued the forces of the German side led by Lettow-Vorbeck around East Africa. Lettow-Vorbeck did not, in the end, surrender until after the armistice that finished the First World War.

After the war we got the League of Nations Mandate to administer the part of German East Africa that became known as Tanganyika.

Thailand

A lot of Britons are hugely fond of Thailand, but relations between the countries have had difficult times as well as good times.

As early as 1826, when we had just finished fighting the Burmese for the first time, we signed a Treaty of Amity and Commerce with the Kingdom of Siam. And in 1855 we signed a Treaty of Friendship and Commerce between the British Empire and the Kingdom of Siam. It all sounds terribly friendly and amicable (with quite a lot of commerce included as well, presumably), except that there was already a sense that growing British power in the region and British desire for commercial and political advantage was putting pressure on Thailand. Indeed, the Anglo-Siamese Treaty of 1909 transferred territory from Siamese to British control.

Nevertheless, Siam joined our side in the First World War in 1917.

In the Second World War, Thailand came under pressure from the Japanese and declared war on Britain. However, there were many Thais who resisted the Japanese presence in Thailand. Then in 1945, with the Japanese retreating, we were planning to invade Thailand, and British and Indian forces mounted attacks into Thailand (like a raid on Phuket in 1945) and advanced across the border in the summer of 1945, but as the war came to an end we abandoned our grandiose schemes for invasion.

In the period after the end of the war, British and Commonwealth troops were deployed in Thailand to help disarm Japanese troops and to assist liberated Allied prisoners of war.

Togo

Togo is a very long, thin country lying to the east of Ghana. It was a major area for the slave trade during the eighteenth century and when we became an anti-slaving instead of a slaving nation, British naval anti-slaving patrols operated off the coast of present-day Togo.

Towards the end of the nineteenth century, the Germans, late entrants into the European competition to build empires in Africa and keen to grab territories not already controlled by their rivals, established the colony of Togoland, slightly wider than present-day Togo.

German control was not to last for long. Hostilities between Britain and Germany began on 4 August 1914. The prospects for the German authorities in Togoland didn't look great. And frankly they weren't that great. They had a British colony to the west and a French colony to the east. There were no German military forces in Togoland, only a police force, and the radio station at Kamina in present-day Togo, designed to be a key part of the German world-wide wireless system, was a major target for the Allies.

British forces quickly advanced and took Lome, the current capital of Togo, while German defenders keen to protect Kamina retreated inland towards it, destroying railway bridges behind them. Despite some fierce clashes, British and French forces were soon advancing on Kamina from a number of directions. On 24 August, the Allies heard loud explosions from Kamina, and on 27 August British and French troops entered Kamina to find the radio station destroyed.

Two hundred Germans surrendered in what was one of the first Allied victories of the war.

German Togoland was separated into two League of Nations Mandates: British Togoland and French Togoland. The residents of British Togoland voted to join independent Ghana in 1957, which is why Togo is now slightly slimmer than German Togoland. French Togoland became independent in 1960.

Tonga

The explorer James Cook visited the Pacific islands of Tonga in 1773, 1774 and 1777.

By 1899, the Germans were taking an (to us) unwelcome interest in Tonga and the Tongans had run up substantial debts to a German trader. We sent in the navy. HMS *Tauranga* arrived and the Tongan king and government agreed to accept British protection.

From 1901 to 1952, Tonga was part of the British Western Pacific territories, though the Tongans always had their own Tongan government throughout the period.

The protectorate ended in 1970 and Tonga joined the Commonwealth.

Trinidad and Tobago

As anybody with some knowledge of Spanish is rapidly going to spot, Trinidad is the Spanish word for 'trinity', and Tobago is the Spanish word for 'tobacco'. Curiously, because we know the name

Trinidad and Tobago so well, the meaning of the words may not actually have occurred to us.

As the names suggest, the first Europeans to reach both these islands were Spanish, but the two islands have rather different histories, so let's start with Trinidad.

Trinidad received some early interest from us when Sir Walter Raleigh on his way to El Dorado (or not as it turned out), dropped in to attack, capture and burn the Spanish settlement of San José de Oruña (now St Joseph) in 1595. After that, there was a period of assorted pirates, smugglers and settlers doing their thing, and there was also something of an influx of French settlers. In 1797, we turned up in force. General Sir Ralph Abercromby and Rear Admiral Henry Harvey arrived with a fleet of ships and the Spanish governor promptly decided to surrender. So, not our most dramatic invasion.

By contrast, things became very confusing in Tobago. As well as the French, Spanish and Brits competing for control, there were also Dutch and Courlanders from modern-day Latvia. The island kept on changing hands. You would think there was hardly time to change the flags on occasions. In 1704, it was declared neutral territory, which was excellent news from a pirate point of view. Then in 1763, the French ceded Tobago to us. The newly independent Americans got in on the act in 1778 by trying to take the island, but HMS *Yarmouth* was able to fight them off. The French invaded yet again in 1781 and caused a lot of destruction. However, we did eventually get the island back. Yet again.

Trinidad and Tobago became independent in 1962.

Tunisia

Tunisia is a lovely country with some amazing scenery and plenty of brilliant archaeology and history. And we, of course, have played a part in that history. From quite early on.

In 1270, the future Edward I arrived off Tunis to join a French Crusade there, just as the French had given up, with their king dead, and were going home.

Then in the seventeenth century, England found itself at war with Tunis in a dispute over passengers sold as slaves. An English squadron happened to be roaming the Mediterranean at the time, so on 4 April 1655, rather than attacking strongly defended Tunis, Admiral Blake destroyed nine warships he happened to come across. Unfortunately for Blake, but not for the ruler of Tunis, the ships turned out to belong to the Ottoman Turks rather than the Tunisians and their destruction had zero effect on the position of the Tunisians. A peace was, however, negotiated in 1658.

In 1675 Sir John Narborough, with another squadron at his back, negotiated another peace with Tunis.

Then in 1796, yet another British squadron dropped by Tunis to recapture the twenty-eight-gun frigate *Nemesis*, which had been captured by the French. Boats slipped into Tunis harbour on the night of 9 March and achieved their objective with almost no opposition and no loss.

In 1816, we were back in Tunis again. This time Lord Exmouth sailed in with a squadron to secure the release of captives and an agreement to abolish slavery.

Our major incursion into Tunisia came in the Second World War. On 15 November 1941, after the Operation Torch landings in Algeria, British forces pushed eastwards along the Mediterranean coast, reaching Tabarka just across the border from Algeria into Tunisia. But as the Allies advanced eastwards, at the same time the Germans and Italians were rushing in reinforcements to try to stop them.

Fighting raged through November and December as the Allies attempted to advance to take Tunis, with among other operations, 1 Commando landing west of Bizerte on 30 November in an attempt to outflank enemy positions, and with a bitter battle at the end of December in an attempt to take Djebel El Ahmera, Longstop Hill. Eventually, the advance was forced back and the Allied push into Tunisia from the west ground to a halt.

In February 1943, Rommel struck back at the Battle of Kasserine Pass with an offensive that surprised the Allies and did some damage, but ultimately came to a standstill in the face of stiffening Allied resistance and because of British advances on the other side of Tunisia.

Here Montgomery's Eighth Army had reached the Mareth Line, an old French line of fortifications designed originally to protect Tunisia from Italian forces in Libya, which had now been occupied and put to use by Tunisia's Axis defenders. On 25 March, X Corps under General Horrocks managed to outflank the Mareth Line, and its defenders were forced to retreat north. American units joined the attack and eventually the Axis defenders were forced all the way back to Enfidaville.

In the west, the Axis forces mounted more attacks, but eventually the Allies regained the initiative and by mid-April the Axis forces were in a desperate position. On 6 May, the British IX Corps began the final assault, and on 7 May, while the Americans entered Bizerte, British tanks entered Tunis. On 13 May, Axis resistance ceased and over 230,000 prisoners of war were taken.

Turkey

Our military involvement with Turkey may have started pretty early, because it was a frequent stopping-off or transit point for Crusaders heading for the Holy Land. However, the Crusades that spent the most time in what is present-day Turkey weren't the ones that seem to have involved the most Brits.

Having said that, there was definitely some English, or at least Anglo-Norman (this is so early on that English in some ways still means Anglo-Saxon as opposed to Norman), participation in the First Crusade. So, for instance, involved in this Crusade along with their retinues were William Percy, who founded Whitby Priory, and Ralph de Gael, former Earl of Norfolk. People have also claimed that the English Edgar Atheling – an interesting character, the last male member of the house of Wessex – was also involved in the First Crusade, or in the Byzantine Empire, or in the Holy Land in some way. It's all frankly a bit hazy and confused. There also seems to have been some kind of English fleet operating somewhere in the area too, as a letter exists from Lucca in Italy stating that Bruno, a Crusader from there, travelled with English ships to Antioch in present-day Turkey in 1098.

There have been times the Eastern Med hasn't been an area of great British activity, but the Napoleonic period saw a big increase. By 1807, it was looking as if we might end up fighting Turkey, so perhaps not entirely tactfully we sent Vice Admiral Duckworth with six ships to sail up the Dardanelles and put a bit of pressure on Istanbul. Duckworth got through the Dardanelles after clashing with Turkish ships and after a Royal Marines landing party had made a raid onto an island to seize guns, but he wasn't able to achieve any-thing significant when he finally reached Istanbul. Instead, on his return journey he came under fire from the Dardanelles guns, the oldest of which had been made in 1453 when the Turks were trying to take Constantinople, before it became Istanbul. An 800lb marble shot (that's a big marble) hit the ship *Windsor Castle*. Also fighting the Turks at this point were the Russians. They were about to start fighting us as well, but that's a different story.

By the mid-nineteenth century, we were fighting on the same side as the Turks, while the Russians were, by this time, on the other side. The Crimean War, which broke out in 1853, was fought on many fronts, though, not surprisingly, a lot of it was fought in the Crimea. One front that's often forgotten nowadays was Turkey's then east-ern border with Russia. This didn't involve many Brits, but did see heroic action by a small number, led by one Colonel (then General) William Fenwick Williams, who ended up leading the gritty Turkish defenders of Kars in a bitter battle against Russian attacks. Kars fell in the end, but not before the Brits had gained a lot of respect.

With the arrival of the First World War we found ourselves back on the same side as the Russians, and back fighting against the Turks in Turkish waters and on Turkish soil.

To begin with, as in the Napoleonic period, the Royal Navy played the main role. As early as November 1914, HMS *Indomitable* and HMS *Indefatigable*, along with French warships, shelled fortresses at the entrance to the Dardanelles. Then in early 1915, the navy started seriously probing Turkish defences of the Dardanelles. On 19 February HMS *Cornwallis* and HMS *Vengeance* engaged in a duel with Turkish batteries, and later in February Royal Marines' demolition parties attacked forts. This all led up to the disastrous (from our point of view) battle of 18 March when we and the French mounted a full-scale assault. Our ships came under heavy fire, but mines caused the major damage. We lost a number of ships, forcing us to withdraw.

The result of all this was that we decided we needed to attack on land next instead. The Dardanelles campaign has been so well covered elsewhere that I won't go into depth here. The idea was that a ground offensive in the Dardanelles/Gallipoli area could clear the way to take Constantinople/Istanbul and open a convenient sea route to our Russian allies.

On 25 April 1915, British troops, including the 29th Division, landed at Cape Helles, while Australian and New Zealand troops landed on the Anzac beaches. A French brigade landed across in Anatolia, but later had to be withdrawn. When, after bitter fighting and heavy losses on both sides, the invading troops failed to make a breakthrough from the existing beachheads, a gamble was taken to make another landing, this time at Suvla Bay on 6 August. This attack, too, became bogged down and eventually it was decided to withdraw. The last British troops left Lancashire Landing on 9 January 1916.

After the Gallipoli debacle, our war against Turkey continued on other fronts. By 25 October 1918, Allenby's forces were advancing rapidly and had taken Aleppo in Syria, less than 50 miles from the current Turkish border. Turkey capitulated on 30 October. After the armistice of Modros, we formed the Army of the Black Sea to supervise the armistice terms. The Allied fleet finally steamed through the straits on 12 November 1918, British occupation troops entered Constantinople/Istanbul the next day, and we also sent troops eastwards towards the Caucasus.

As the situation in Turkey became steadily more tense in the period after the First World War, with resentment of the Allies rising and Greek forces fighting a war against Turkish forces, the position of the occupation troops was not always an easy one. For instance, in June 1920 Turkish Nationalist forces clashed with elements of the 24th Punjabis at Ismid and HMS *Ramillies* ended up engaging assorted targets with its guns.

Then in September 1922 we almost declared war on Turkey yet again, in the Chanak Crisis, when it looked like Turkish troops might advance on our troops guarding the Dardanelles. Finally, another deal was done and British troops eventually departed from Constantinople/Istanbul in September 1923.

Turkmenistan

Here is another huge country that most Brits know little about. But we have invaded parts of what is now its territory.

In the late nineteenth century we were sort of there by proxy as part of the Great Game. Our Afghan allies were in control with our support of the oasis of Panjdeh (or Pandjeh), in what is now

Turkmenistan, a strategic area controlling the approach to Herat in Afghanistan, but the Russians also claimed it because they controlled Merv. In March 1885, the commander of local Russian forces, General Komarov, demanded that Afghan forces withdraw. We immediately told the Afghans to send reinforcements to Panjdeh, demanded assurances from the Russians that they wouldn't attack unless attacked and mobilised two corps of the army in India to march north if necessary. Our General Lumsden sent three engineers from his staff to Herat to work out how it could best be defended. We seemed to be on the brink of war with Russia.

The Russians sensed what could occur and gave the assurances we asked for, which left them a problem since they still wanted Panjdeh. Komarov's only chance was to provoke the Afghans into starting a fight. General Lumsden warned the local Afghan commander not to react, but finally, according to the Russian account, the Afghans fired first and after bitter fighting and many dead, particularly on the Afghan side, the Russians pushed the Afghans out of Panjdeh. In London, preparations were made for war. The Royal Navy was placed on alert and told to occupy Port Hamilton in Korea in readiness for an attack on Russia in the east, while the Foreign Office prepared an official announcement of war. And then, on the very brink of a devastating war, Afghans, Brits and Russians all decided they didn't actually want one. A border commission was established which gave the Russians (and hence, today, Turkmenistan) Panjdeh in return for land elsewhere.

After the Russian Revolution in 1917, we tried our hand again in Turkmenistan. In 1918, General Malleson was sent with a force from India to the area. His initial mission was to counter Turkish and German influence and moves there, but it soon turned into a bitter fight against local Bolshevik forces, in which our troops ended up supporting a local anti-Bolshevik regime, the Ashkhabad Committee, that controlled the Transcaspian Government. Mallesons' force pushed into Turkmenistan and had some success against the Bolsheviks, including defeating them at the Battle of Dushak. Eventually, the TransCaspian Force occupied Merv, a key Russian possession in the Panjdeh crisis. However, by the end of 1918, with the First World War finished and with the local support for the British intervention weakening, a decision was made to pull out Malleson and his men. By 1919 they were gone.

Tuvalu

Tuvalu apparently means 'eight together', which seems a reasonable name when you know that it's a reference to the eight Tuvaluan atolls that were originally populated. Though it's got nine stars on the actual flag.

In terms of landmass, Tuvalu is the fourth smallest country in the world, after the Vatican City, Monaco and Nauru.

In 1819, Arent Schuyler de Peyster turned up, sighting Funafuti Island. He happened to be captain of an armed brigantine *Rebecca*, which was sailing under a British flag. The owner of his cargo was one Edward Ellice, MP for Coventry, so, being more interested in what his client thought than what the inhabitants of the island thought, he called it Ellice's Island. And to us Brits the whole group became known as The Ellice Islands. All because Ellice had sent a cargo.

Ultimately, Tuvalu came under British control in a very friendly sort of invasion, if you can call it an invasion at all. Captain Davis in HMS *Royalist* had been sent to the nearby Gilbert Islands (Kiribati) to declare them a protectorate to prevent the Germans or Americans getting their hands on them, and he dropped in on Tuvalu too. The kings allegedly had said they wanted to be part of a British Protectorate as well. So Captain Gibson in HMS *Curacao* spent 9–16 October 1892 touring the islands telling each king that we had arrived and they were now under our protection.

Tuvalu almost got invaded by the Japanese in the Second World War. Fortunately, the Battle of Midway cooled Japan's enthusiasm for the idea and the Americans turned up first to help.

Tuvalu became fully independent in 1978.

11

UGANDA TO VIETNAM

Uganda

I've long thought Uganda has a rather jolly flag. Apparently the bird in the centre of it is the Grey Crowned Crane, the national symbol. I'm not quite sure why they've got two bands of each colour, though I guess with only one band it would have looked a bit like the German flag.

Uganda has had a fairly eventful history at times, and inevitably we have played quite a large role in making it eventful.

John Hanning Speke was an officer in the British Indian Army who spent much of his life exploring Africa instead. He turned up in 1862 in what is now Uganda, searching for the source of the Nile, and setting off the famous Burton-Speke controversy.

Henry Morton Stanley turned up in 1875, and in his wake a couple of years later came missionaries from the Church Missionary Society in London. Two years later, French Catholic White Fathers arrived.

Then as politics, religious rivalry, local rivalry and competition by European powers began to combine in a toxic cocktail, things began to get really messy.

Mwanga, the ruler of Buganda, the largest kingdom in what is now Uganda, launched a campaign of repression against Christians and a number were killed, including local Christians and the Anglican Bishop James Hannington. Eventually, Mwanga was forced off the throne and a period of conflict ensued involving Christians, Muslims and others.

By 1889, Mwanga was back as ruler. In February 1890, the Germans persuaded him to sign a treaty with them. In the summer of 1890, we did a deal with the Germans whereby we got various bits of Africa, including Buganda, and we gave the Germans Heligoland which, yes, surprising as it now seems, we were in control of at that time (see Germany). By December 1890, Frederick Lugard, in the service of the Imperial British East Africa Company, had turned up with a column of men and a Maxim gun, and had negotiated a treaty with Mwanga, his negotiating tactics including threatening to use the Maxim.

The Germans were now to a certain extent out of the competition to be the main European power in the area, but the French weren't. Gradually, tensions between the French and local Catholic converts on one side and the British and local Protestant converts on the other side rose. In January 1892, fighting broke out with the Battle of Mengo, which was won by the British and local pro-British Protestants. The Maxim created a terrible slaughter, and in the aftermath of the battle the French bishop fled and the French Catholic Mission was attacked. Not surprisingly this caused a lot of anger in France and the British government ended up paying compensation.

Nevertheless, British control of Buganda was established, and after that we pressed on to conquer the rest of what is now Uganda, including places like the Bunyoro territory and the land of the Acholi. In 1894, Uganda formally became a British protectorate.

Uganda gained independence from Britain in 1962.

Ukraine

Part of the territory of the Ukraine is the Crimean peninsula so, yes, this is going to be mainly about the Crimean War. The name of the Crimean War is such a familiar one, with its overtones of Charge of the Light Brigade and Florence Nightingale and so on, that it's sometimes easy to forget that the Crimea isn't one of the usual battlefields we've been fighting on for centuries. It's right in the north of the Black Sea.

Nevertheless, the details of the main fighting in the Crimea and surrounding territory, unlike some of the fighting on other fronts, like the Baltic, are well known, so I'll cover it only in brief here.

To begin with, the Russians had been pushing back the Turks in Europe and we weren't very happy about the growth in Russian power and its increasing proximity to the Med. So we and the

French demanded the Russians get out of Moldavia (Moldova) and Wallachia (part of Romania; it sounds like the kind of place vampires might hang out, so it won't come as a huge surprise that Vlad III Dracula was indeed Voivode of Wallachia).

We ended up declaring war on Russia, and when it didn't look like we could give the Russians a knockout punch in the Balkans (very painful) or in the Baltics (also very painful) we decided on the bold, and, as it turned out, too bold, move of invading the Crimea.

On 24 September 1854 we won the Battle of the Alma, but didn't succeed in pressing on and taking the key strategic target Sevastopol. The Russians then hit back with the Battle of Sevastopol on 24 October (which included the Charge of the Light Brigade) and the Battle of Inkerman on 5 November. Plenty of fireworks on that day. The Russians lost both battles, but we lost significant numbers of men. While not totally disastrous for us, it still was all looking rather grim and miserable, and it started looking even grimmer and more miserable when winter arrived.

In May 1855, we made another landing in the Crimea, this time at Kerch, but that didn't lead to a breakthrough either. Eventually, in August, the Russians lost the Battle of Tchernaya, and in September, after the French had finally taken the fortifications on Malakoff Hill, Sevastopol fell.

Both sides in the war were sick of it by now, and in 1856 a peace was signed in which Russia gave in on a number of key points, including reinstating Turkish control over the mouth of the Danube.

Small numbers of our troops, in the shape of an armoured car squadron, were back in action in Ukraine in the First World War. This time they were fighting on the same side as the Russians, not against them, and in this case they were trying to invade territory held by the Austrians.

United Arab Emirates

This is a federation of seven Gulf emirates. The two best known to many Brits are Dubai and Abu Dhabi.

When we first got involved with the area, our major concern was raids on our shipping. During the period of the Napoleonic Wars we launched several campaigns against raiders in the area of the current United Arab Emirates. In 1809, for instance, fearing the spread of French influence in the area and keen to suppress the raiders, a substantial force was gathered at Bombay (Mumbai) with a large contingent of small East India Company warships, plus the bomb vessel *Stromboli* and the British naval frigates HMS *Caroline* and HMS *Chiffone*. A substantial body of troops was also involved in the expedition, including a battalion of the 65th Foot.

The force arrived at Ras al-Khaimah (one of the seven emirates that today make up the UAE) and, after bombarding the town, a diversionary landing was made to the north, while the main landing was made to the south. Our troops advanced with fixed bayonets and house-to-house fighting ensued as they pushed into the burning town and took the sheikh's palace. After the town had fallen, we burnt fifty of the raiding craft in the bay.

In 1819 we were back again. Collier led another joint navy and East India Company squadron to the gulf with 3,000 troops in transport, commanded by Major General Sir William Keir. Again we attacked Ras al-Khaimah, capturing and razing fortifications and destroying ships. We occupied Ras al-Khaimah until 1821, and finally we signed a General Treaty of Peace with sheikhs in the area.

In 1835 we got the locals to sign a Maritime Truce and in 1853 this turned into the rather grand Treaty of Peace in Perpetuity by which we got to arbitrate disputes between the sheikhs of the area. In 1892 we won control of the foreign affairs of the sheikhs, in return for us committing to protect them.

Britain's protectorate over the seven emirates ended on 1 December 1971.

United States of America

We have with the USA a record of invading the area both before it became independent *and* afterwards as well.

The story of our invasion and colonisation of the eastern part of what is now the United States is a huge and complex one. It's also a relatively well-known one so I'm going to cover it pretty quickly.

In the early years of the European exploration and settlement we were mainly up against the Spanish, French and Dutch. The first

successful English settlement was established at Jamestown in 1607
(the Virginia Colony), and then in 1620 came the Pilgrims' Plymouth
Colony (together with the origins of America's modern Thanksgiving
Day and so on). In 1628, the Massachusetts Bay Colony received its
charter and things really got moving on the English settlement front.

Some of the locals we persuaded to work with us, others resisted
us, particularly once it became clear that our colonists were there to
stay and that more and more colonists would arrive and want more
and more land.

There was, for example, plenty of conflict with the Powhatan
Confederacy, including the capture of Pocohontas herself.
Metacomet's War of 1675–78 was a bitter confrontation in which
many died, and so was the Yamasee War of 1715–17.

The European battle for control of North America was something of a knock-out competition and first out of the major players
were the Dutch. In 1664, we had sailed into the harbour of New
Amsterdam and demanded its surrender, and in 1665 we changed
the name to New York. Then the Dutch took it back and renamed it
New Orange. But in 1674 the Dutch ceded all their American territory to us. It was goodbye New Orange, hello New York.

With the Dutch out of the picture, the conflict between the British
and the French gathered intensity. As we have already seen in the case
of Canada, the late seventeenth century and the eighteenth century
saw a series of wars in North America, generally as part of wider
conflicts between us and our local allies on one side and the French
with their local allies on the other. And the Spanish were in there
sometimes too.

King William's War of 1688–97 saw clashes with the French and
their allies in the New England area, particularly in Maine.

In Queen Anne's War of 1702–13 there were clashes again
with the French in same area, with events including the raid
on Deerfield in 1704. And in the south, our Province of Carolina
fought against the Spanish Florida. Plenty of destruction and death
resulted from this war, but there wasn't much in the way of major
territorial changes.

Father Rale's War saw conflict with the Wabanaki Confederacy,
which had French support, as we tried to expand our control
north. Fighting again took place in Maine, as well as Massachusetts
and Vermont.

King George's War of 1744–48 saw fighting with the French and their local allies in New York, New Hampshire and Massachusetts.

Assorted other fighting followed and finally came the French and Indian War of 1754–63. There was fighting with the French and their allies from Virginia in the south to Nova Scotia in the north. We had some rather bad times during the conflict, in fact some disastrous times really, but eventually we reinforced, regrouped and won the war. The Treaty of Paris in 1763 officially ended it, and pretty much ended the French presence in North America as well. France hung on to Saint Pierre and Miquelon, but ceded much of its territory to us and the rest it gave to Spain to compensate Spain for the fact that it had to give Florida to us to get back from us the territory we had gained in Cuba. Complicated, eh.

We had achieved a near complete victory in the European battle for control of the eastern part of what is now the United States. We didn't get to enjoy that victory for too long because, partly as a result of the 1765 Stamp Act designed to help pay for British troops in North America, relations between us and many of the colonists went downhill fast. In 1776, the Thirteen Colonies declared their independence as the United States of America. George Washington played a major role in our subsequent defeat and the French and the Spanish got a bit of a revenge helping the rebels. The Spanish even got Florida back.

But, of course, the American War of Independence wasn't the end of our military activity in the United States. In 1812 we were back.

In fact, it was the Americans who declared war on us at a time when we were deeply involved in the war against Napoleon. They had assorted grievances against us and invaded Canada. With our main focus elsewhere, we concentrated initially on defending Canada, which we did fairly successfully against multiple US attacks. Finally, in 1814, with Napoleon (at least temporarily) defeated we could strike back. After victory at the Battle of Bladensburg in August 1814 we captured and burned Washington DC. But the Americans had their victories too, turning back our attacks on New Orleans, Baltimore and New York. Indeed, it was the events linked to the Battle of Baltimore in 1814 that inspired the words for the US national anthem. There was also plenty of naval activity. Finally, peace came and assorted treaties were signed.

We should also mention the Caroline Affair of 1837 when Canadian militia crossed the US border in pursuit of rebels. And there was the Aroostook War over timber and land in which, it's good to know, nobody died.

Let's not forget our five-month occupation in 1843 of what is now a US State. The British Union Flag is still part of the US state flag in question. Which one? Hawaii. This use of our flag represents the early tradition of close links between Hawaii and Britain. In February 1843, in a dispute over land and influence, Captain Lord George Paulet of HMS *Carysfort* took over control of the islands for six months, destroying Hawaiian flags and raising the British one. In July, Admiral Thomas in HMS *Dublin* arrived to resolve the issue diplomatically and restore Hawaiian freedom. Thomas Square in Honolulu was named in his honour and laid out in the shape of a British flag.

And how could we not mention the Pig War of 1859? Due to ambiguities in a treaty, the San Juan Islands lying between Vancouver Island and the North American mainland were disputed territory between Britain and the United States. In 1859, an American farmer on the island shot a pig he found in his garden. It turned out the pig belonged to an employee of the Hudson's Bay Company and he wasn't happy (that is, the employee wasn't happy, though under the circumstances, I think we can conclude the pig was none too happy about it all either). The conflict escalated, with US troops landing on the island, British warships arriving soon after, and a tense stand-off developing. Eventually, US and UK governments managed to calm things down, the matter went to arbitration and the islands were awarded to the US. In 1872, the Royal Marines stationed on the island finally departed.

Uruguay

Many Brits probably confuse Uruguay and Paraguay. Uruguay is not a huge country by South American standards; it's situated on the east coast, sandwiched between Argentina and Brazil.

The current area of Uruguay was for a time a place where the Spanish and Portuguese competed for control. Then in 1807 we got involved. We don't tend to think of South America as an area of major British imperial interest, but during the late eighteenth century a number of schemes were discussed with the intention of putting large chunks of Spanish-controlled South America under

British rule instead. Finally in 1806, we started trying to put one of them into practice.

In 1806 we attacked Buenos Aires (see Argentina). In 1807, it was the turn of Montevideo, the capital of Uruguay. On 20 January, we won the Battle of Cardal. And on 3 February, 3,000 British troops under the command of General Sir Samuel Auchmuty launched an assault on the city itself. After ferocious fighting from both sides, the defenders finally surrendered and we occupied the city. We stayed until September 1807, when we were forced to withdraw due to events further south in Buenos Aires.

However, we returned briefly in 1845. There was a civil war going on in Uruguay, which confusingly included people like Garibaldi, linked in a lot of Brits' minds with Italy (linked also in a lot of Brits' minds with biscuits). And it included us. And the French. We intervened to save besieged Montevideo, and then we did a certain amount of sending boats up assorted waterways, including the Uruguay River. By 1850, though, we had had enough, signed a treaty with the other side and went home. Yet again.

Uzbekistan

Uzbekistan is another of those Central Asian countries that we never quite got round to invading during the Great Game. But that didn't stop us window-shopping.

In the early nineteenth century, Captain Alexander Burnes acquired the rather unimaginative nickname of Bukhara Burnes for having made it as far as, you guessed it, Bukhara.

Colonel Charles Stoddart made it to Bukhara a few years later and had a rather less happy time of it. He was taken prisoner by the Emir of Bukhara, Nasrullah Khan. Captain Arthur Conolly, the man who invented the term the Great Game, headed to Bukhara to try to persuade the emir to release Stoddart, and both men were eventually beheaded in 1842 as British spies.

The arrival of heavy Russian influence in the area later in the nineteenth century somewhat curtailed our efforts in the region, but we were still interested in it.

In 1918, after the Russian Revolution, Frederick Marshman Bailey, a British intelligence officer, was sent on a mission to

Tashkent (the capital of Uzbekistan) to see if some understanding could be reached with the head of the Tashkent Soviet. When that proved impossible Bailey went underground, making contact with opposition groups. He even ended up posing as an Austrian POW and joining the local Cheka to search for a foreign spy, in this instance himself. When he finally escaped from Taskhent, he did so via Bukhara, but with more luck than Stoddart and Conolly. He got out safely and wrote a book about his adventures.

Meanwhile, our General Malleson, facing the Bolsheviks in Turkmenistan, had also been in contact with the Bukharans. The emir had sent him an envoy to discuss possible cooperation. Malleson had been cautious and the meeting concluded with the emir sending Malleson two Bukharan carpets plus a silk robe, and Malleson sending the emir two sporting rifles.

After the meeting, Malleson was given permission to send a small supply of weapons to the emir.

Eventually, Malleson's men withdrew and the Soviets took over in Bukhara and the rest of what is today independent Uzbekistan.

Vanuatu

Vanuatu is an island nation in the South Pacific, about 1,000 miles east of northern Australia and north of, but also a bit west of, New Zealand.

The first Brits to arrive on the islands were Captain Cook and his men in 1774. He called them the New Hebrides. Not that they seem to look that much like the original Hebrides. I mean they are islands it's true, but lovely though the original Hebrides are, the New Hebrides/Vanuatu seem, frankly, to have a lot more of the Pacific island thing going on.

Anyway, you can still see the name New Hebrides displayed on old stamps from the islands.

During the nineteenth century, more and more Brits and French arrived here, so that there was pressure for Britain to annexe the islands and pressure for the French to do so too.

In 1887, Britain and France agreed on a joint naval commission for the islands, but nothing more. Then, eventually, in an unusual arrangement, Britain and France decided in 1906 to share control of the islands between them and run two separate administrations united by a combined court. This was known as the British-French Condominium and had nothing to do with apartments, let alone any form of birth control. It was also rather quiet as invasions go, but we were still ruling the islands or at least co-ruling them.

Vanuatu became fully independent within the Commonwealth on 30 July 1980.

Vatican City

The Vatican City State is a country, but it's not a member of the United Nations.

These days you wouldn't associate the Vatican with armed conflict. The Swiss Guard, for instance, don't, in a military era of camouflage and automatic guns, look hugely threatening with their pikes and brightly coloured costumes. But the Vatican has played a significant role in armed conflicts in the past, and armed Brits have been involved. It's not exactly an invasion, but still a story worth mentioning.

We've come across English mercenaries before and John Hawkwood is one of the most interesting. He seems to have fought in the early stages of the Hundred Years War under Edward III and he is best known for his exploits as a mercenary leader in Italy, in the late fourteenth century. He became leader of a mercenary band known as the White Company, or the Great Company of English and Germans, or simply the English Company.

In the course of his long career, as well as working for other masters, he served both on the side of the Pope and against him. In the end he rose so high that he was appointed ambassador to the Vatican by Richard II in 1381, and in 1436 the Florentines commissioned Ucello to design a funerary monument to him. The fresco still stands in the *duomo* in Florence.

In the seventeenth century, in the time of Cromwell, when Admiral Blake and his English fleet arrived off Leghorn (Livorno), it is said that there was nervousness in Catholic Church circles in Rome that Blake might attack the city. But he never did. And when, during the Second World War, the Allies entered Rome in 1944, great efforts were made to respect the Vatican's neutrality.

Venezuela

In the early period, Venezuela, then under Spanish control, received a fair amount of attention from British pirates and privateers. One such was Henry Morgan (him again, see Nicaragua and Panama) who, in a varied career, even picked up the rank of admiral in the Royal Navy. On one raid in 1669, Morgan sacked Maracaibo, now Venezuela's second city, then he pressed on into Lake Maracaibo, looking for more loot. On his return to the coast shortly afterwards, Morgan encountered a defended Spanish fort and three Spanish ships. He destroyed one ship, blew up another by getting a boat packed with gunpowder close to it, and the third ship decided it had had enough and surrendered. Then Morgan pretended to attack the fort from land and while the garrison were distracted he got his sea force past it to safety.

In the eighteenth century, the Royal Navy had a go at the Venezuelan coast. Not very successfully, though. In fact, quite unsuccessfully. During the delightfully named War of Jenkins' Ear in 1743, Commodore Charles Knowles, with the seventy-gun HMS *Suffolk*, was sent to attack Puerto Cabello and La Guaira. Unfortunately for Knowles, the defenders seem to have known he was coming and his attacks were repelled.

During the fight to free Venezuela (from Spanish rule), as elsewhere, British volunteers played a crucial role. In particular, at the Battle of Carabobo on 24 June 1821, the British Legions fought with tremendous courage, capturing enemy positions on vital hills and suffering heavy casualties, before Bolivar's army finally crushed the main enemy force in Venezuela, thus guaranteeing independence.

Since Venezuela became independent from Spain, we've had a couple more brushes with the country. The Venezuelan Crisis of 1895 saw the border between Venezuela and British Guiana finally defined after some very tense times, in which eventually we accepted that the US had a right to intervene in events in the area under the Monroe Doctrine.

Then in 1902–03 there was another Venezuelan Crisis and this time we invaded. We wanted debts and damages paid. In a slightly unlikely alliance of Britain, Germany and Italy, we sent ships to recover our money. Kipling was so upset about us getting too close to Germany on this mission that he wrote a poem, *The Rowers*, with reference to the event. President Castro (not the Cuban one) seems to have reckoned that after the crisis of 1895 he might have the US on his side this time. It was a bad miscalculation. With our allies, we launched a blockade of Venezuela, and among a range of other actions, brushed aside or sank the Venezuelan navy, landed troops to rescue our citizens and bombarded the Venezuelan fortifications at Puerto Cabello. Eventually, we got the money we believed we were owed.

Vietnam

We're so used to thinking of America's war in Vietnam that we often tend to forget our own presence there. And Brits have been in action there.

Inevitably, over the centuries, Vietnam has had some attention from ships with armed Brits abroad. For instance, in the late seventeenth century, privateer William Dampier dropped in.

An early experience on Vietnamese soil, though, was not a happy one for us. Côn Son Island is situated off the coast of Vietnam. It has also been known by the name Poulo Condor, a French version of its Malay name. In 1702 one Allan, or Allen, Ketchpole, or Catchpole, working for the British East India Company, is supposed to have set up a settlement here, but it wasn't a success.

In 1945, we arrived in mainland Vietnam in force.

During the Second World War, Vietnam, as then part of French Indo-China, went through a similar process to Cambodia and Laos, with Vichy French and Japanese at first collaborating, and then in March 1945 with the Japanese taking full control. In the meantime, local pro-independence activists were trying to take advantage of the situation to end French control forever. In 1944, the RAF parachuted in Vietnamese communists who had been previously interned by the French in Madagascar, and in 1945 we started running, with French support, commando operations against the Japanese in Vietnam's northern mountains.

In August 1945 the Japanese surrendered, and on 2 September 1945 Ho Chi Minh declared Vietnamese independence from France. The French, to put it mildly, weren't happy.

Into this highly charged situation we launched Operation Masterdom.

Major General Gracey arrived in Saigon to find the Communist Viet Minh largely in control, but his orders were to disarm the Japanese troops and restore French control. Gradually, his units took control from the Viet Minh and then handed control to incoming French troops. Realising that this was a serious attempt to reimpose French rule, the Vietnamese rioted and the Viet Minh attacked Tan Son Nhut Airfield, which was later to become well known during America's war. A British soldier was killed driving off the attackers.

From this point the situation rapidly deteriorated as a bitter little war broke out between Britain and the Viet Minh. Gracey received reinforcements, but he also ended up in the bizarre situation of using our former enemies, still armed Japanese units, to fight alongside British and Commonwealth troops against the Viet Minh. Gateforce formed under Lieutenant Colonel Gate, consisted of Indian infantry, armoured cars and artillery, but also had an entire Japanese infantry battalion attached to it.

Eventually we pushed the Viet Minh out of Saigon and handed increasing control and responsibility to the French.

Our last big battle with the Viet Minh was at Bien Hoa on 3 January 1945 when British/Indian troops, without any loss to themselves, killed about 100 from an attacking force of roughly 900 Viet Minh, mainly through machine-gun crossfire.

By the summer of 1946 all British troops were gone from Vietnam.

12

YEMEN TO ZIMBABWE

Yemen

Now that Yugoslavia has gone, if you want a country that starts with a 'Y' in English, then Yemen's pretty much it.

And we've played quite a large role in Yemeni history, because of Aden.

Readers who were around in the late 1960s will remember the bitter campaign that British forces fought against local fighters here before our final withdrawal on 30 November 1967. But this came at the end of many decades of British control of the area.

Aden sits in an obvious strategic location on the sealanes between the Gulf of Aden and the Red Sea, and has long been known to British sailors. In the late seventeenth century English pirates made use of it.

Then, in 1798 Napoleon invaded Egypt and we started getting nervous about French influence in the region. So we decided to establish a strategic base in the area, and in 1799 took control of the Yemeni island of Perim, at the southern entrance to the Red Sea. But after a short while we started looking for a more convenient spot to station the troops and we settled for Aden, with the agreement of the local sultan. The troops remained there until the danger from the French had passed.

In 1820, we bombarded nearby Mocha (yes, that Mocha) and imposed a commercial treaty upon it. And in 1827 we imposed a blockade on nearby Berbera as well, after an attack on a British ship.

In the 1830s, Aden was being used as a coaling station and the local sultan had subsequently agreed to let us take control here.

But the sultan's successor wasn't too keen on the agreement, so we decided to take control of Aden anyway. Captain Smith on HMS *Volage* was sent in with three smaller ships and some transports. On 19 January 1839, the force bombarded Aden, and then landed troops, and after some brief resistance from the sultan's army, our flag was hoisted. Today, in the Tower of London, you can see a souvenir taken by Captain Smith in the capture of Aden. Rather more impressive than the average souvenir today, it's a cannon of Suleiman the Magnificent founded by Mohammed ibn Hamza in 1530–31.

British influence then spread further in the region with the establishment of the Aden Protectorate.

There was some fighting in the area in the First World War and just before the war ended, our cruisers HMS *Proserpine*, HMS *Juno* and HMS *Suva* covered the 101st Bombay Grenadiers as they landed at Hodeida in Yemen and took it from Ottoman forces.

Zambia

The explorer David Livingstone turned up here in 1855 and ended up visiting the Victoria Falls, though that's not what the locals called them at the time.

In 1888, Cecil Rhodes' British South Africa Company (BSAC) secured some local mineral rights, and in 1890 Lewanika, King of Barotseland, made a deal with Rhodes to accept protection. In 1891, the British government also accepted BSAC control of the area.

The Portuguese, meanwhile, hadn't been too keen on British control of the area, since they themselves wanted it as part of the link between their territories on the east coast of Africa and their territories on the west coast. In the Anglo-Portuguese Crisis of 1889–90 they lost out to us.

We got control over other parts of what is now Zambia in different ways. For instance, in 1898–99, a succession crisis in the Bemba tribe in the northern part of what is now Zambia led to us taking control there.

In 1964 Northern Rhodesia, as we had called it, became independent as Zambia.

Zimbabwe

In 1888, Cecil Rhodes arrived in the area and got King Lobengula of the Ndebele to grant him mining rights. From that starting point, Rhodes then persuaded the British government in 1889 to grant his British South Africa Company control of the area.

In 1890, he decided to put this theoretical control into effect, sending the Pioneer Column of settlers north to found Fort Salisbury (now Harare). In 1893, an attack by Ndebele raiders on Shona tribesman allowed Rhodes to set up a war.

British forces, along with their local allies, advanced on Lobengula's capital and, though there were plenty of Ndebele resisting, they didn't have the Maxim guns of the British forces. The Ndebele were mown down by the Maxims, Bulawayo was mostly destroyed and Lobengula fled, eventually dying the following year. Between 1896 and 1897 both Ndebele and Shona rose in rebellion, but the rebels were crushed.

Ian Smith's government issued a Unilateral Declaration of Independence from Britain in 1965, which led to a long guerrilla war of liberation by ZANU and ZAPU.

On 1 December 1979, the Lancaster House Agreement was signed to end the war, and we temporarily returned to Zimbabwe, with Lord Soames briefly becoming governor, to oversee elections in 1980 and with the British Army supervising the demobilisation of guerrillas.

CONCLUSION

So there you have it, from Afghanistan to Zimbabwe, a story of how, under arms, we have roamed the world, reaching almost every country in it and in some way, small or big, changing the history of those places. I hope that you have found it as fascinating, amazing and eye-opening to read as I found writing it. And I hope that my, doubtless in many ways imperfect, attempt to tell this vast and complex story will encourage you to explore further those aspects that interest and intrigue you most.

It is a story that has cost many lives, that has seen dreams achieved, as well as dreams crushed, that has included great wrong as well as great good and that has featured disastrous mistakes as well as brilliant triumphs. All of it, though, is worth knowing about, because ultimately, if you're a part of this country, of the United Kingdom, then all of this amazing and unique heritage is a part of who you are today. It's your heritage. It's our heritage.

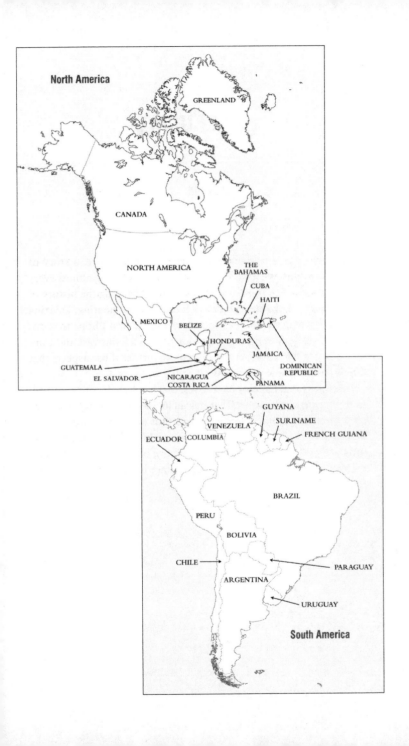

Europe

ICELAND

NORTHERN
IRELAND

UNITED
KINGDOM

PORTUGAL

SPAIN

FRANCE

LUXEMBOURG

BELGIUM

THE
NETHERLANDS

GERMANY

NORWAY

SWEDEN

FINLAND

ESTONIA

LATVIA

LITHUANIA

BELARUS

POLAND

CZECH

SLOVAKIA

AUSTRIA HUNGARY

SWITZERLAND

ITALY

SLOVENIA

CROATIA

SERBIA

ROMANIA

UKRAINE

BULGARIA

MALTA

ALBANIA

BOSNIA
&
HERZEGOVINA

MACEDONIA

GREECE

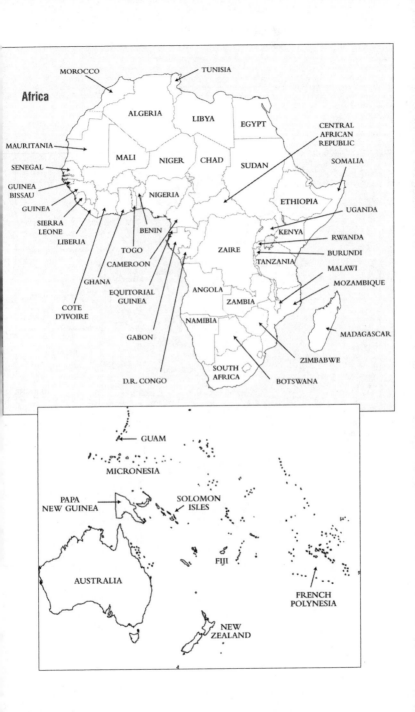

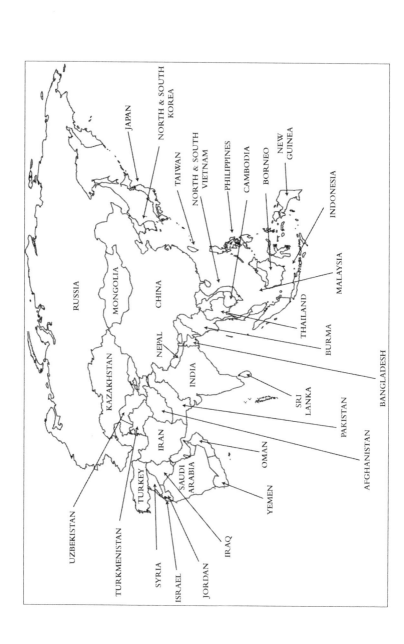